ANIM(O)SITY™

VOLUME
6

KING OF TEXAS

MARGUERITE BENNETT

ELTON THOMASI

RAFAEL DE LATORRE

ROB SCHWAGER

JUANCHO!

TAYLOR ESPOSITO

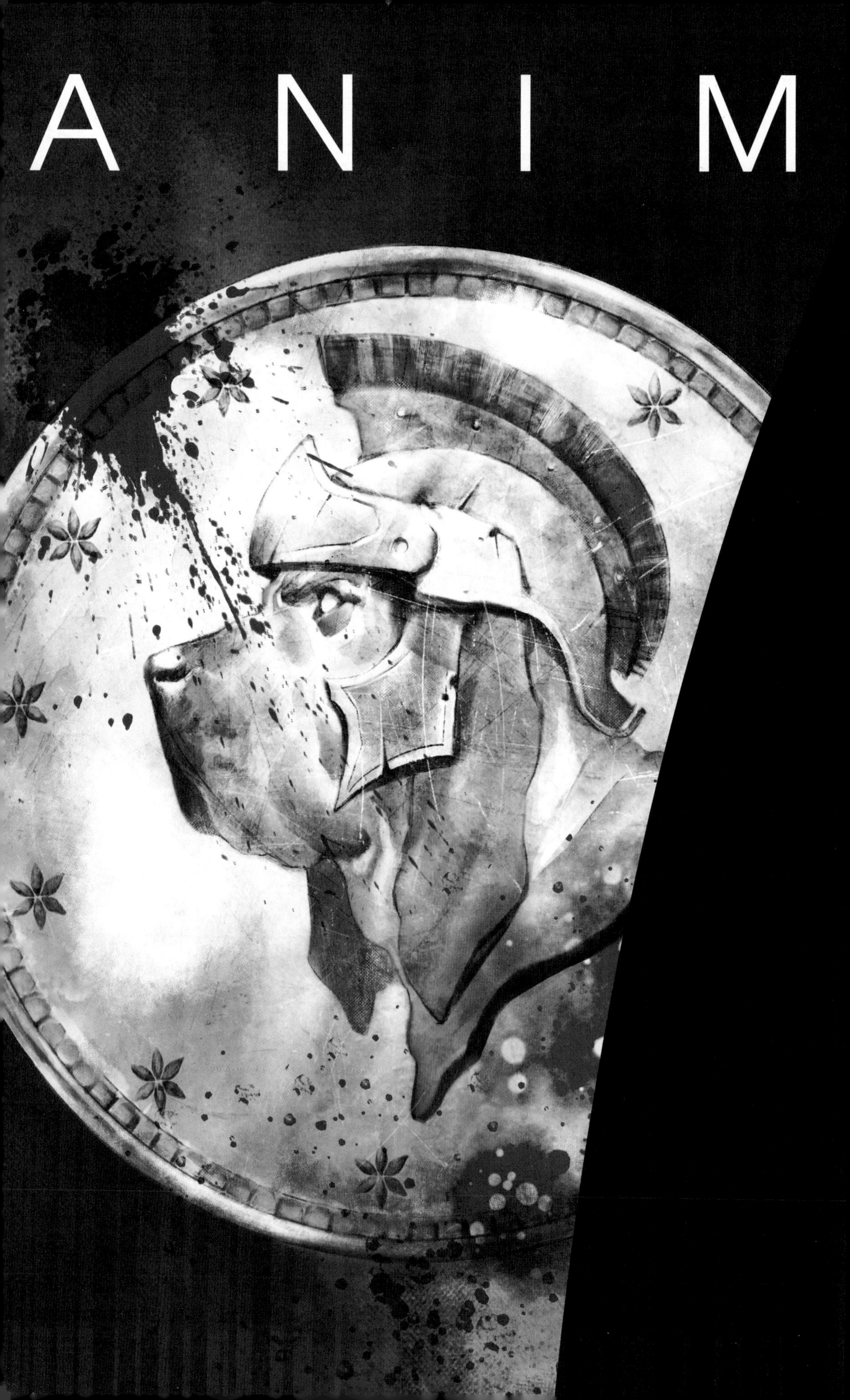
A N I M

O S I T Y
V O L U M E   6
K I N G   O F   T E X A S

MARGUERITE BENNETT writer

ELTON THOMASI & **RAFAEL DE LATORRE** artists

ROB SCHWAGER & **JUANCHO!** colorists

TAYLOR ESPOSITO letterer

RAFAEL DE LATORRE w/ **MARCELO MAIOLO** front & original series covers

JOHN J. HILL logo designer

COREY BREEN book designer

MIKE MARTS editor

created by **MARGUERITE BENNETT**

AFTERSHOCK

MIKE MARTS - Editor-in-Chief • JOE PRUETT - Publisher/CCO • LEE KRAMER - President • JON KRAMER - Chief Executive Officer
STEVE ROTTERDAM - SVP, Sales & Marketing • DAN SHIRES - VP, Film & Television UK • CHRISTINA HARRINGTON - Managing Editor
MARC HAMMOND - Sr. Retail Sales Development Manager • RUTHANN THOMPSON - Sr. Retailer Relations Manager
KATHERINE JAMISON - Marketing Manager • KELLY DIODATI - Ambassador Outreach Manager • BLAKE STOCKER - Director of Finance
AARON MARION - Publicist • LISA MOODY - Finance • RYAN CARROLL - Development Coordinator • JAWAD QURESHI - Technology Advisor/Strategist
RACHEL PINNELAS - Social Community Manager • CHARLES PRITCHETT - Design & Production Manager • COREY BREEN - Collections Production
TEDDY LEO - Editorial Assistant • STEPHANIE CASEBIER & SARAH PRUETT - Publishing Assistants

AfterShock Logo Design by COMICRAFT
Publicity: contact AARON MARION (aaron@publichausagency.com) & RYAN CROY (ryan@publichausagency.com) at PUBLICHAUS
Special thanks to: ATOM! FREEMAN, IRA KURGAN, MARINE KSADZHIKYAN & ANTONIA LIANOS

I N T R O D U C T I O N

There are very few stories that make significant statements about society, civilization and future generations of mankind. George Orwell's *Animal Farm* is one of those rare tales that hits all of those marks and then some. Beyond the very obvious ideological surface conflicts in *Animal Farm*, Orwell digs deeper and shows us there is a very basic war between humans and animals that has transpired for thousands of years.

When I first read his book at a young age, I reflected that what transpired at Mr. Jones' farm was a good thing...a once-in-a-lifetime experience. That gave me peace...and relief about the whole man vs. animal conflict.

UNTIL I was invited to be the colorist of Marguerite Bennett and Rafael De Latorre's ANIMOSITY covers. Right then and there whatever peace I had achieved ENDED, for Marguerite and Rafael had elevated Orwell's tale to a global scale! Animals are no longer safely caged in petting zoos or sitting securely in their pens. They're no longer items to be purchased from the butcher shop. No, that type of social distancing with animals doesn't exist in ANIMOSITY!

Danger lurks in all places now...EVERYWHERE! Our pets, strays outside, the creatures in the sewers, the ones flying in the air...ALL OF THEM. All conscious now! All thinking. All making decisions. All plotting REVENGE.

ANIMOSITY is a great tale that will surely stand the test of time...one that will always make us think about how we react to the environment around us. After ANIMOSITY, we may never look at that seemingly innocent little kitten sitting next to us the same way ever again! For the cat may be thinking: "Whatever stands upon two legs is my enemy..."

MARCELO MAIOLO
September 2020

25

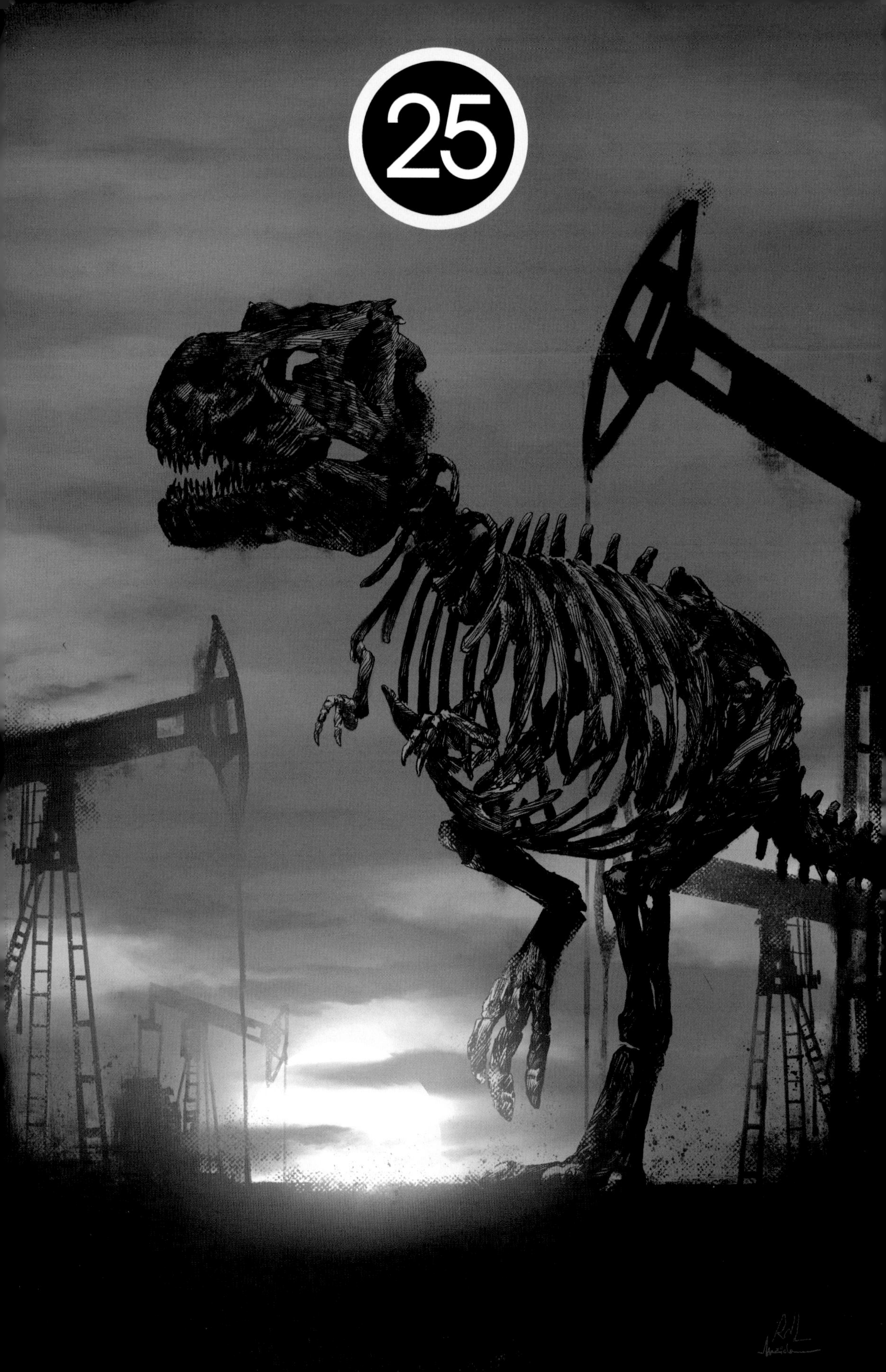

KING OF TEXAS, PART ONE

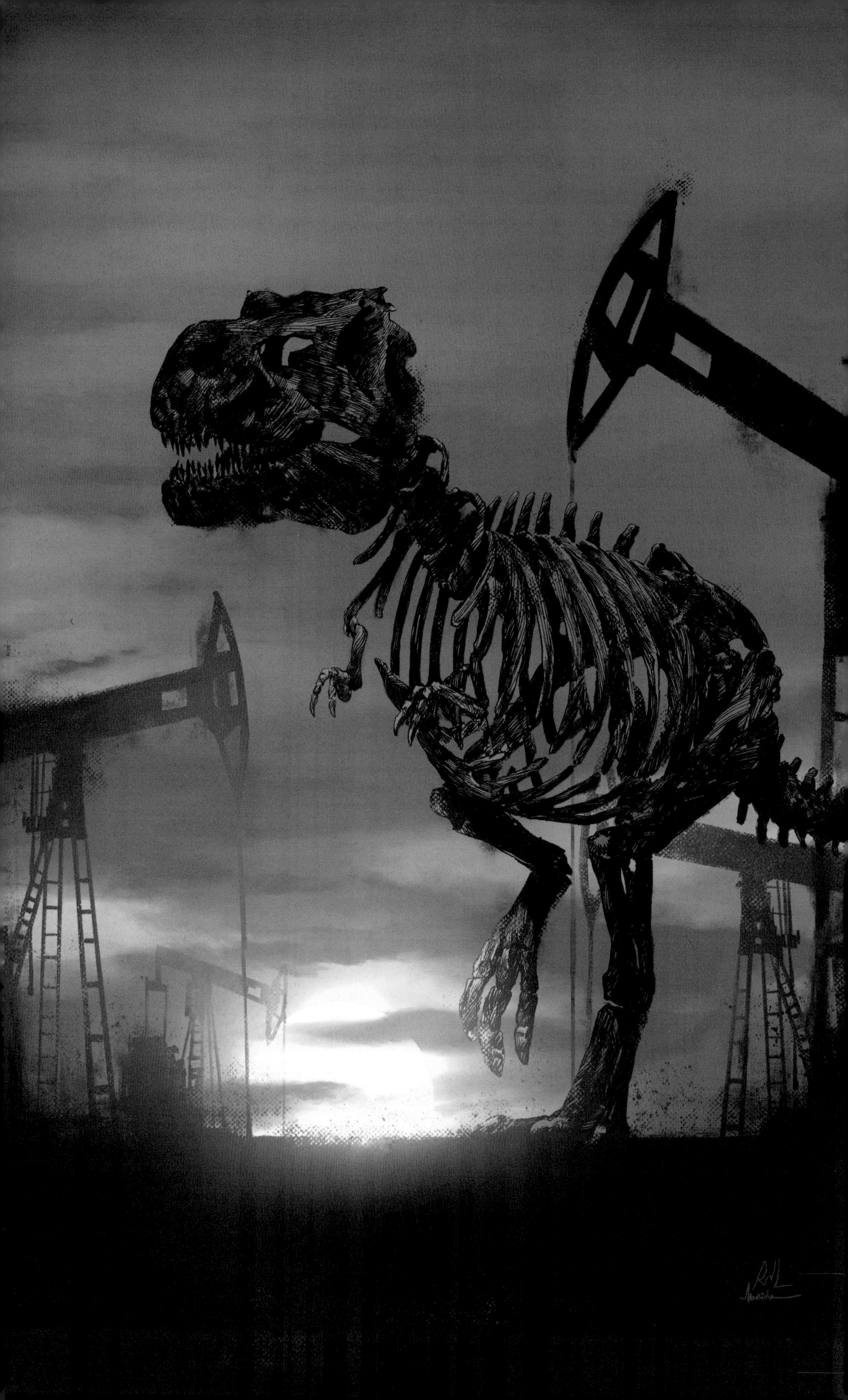

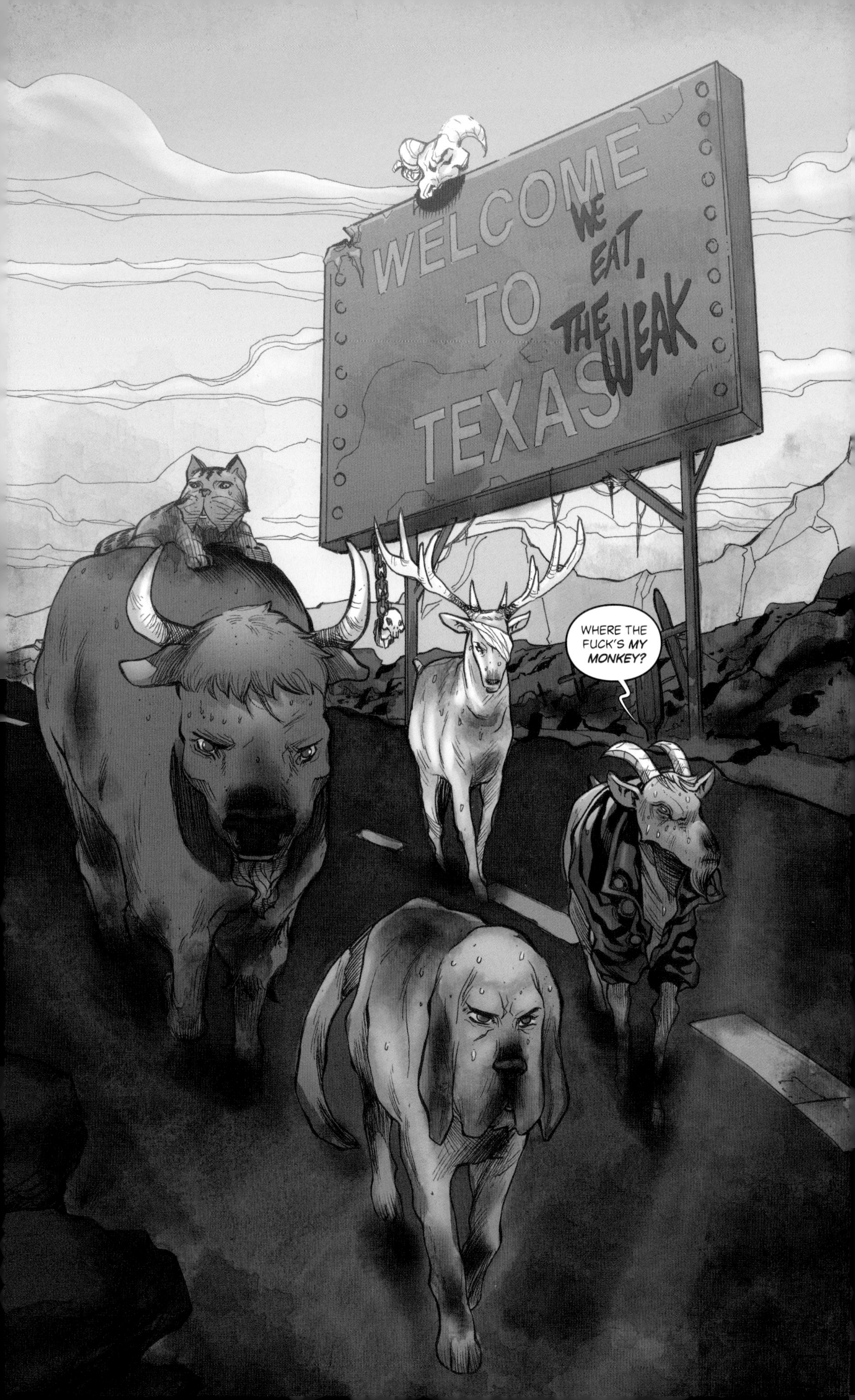
WELCOME TO TEXAS
WE EAT THE WEAK
WHERE THE FUCK'S MY MONKEY?

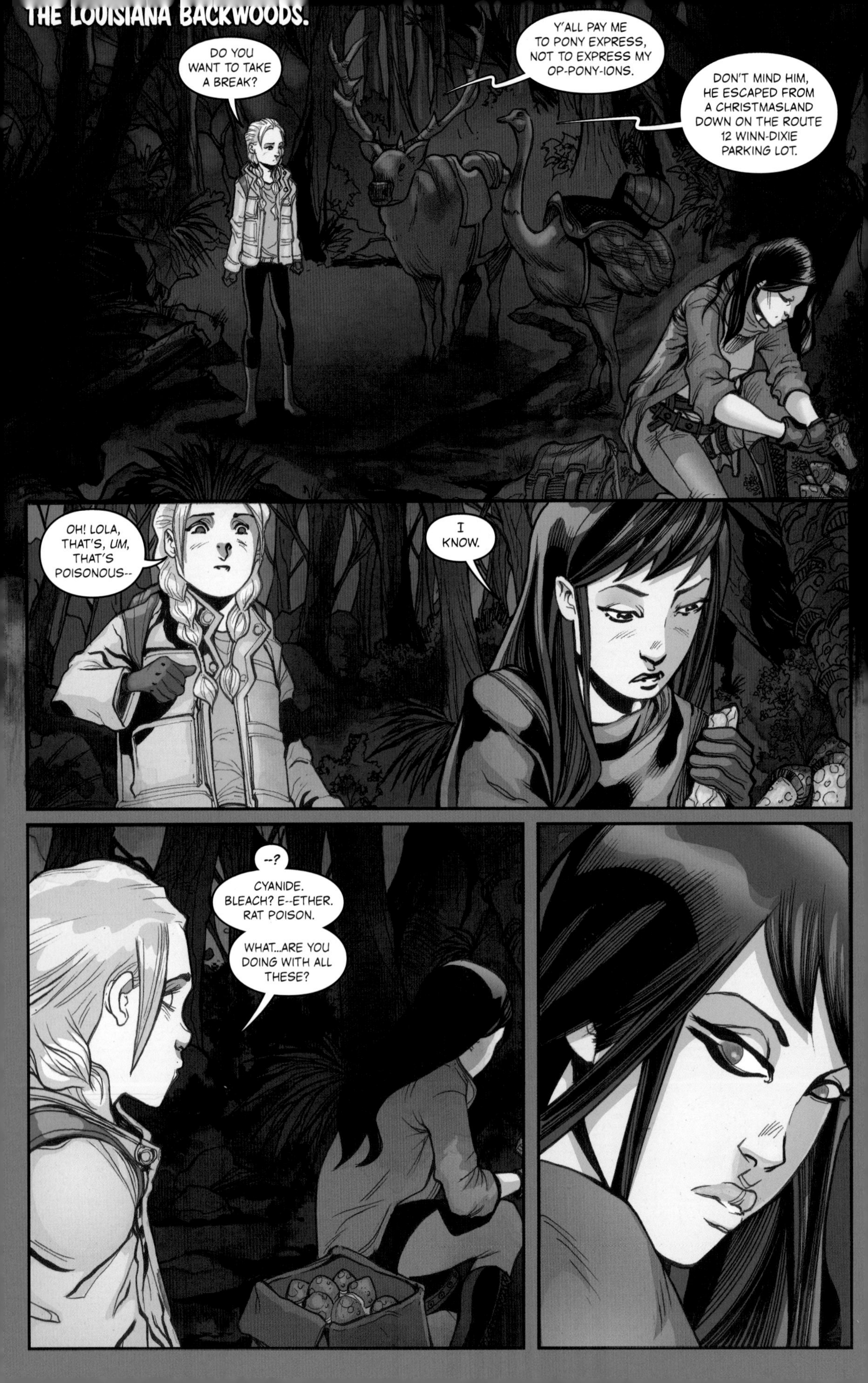
THE LOUISIANA BACKWOODS.
DO YOU WANT TO TAKE A BREAK?
Y'ALL PAY ME TO PONY EXPRESS, NOT TO EXPRESS MY OP-PONY-IONS.
DON'T MIND HIM, HE ESCAPED FROM A CHRISTMASLAND DOWN ON THE ROUTE 12 WINN-DIXIE PARKING LOT.
OH! LOLA, THAT'S, UM, THAT'S POISONOUS--
I KNOW.
--?
CYANIDE. BLEACH? E--ETHER. RAT POISON.
WHAT...ARE YOU DOING WITH ALL THESE?

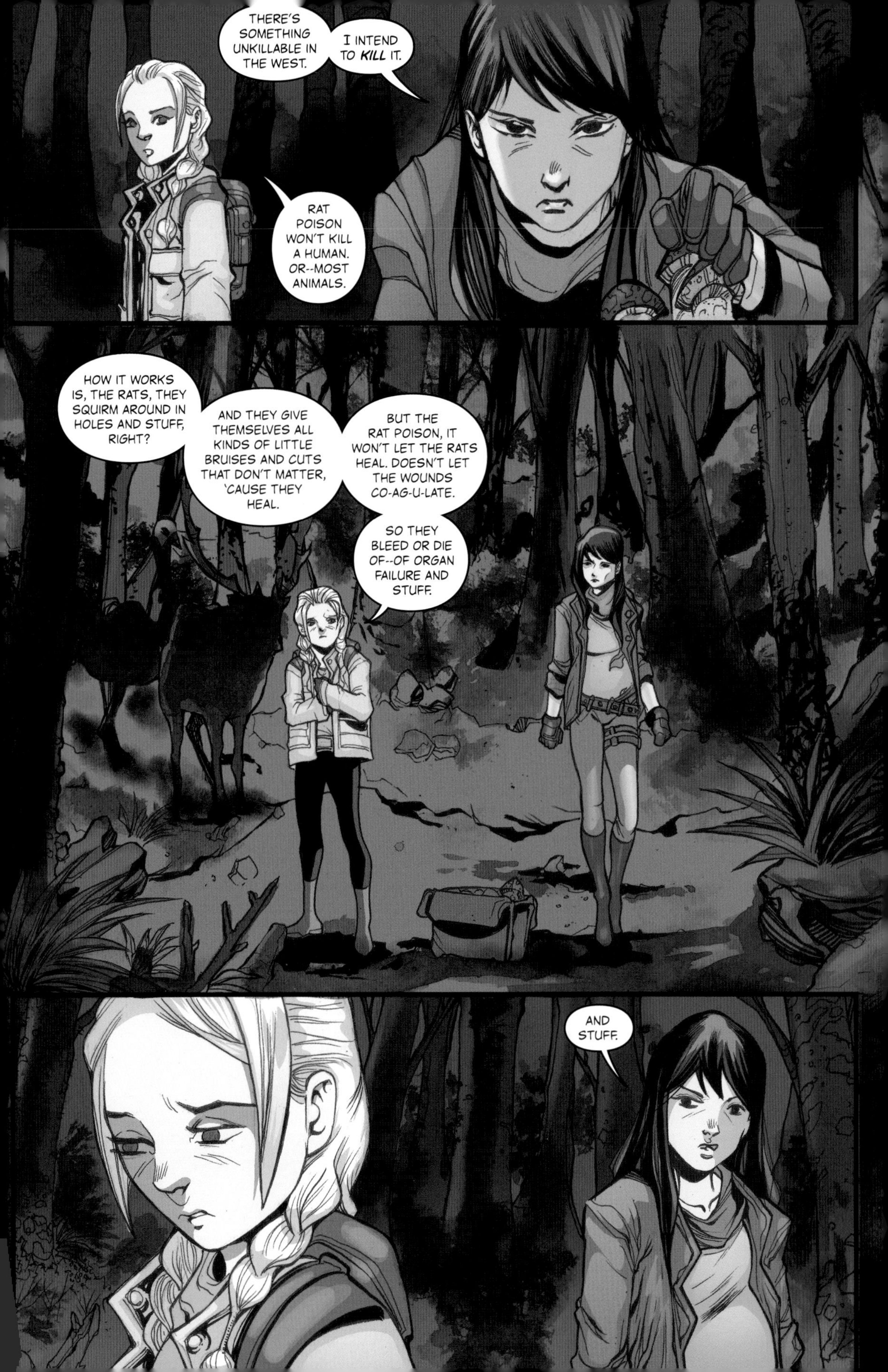
THERE'S SOMETHING UNKILLABLE IN THE WEST.
I INTEND TO ***KILL*** IT.
RAT POISON WON'T KILL A HUMAN. OR--MOST ANIMALS.
HOW IT WORKS IS, THE RATS, THEY SQUIRM AROUND IN HOLES AND STUFF, RIGHT?
AND THEY GIVE THEMSELVES ALL KINDS OF LITTLE BRUISES AND CUTS THAT DON'T MATTER, 'CAUSE THEY HEAL.
BUT THE RAT POISON, IT WON'T LET THE RATS HEAL. DOESN'T LET THE WOUNDS CO-AG-U-LATE.
SO THEY BLEED OR DIE OF--OF ORGAN FAILURE AND STUFF.
AND STUFF.

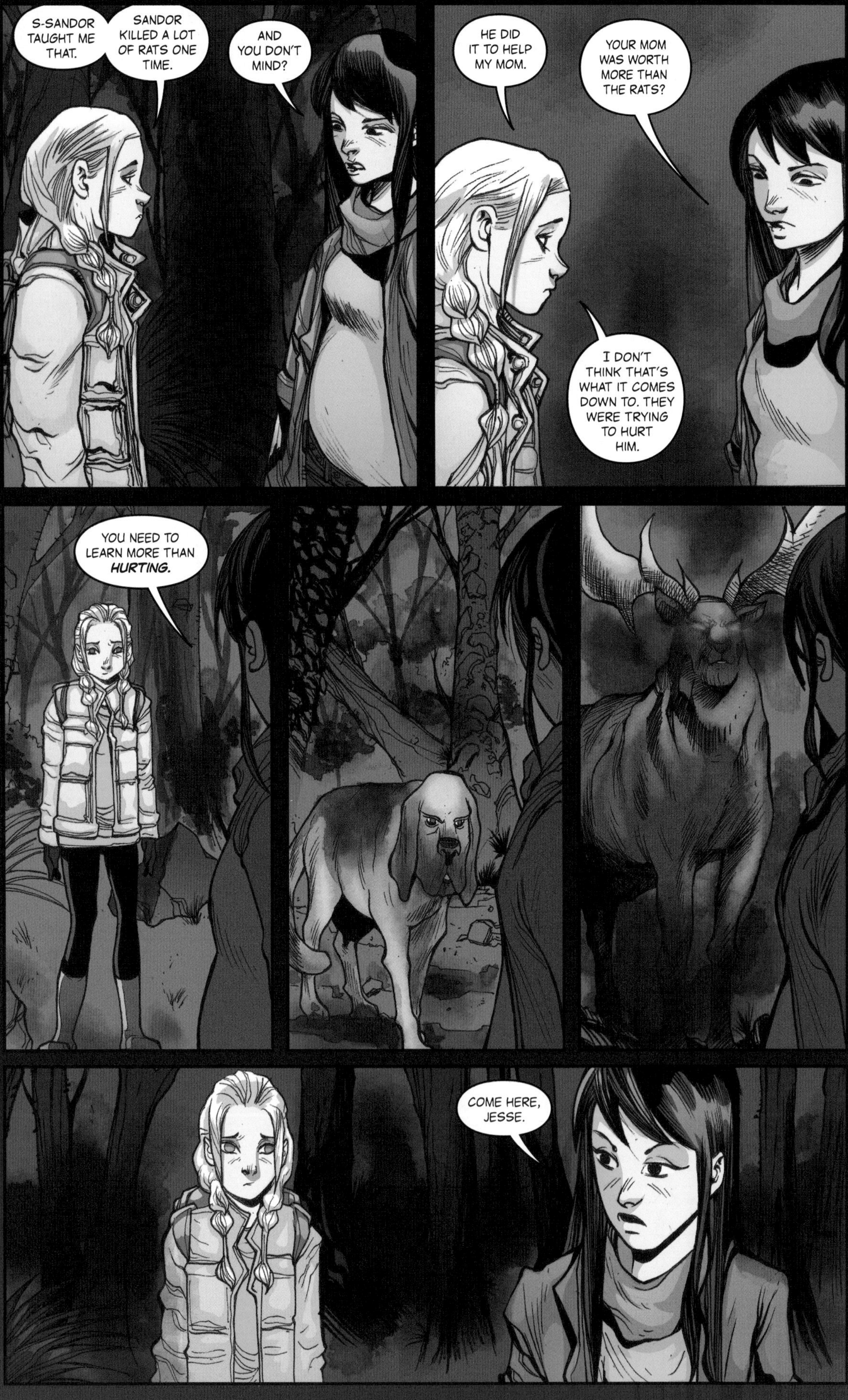
S-SANDOR TAUGHT ME THAT.
SANDOR KILLED A LOT OF RATS ONE TIME.
AND YOU DON'T MIND?
HE DID IT TO HELP MY MOM.
YOUR MOM WAS WORTH MORE THAN THE RATS?
I DON'T THINK THAT'S WHAT IT COMES DOWN TO. THEY WERE TRYING TO HURT HIM.
YOU NEED TO LEARN MORE THAN ***HURTING.***
COME HERE, JESSE.

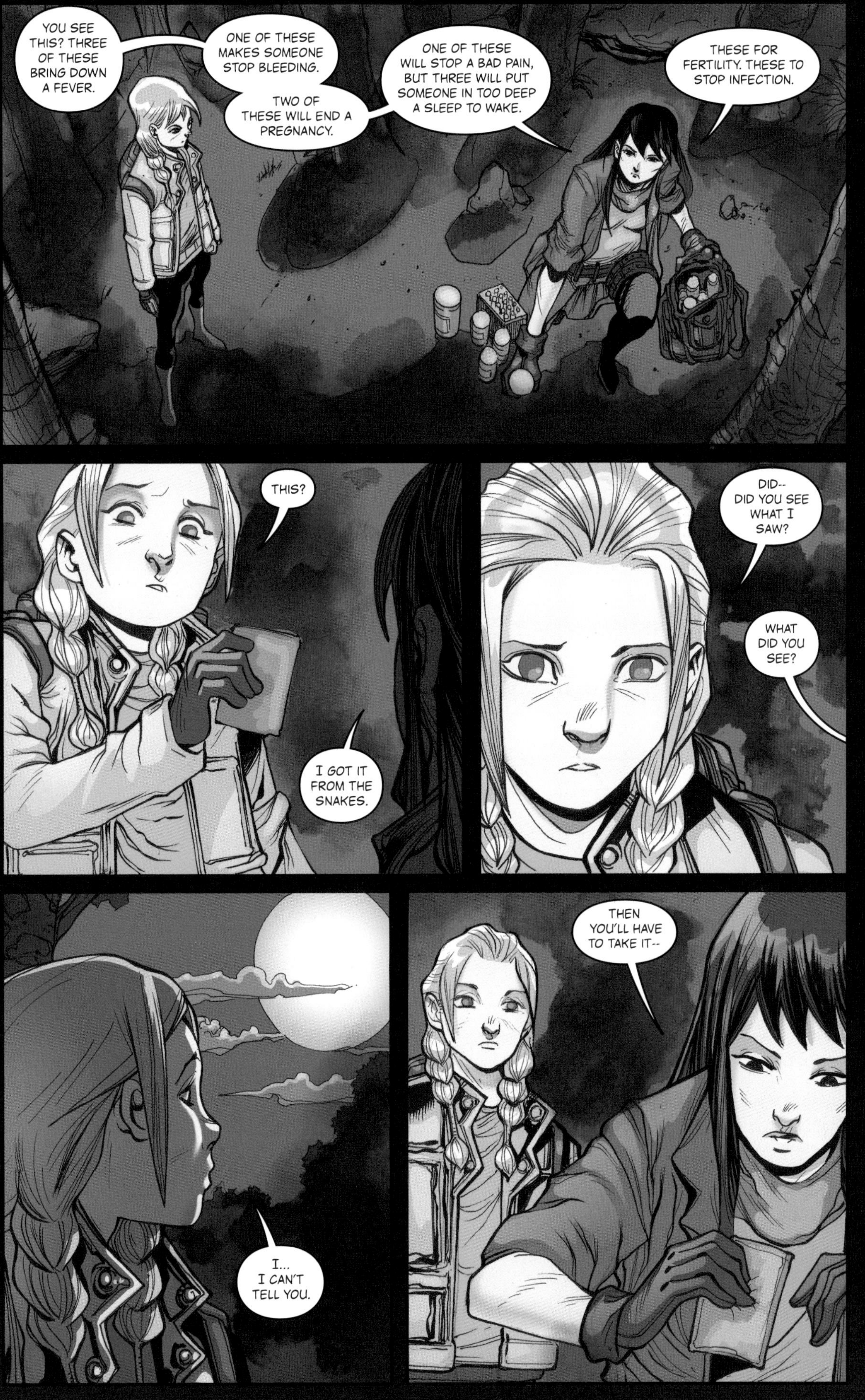
YOU SEE THIS? THREE OF THESE BRING DOWN A FEVER.
ONE OF THESE MAKES SOMEONE STOP BLEEDING.
TWO OF THESE WILL END A PREGNANCY.
ONE OF THESE WILL STOP A BAD PAIN, BUT THREE WILL PUT SOMEONE IN TOO DEEP A SLEEP TO WAKE.
THESE FOR FERTILITY. THESE TO STOP INFECTION.
THIS?
I GOT IT FROM THE SNAKES.
DID-- DID YOU SEE WHAT I SAW?
WHAT DID YOU SEE?
I... I CAN'T TELL YOU.
THEN YOU'LL HAVE TO TAKE IT--

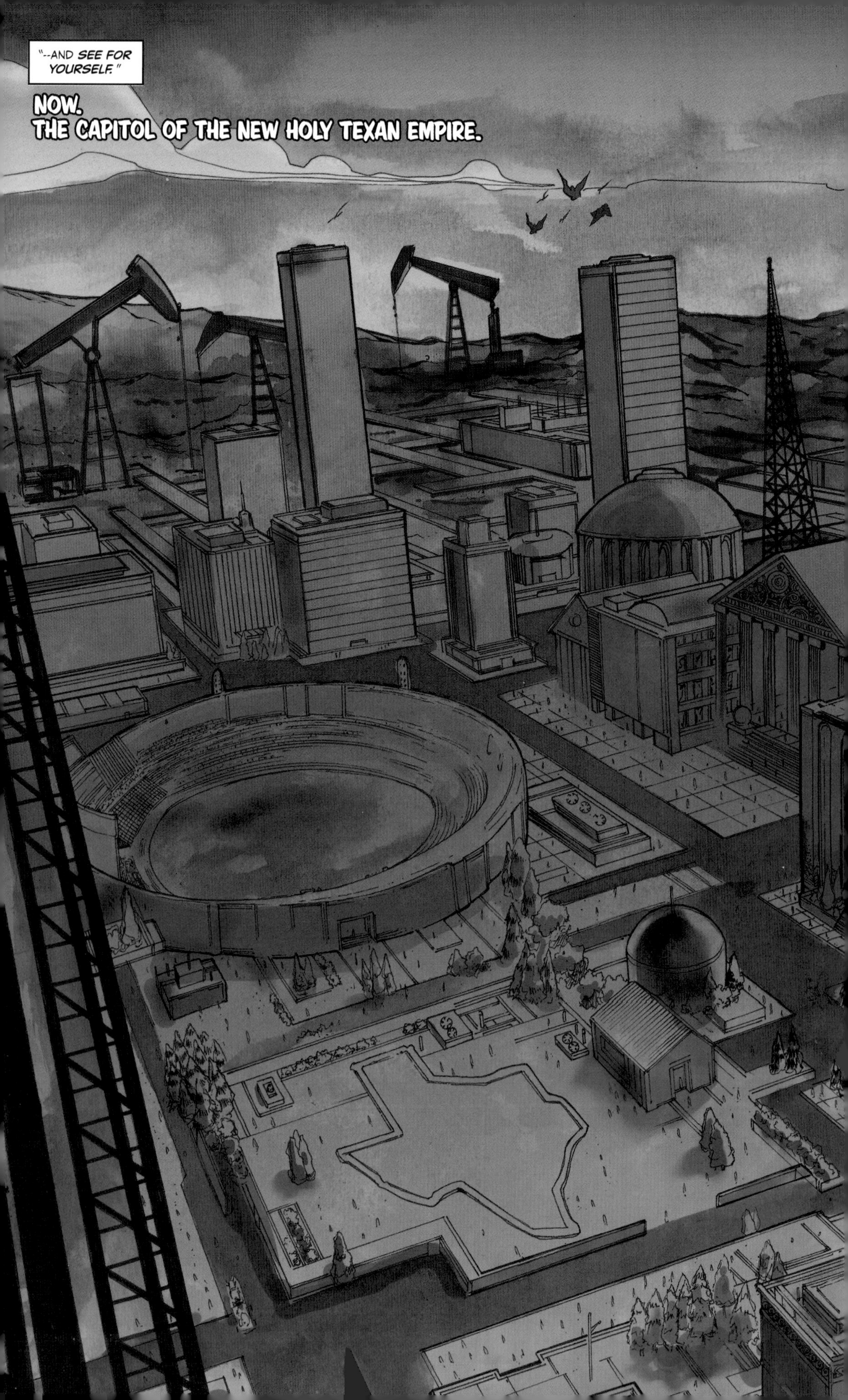
"--AND SEE FOR YOURSELF."
NOW.
THE CAPITOL OF THE NEW HOLY TEXAN EMPIRE.

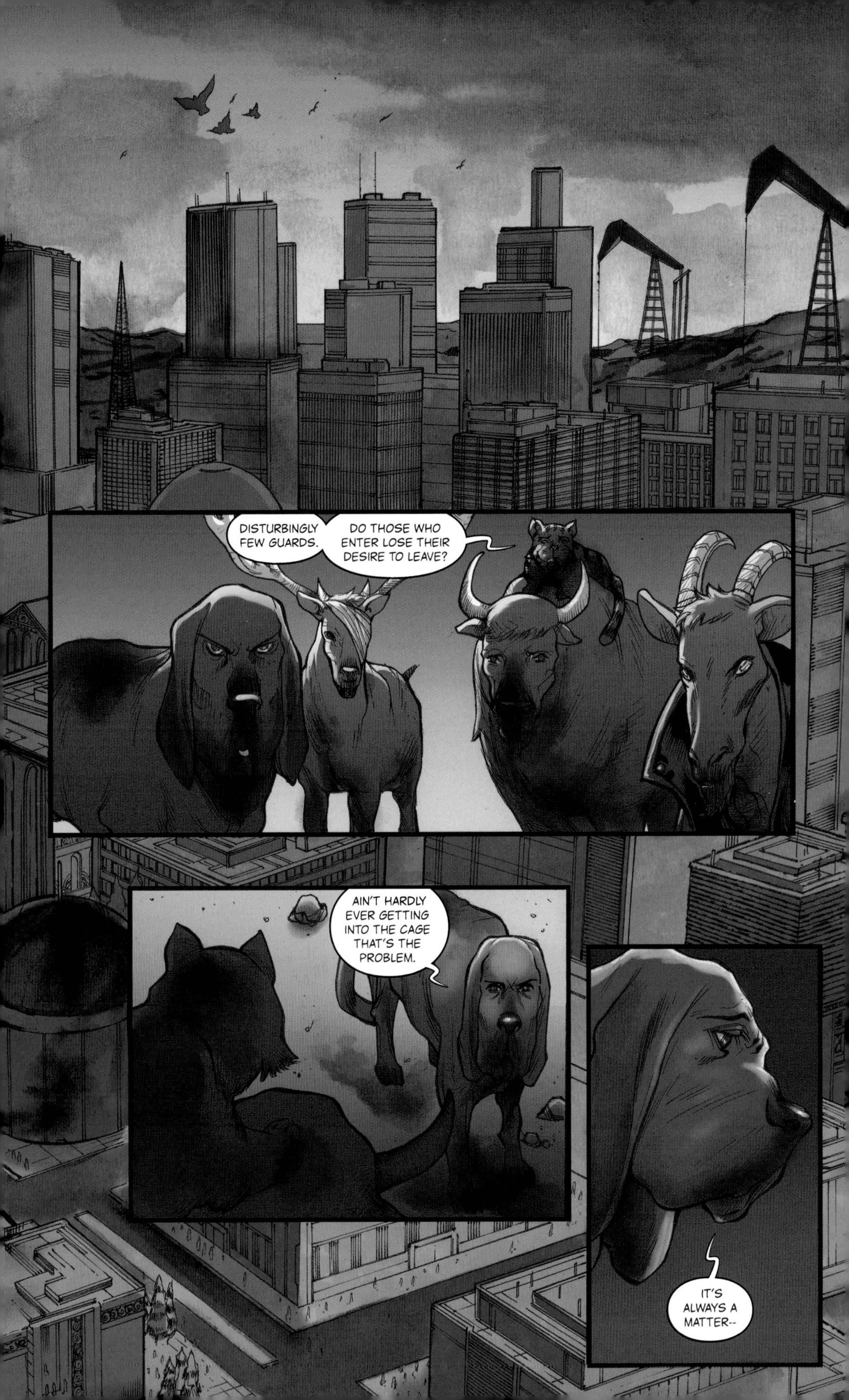
DISTURBINGLY FEW GUARDS.
DO THOSE WHO ENTER LOSE THEIR DESIRE TO LEAVE?
AIN'T HARDLY EVER GETTING INTO THE CAGE THAT'S THE PROBLEM.
IT'S ALWAYS A MATTER--

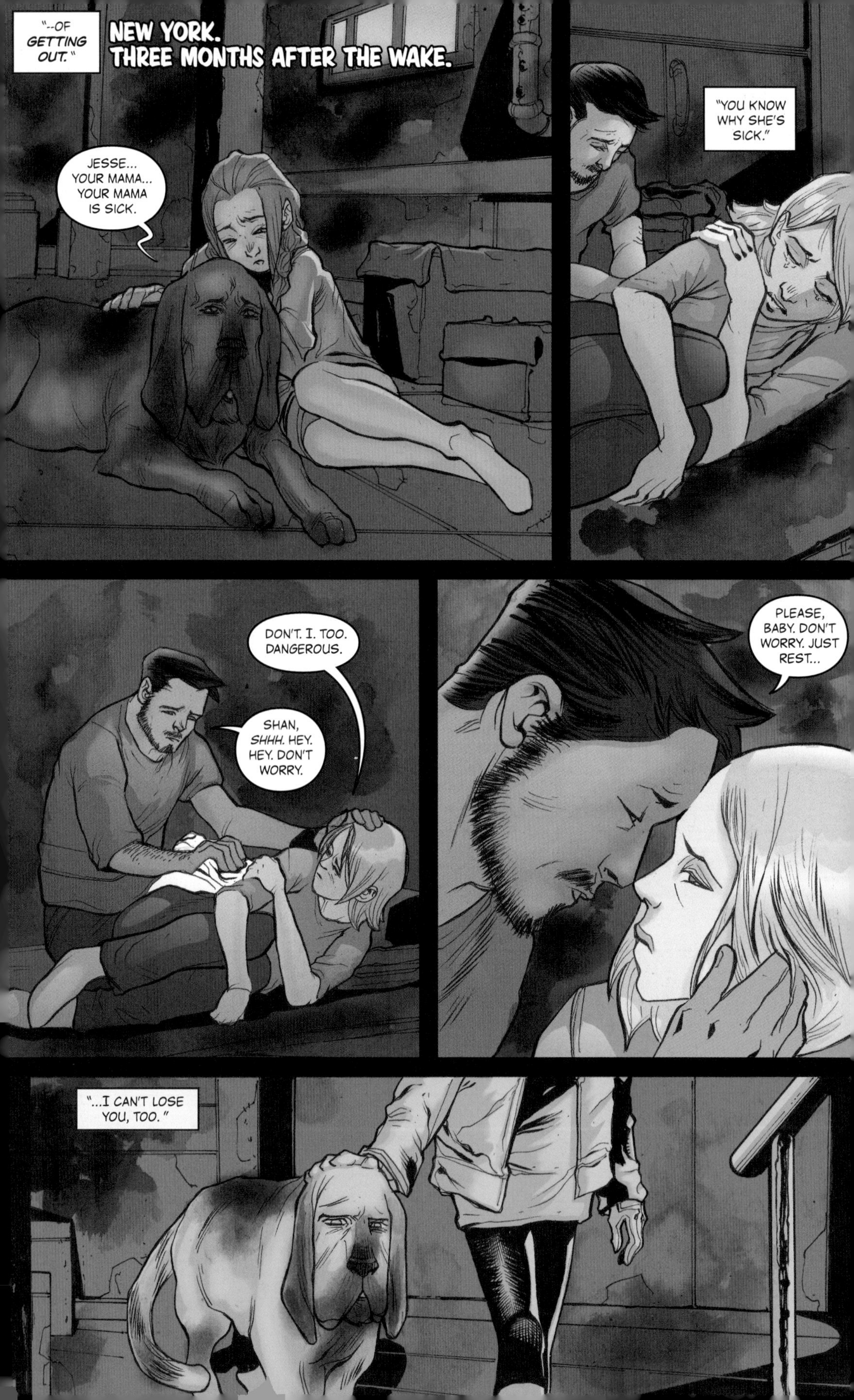
"--OF GETTING OUT."
NEW YORK. THREE MONTHS AFTER THE WAKE.
JESSE... YOUR MAMA... YOUR MAMA IS SICK.
"YOU KNOW WHY SHE'S SICK."
DON'T. I. TOO. DANGEROUS.
SHAN, SHHH. HEY. HEY. DON'T WORRY.
PLEASE, BABY. DON'T WORRY. JUST REST...
"...I CAN'T LOSE YOU, TOO."

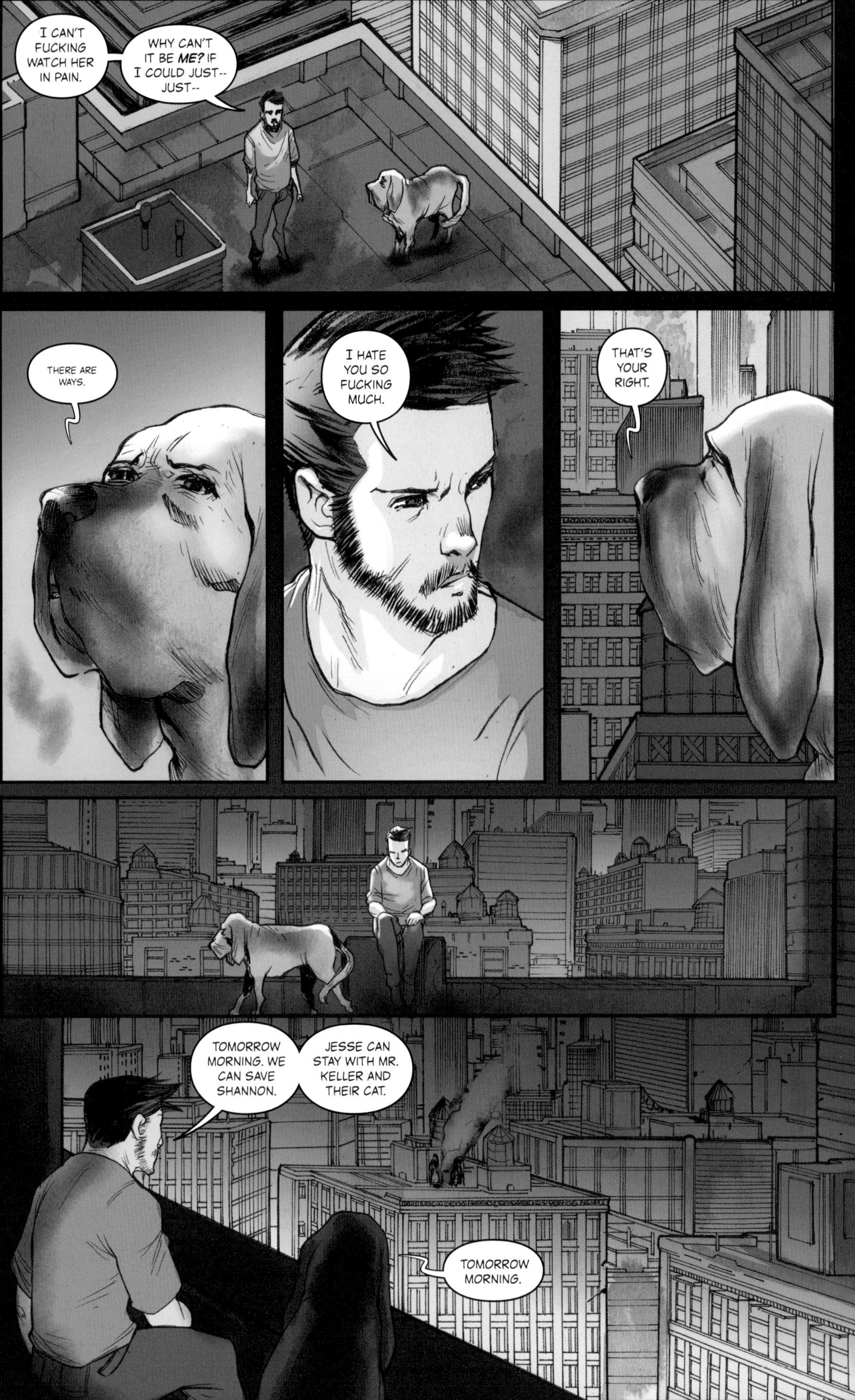
I CAN'T FUCKING WATCH HER IN PAIN.
WHY CAN'T IT BE ME? IF I COULD JUST-- JUST--
THERE ARE WAYS.
I HATE YOU SO FUCKING MUCH.
THAT'S YOUR RIGHT.
TOMORROW MORNING. WE CAN SAVE SHANNON.
JESSE CAN STAY WITH MR. KELLER AND THEIR CAT.
TOMORROW MORNING.

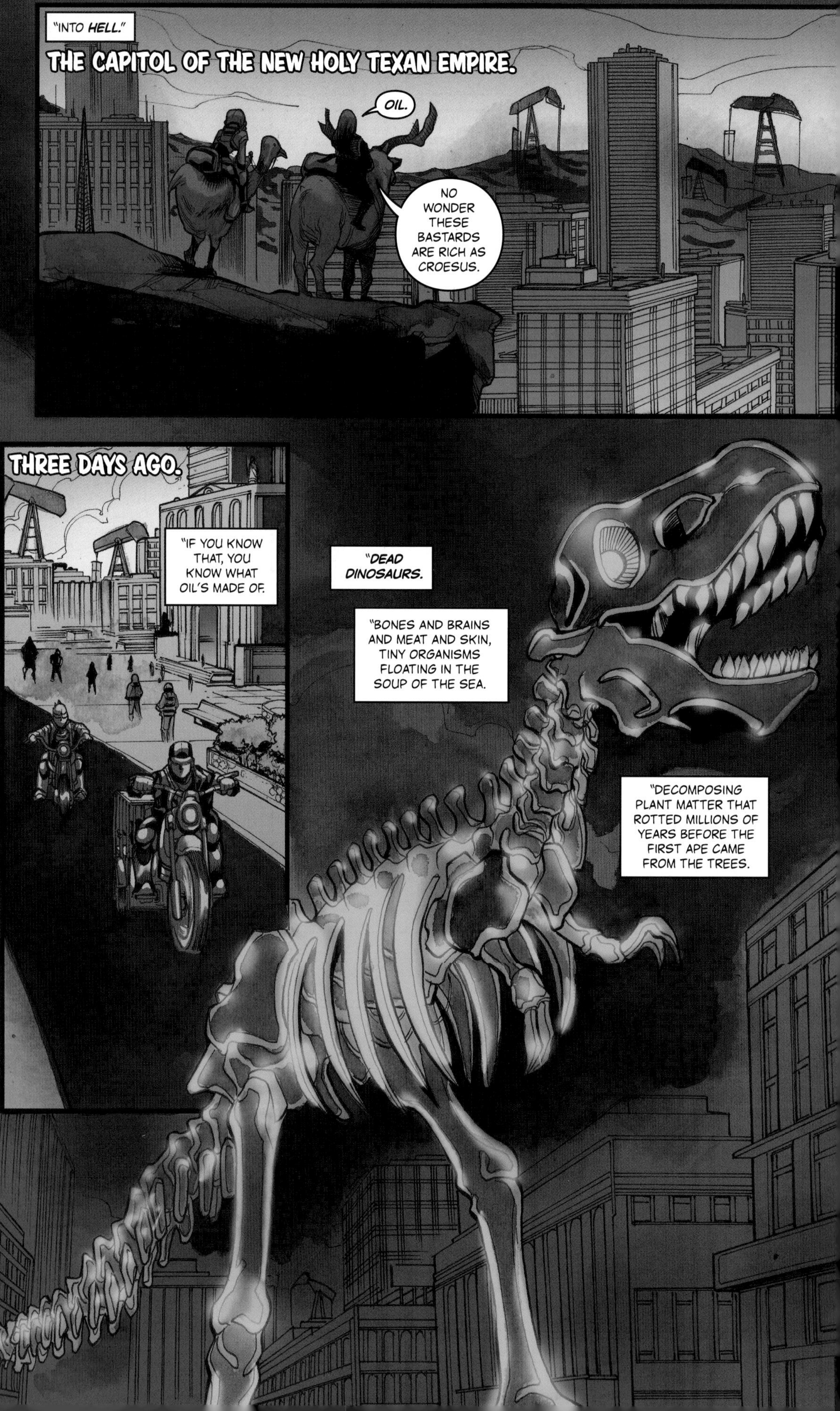
"INTO *HELL.*"
THE CAPITOL OF THE NEW HOLY TEXAN EMPIRE.
OIL.
NO WONDER THESE BASTARDS ARE RICH AS CROESUS.
THREE DAYS AGO.
"IF YOU KNOW THAT, YOU KNOW WHAT OIL'S MADE OF.
"*DEAD DINOSAURS.*
"BONES AND BRAINS AND MEAT AND SKIN, TINY ORGANISMS FLOATING IN THE SOUP OF THE SEA.
"DECOMPOSING PLANT MATTER THAT ROTTED MILLIONS OF YEARS BEFORE THE FIRST APE CAME FROM THE TREES.

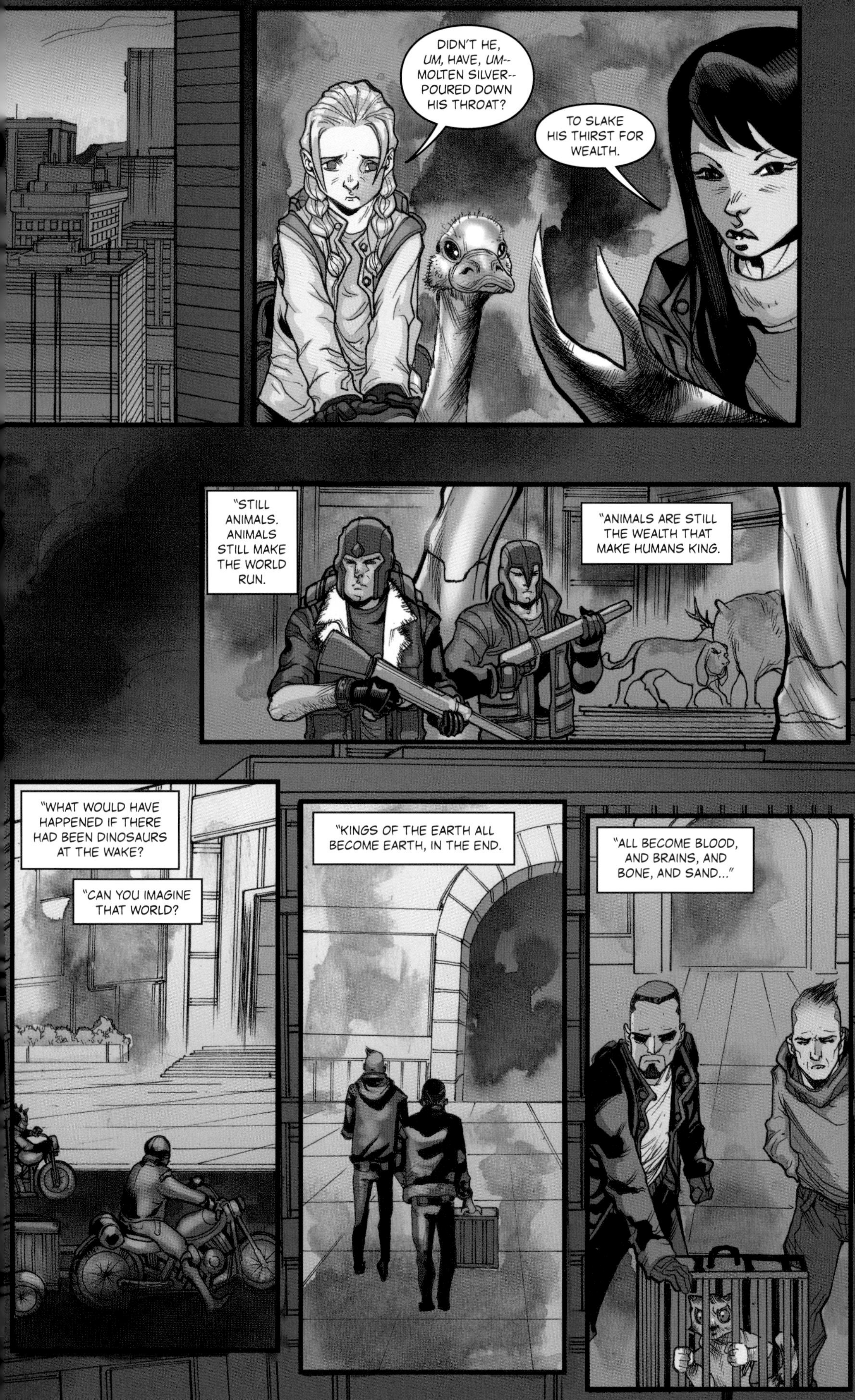
DIDN'T HE, UM, HAVE, UM-- MOLTEN SILVER-- POURED DOWN HIS THROAT?
TO SLAKE HIS THIRST FOR WEALTH.
"STILL ANIMALS. ANIMALS STILL MAKE THE WORLD RUN.
"ANIMALS ARE STILL THE WEALTH THAT MAKE HUMANS KING.
"WHAT WOULD HAVE HAPPENED IF THERE HAD BEEN DINOSAURS AT THE WAKE?
"CAN YOU IMAGINE THAT WORLD?
"KINGS OF THE EARTH ALL BECOME EARTH, IN THE END.
"ALL BECOME BLOOD, AND BRAINS, AND BONE, AND SAND..."

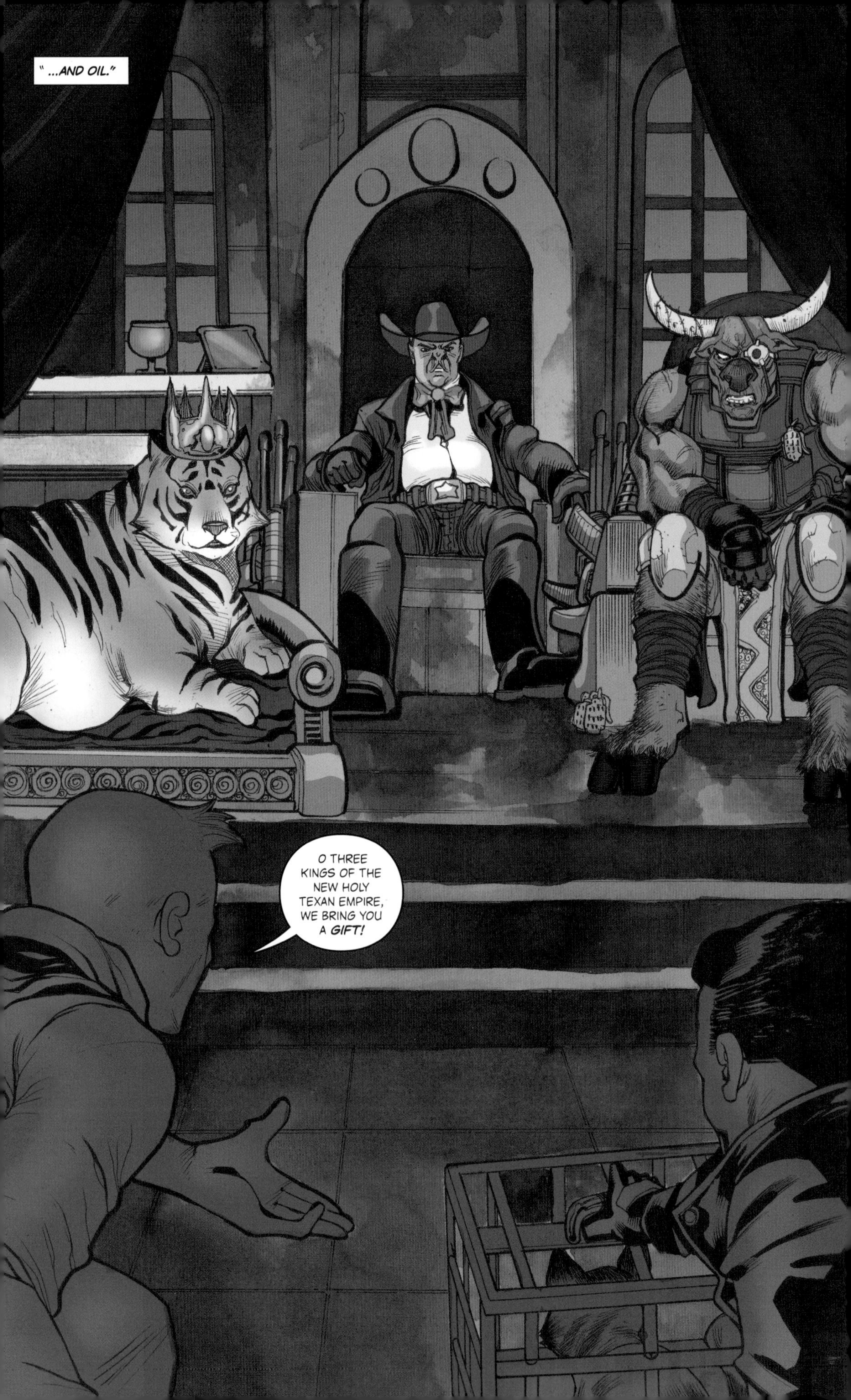
" ...AND OIL."
O THREE KINGS OF THE NEW HOLY TEXAN EMPIRE, WE BRING YOU A *GIFT!*

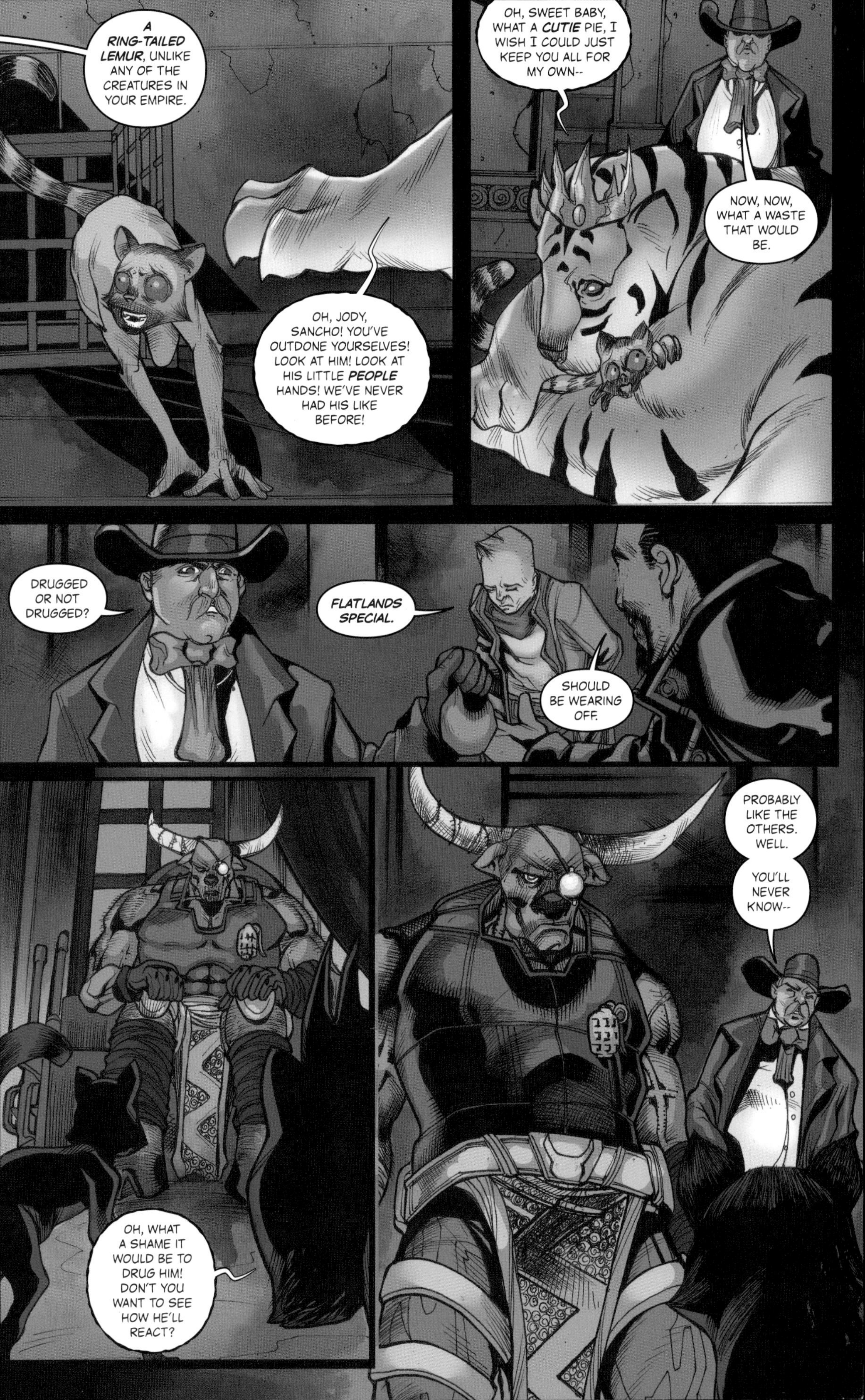
A RING-TAILED LEMUR, UNLIKE ANY OF THE CREATURES IN YOUR EMPIRE.
OH, JODY, SANCHO! YOU'VE OUTDONE YOURSELVES! LOOK AT HIM! LOOK AT HIS LITTLE PEOPLE HANDS! WE'VE NEVER HAD HIS LIKE BEFORE!
OH, SWEET BABY, WHAT A CUTIE PIE, I WISH I COULD JUST KEEP YOU ALL FOR MY OWN--
NOW, NOW, WHAT A WASTE THAT WOULD BE.
DRUGGED OR NOT DRUGGED?
FLATLANDS SPECIAL.
SHOULD BE WEARING OFF.
OH, WHAT A SHAME IT WOULD BE TO DRUG HIM! DON'T YOU WANT TO SEE HOW HE'LL REACT?
PROBABLY LIKE THE OTHERS. WELL.
YOU'LL NEVER KNOW--

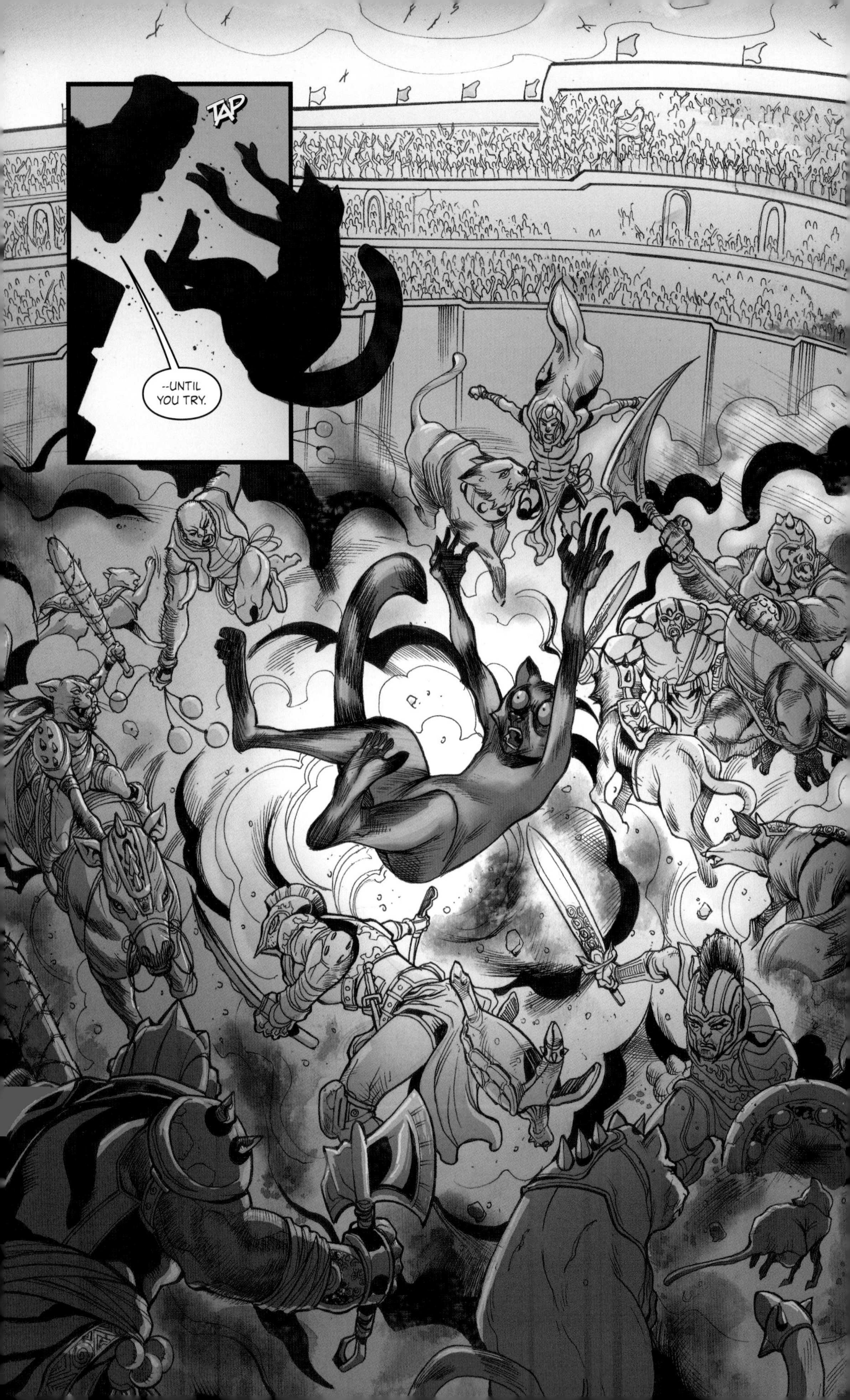
TAP
--UNTIL YOU TRY.

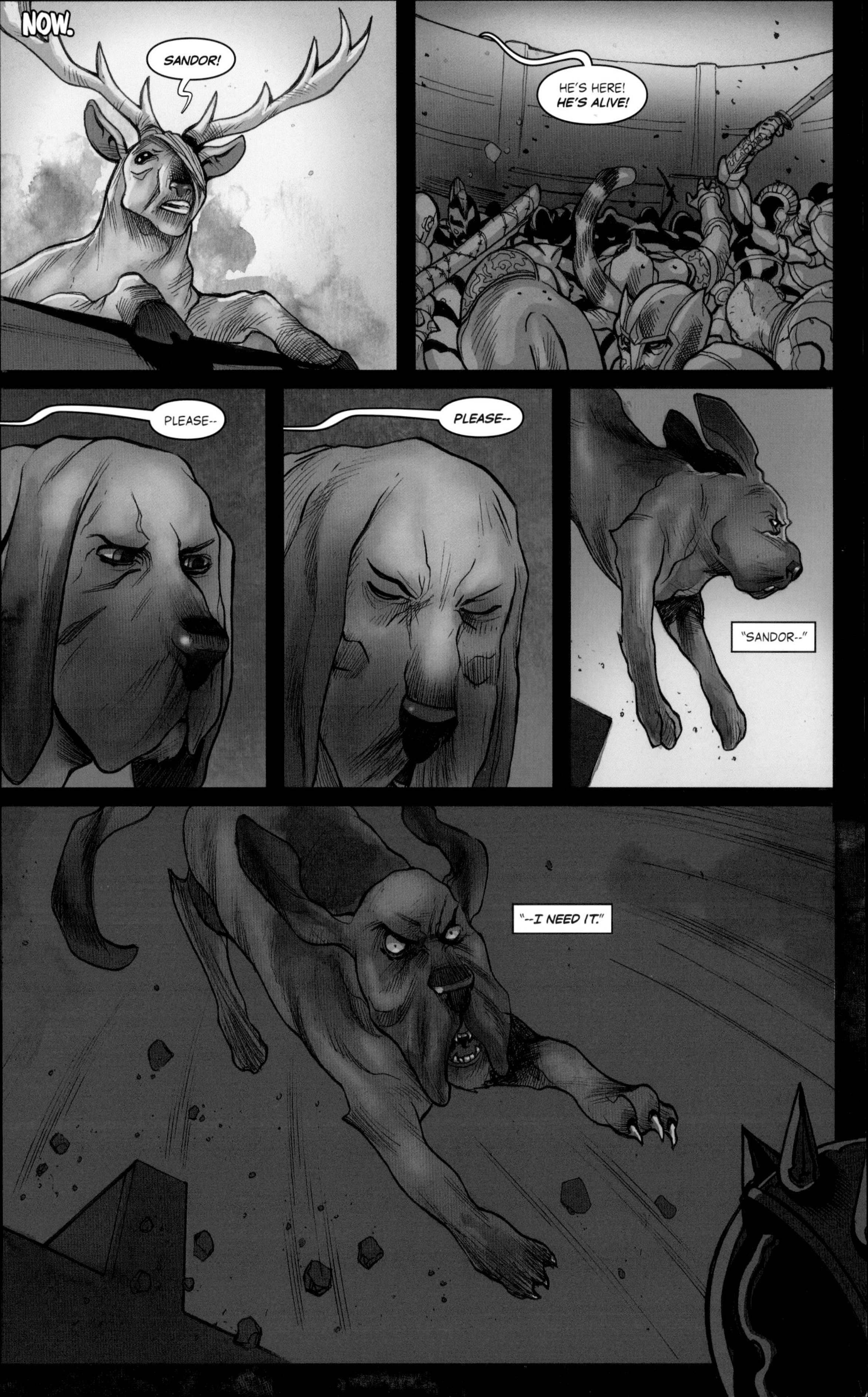
NOW.
SANDOR!
HE'S HERE! HE'S ALIVE!
PLEASE--
PLEASE--
"SANDOR--"
"--I NEED IT."

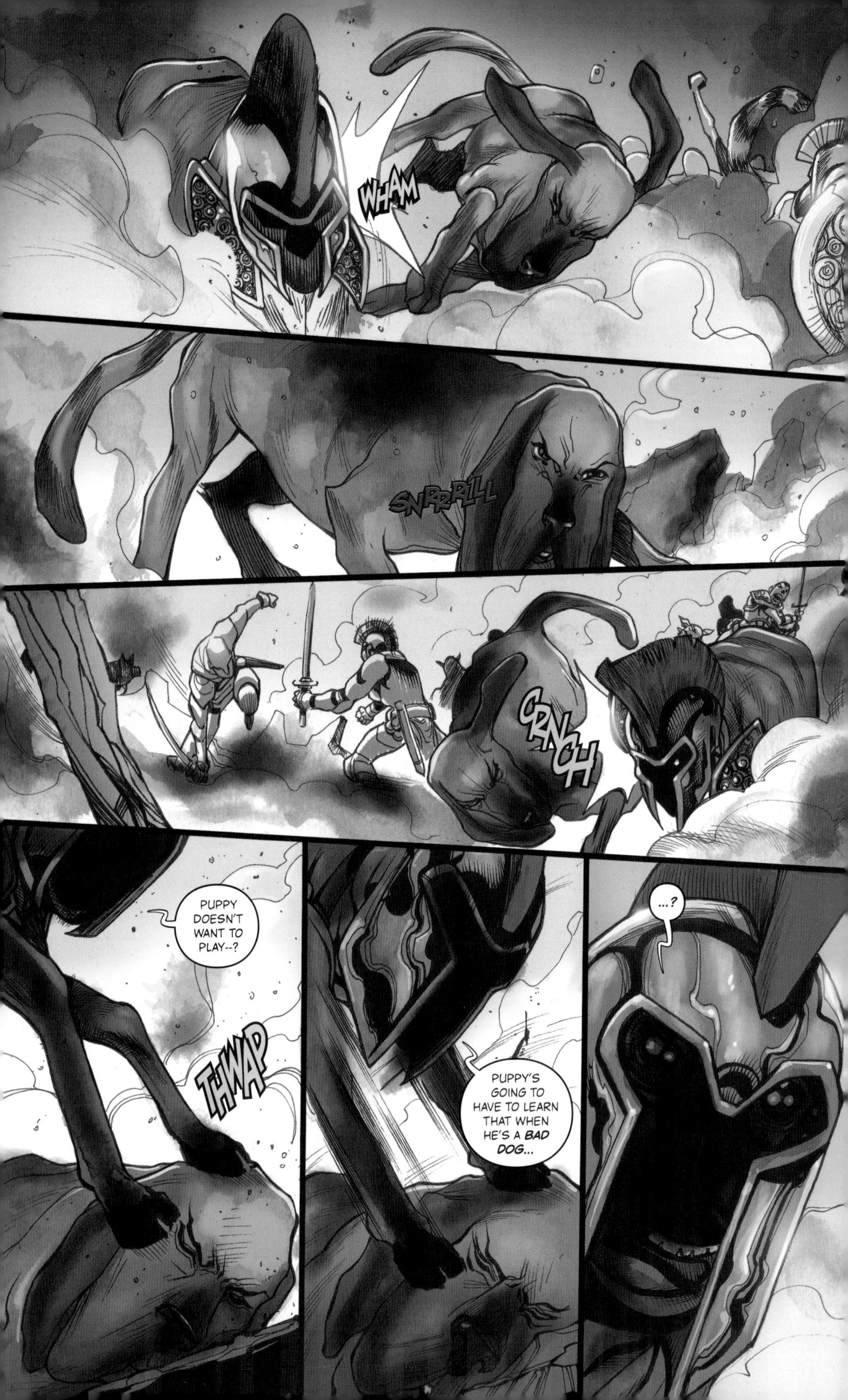
WHAM
SNRRRLLL
CRNCH
PUPPY DOESN'T WANT TO PLAY--?
THWAP
PUPPY'S GOING TO HAVE TO LEARN THAT WHEN HE'S A *BAD DOG*...
...?

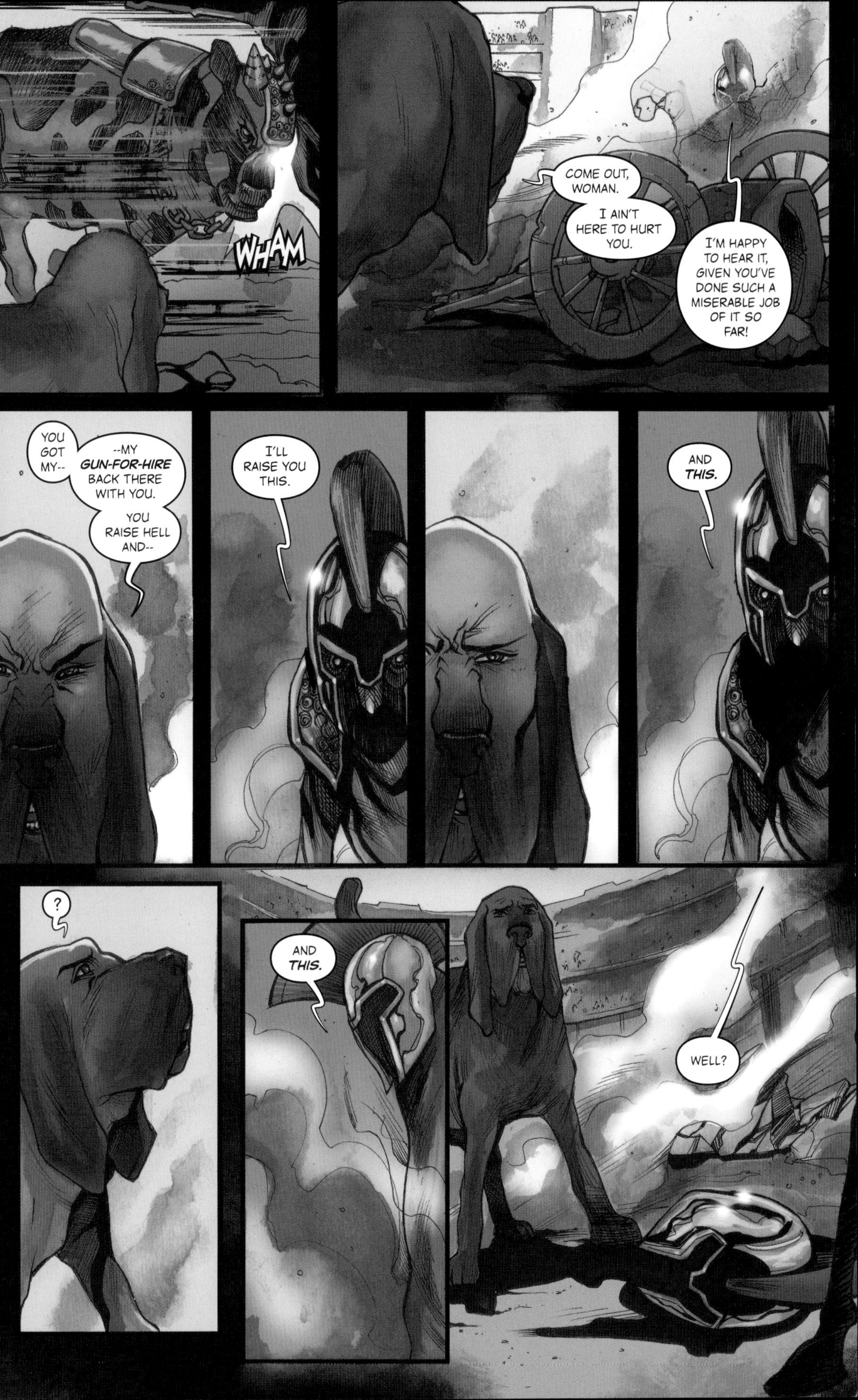
WHAM
COME OUT, WOMAN.
I AIN'T HERE TO HURT YOU.
I'M HAPPY TO HEAR IT, GIVEN YOU'VE DONE SUCH A MISERABLE JOB OF IT SO FAR!
YOU GOT MY--
--MY GUN-FOR-HIRE BACK THERE WITH YOU.
YOU RAISE HELL AND--
I'LL RAISE YOU THIS.
AND THIS.
?
AND THIS.
WELL?

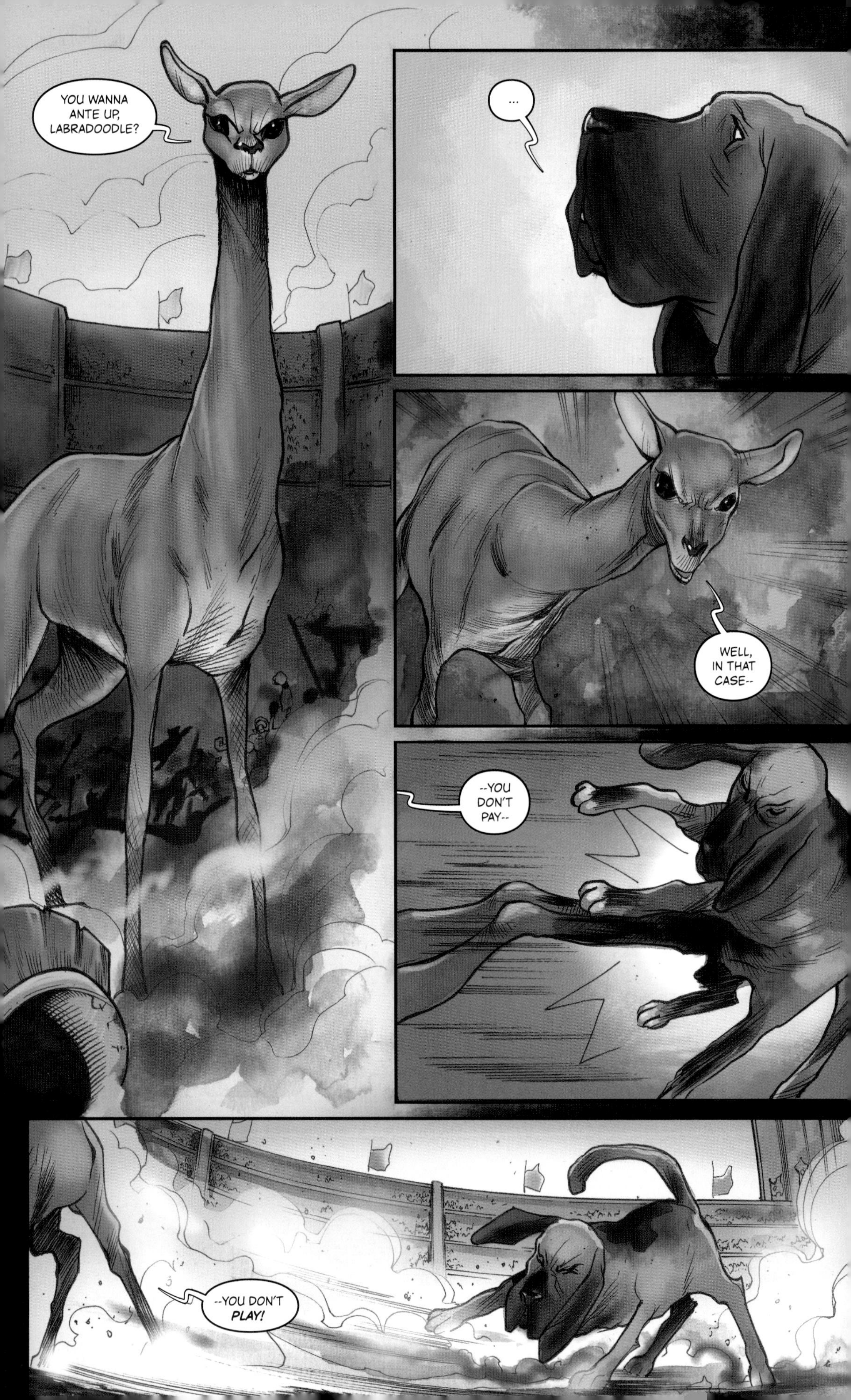
YOU WANNA ANTE UP, LABRADOODLE?
...
WELL, IN THAT CASE--
--YOU DON'T PAY--
--YOU DON'T PLAY!

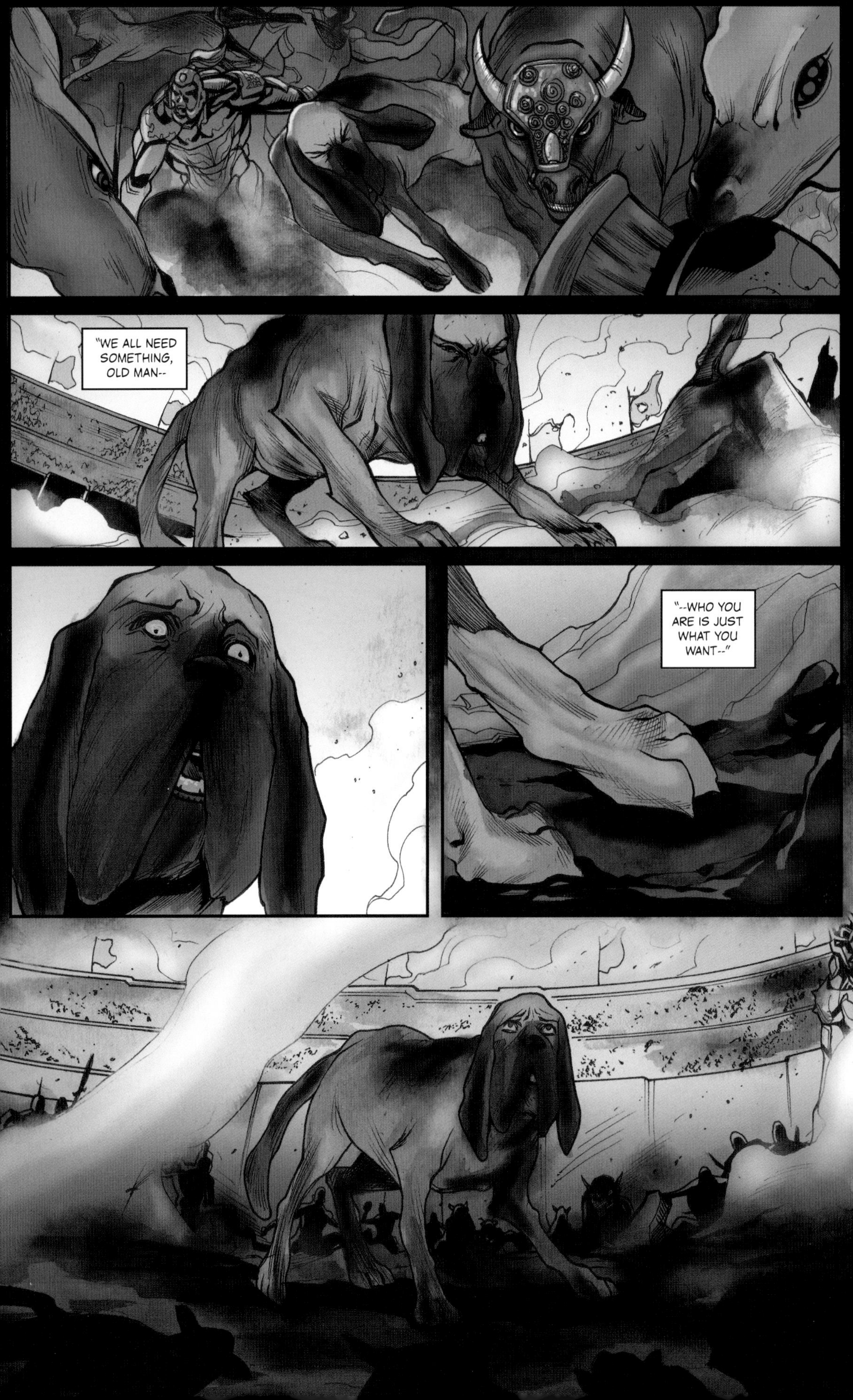
"WE ALL NEED SOMETHING, OLD MAN--
"--WHO YOU ARE IS JUST WHAT YOU WANT--"

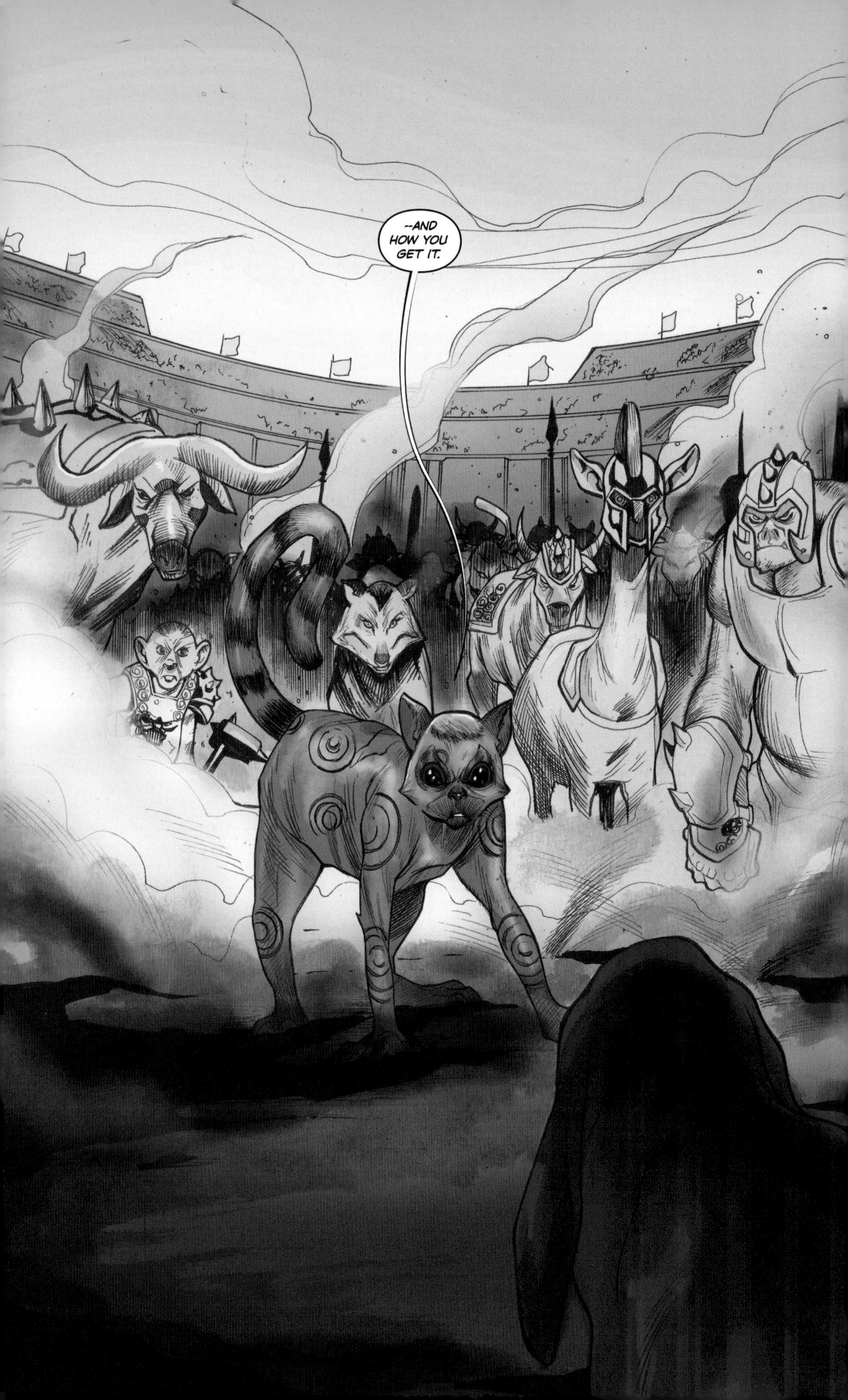
--AND HOW YOU GET IT.

26

KING OF TEXAS, PART TWO

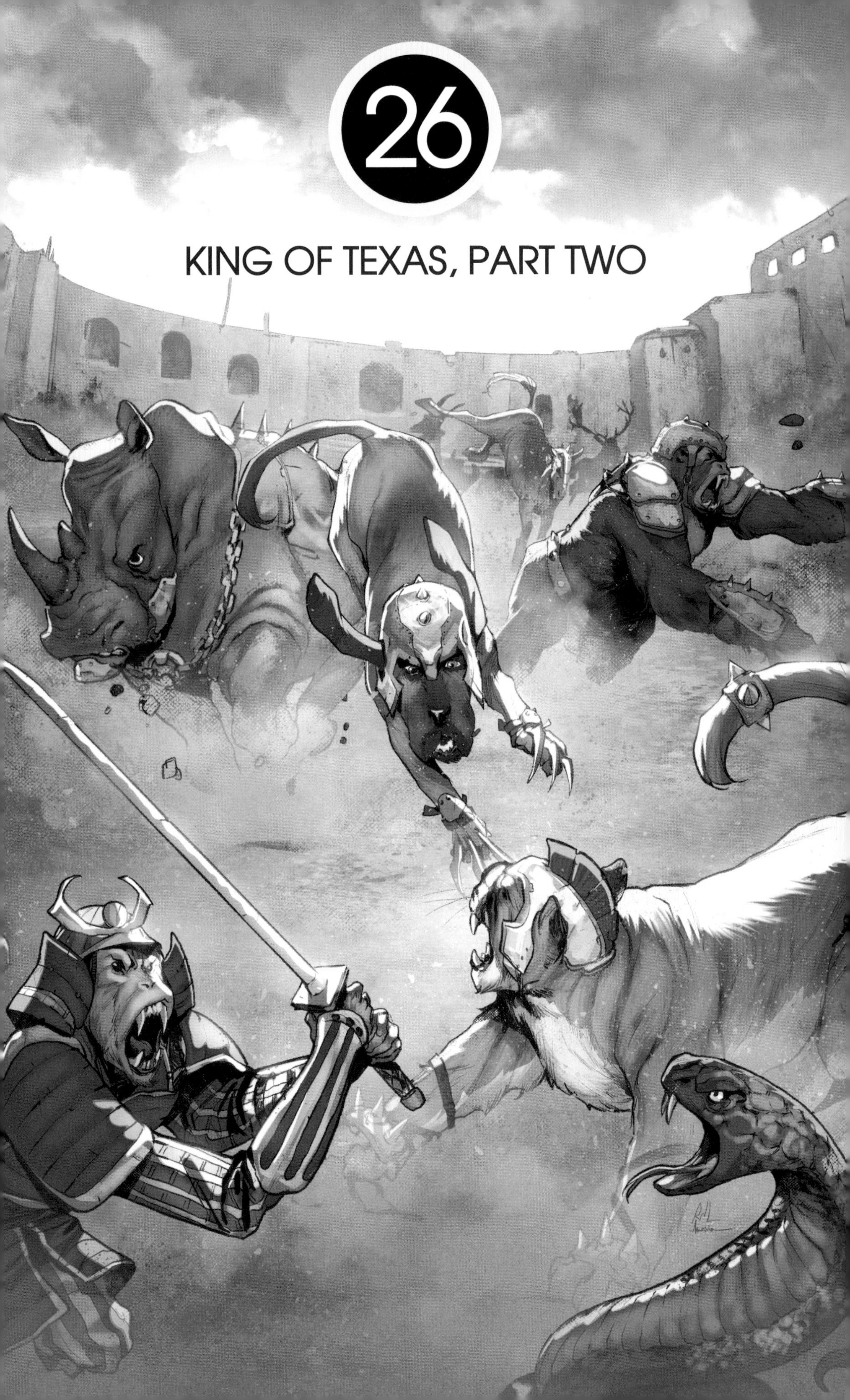

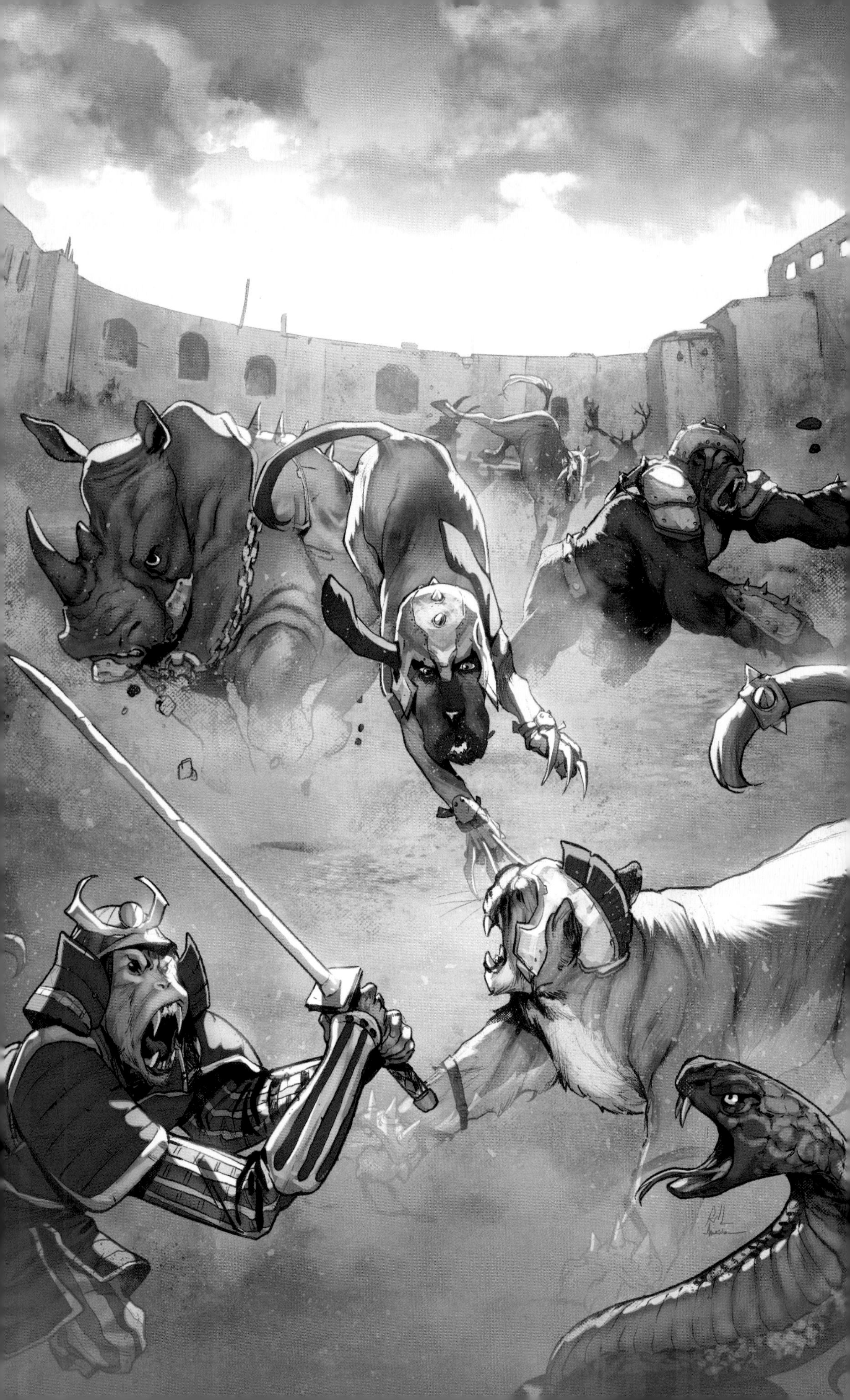

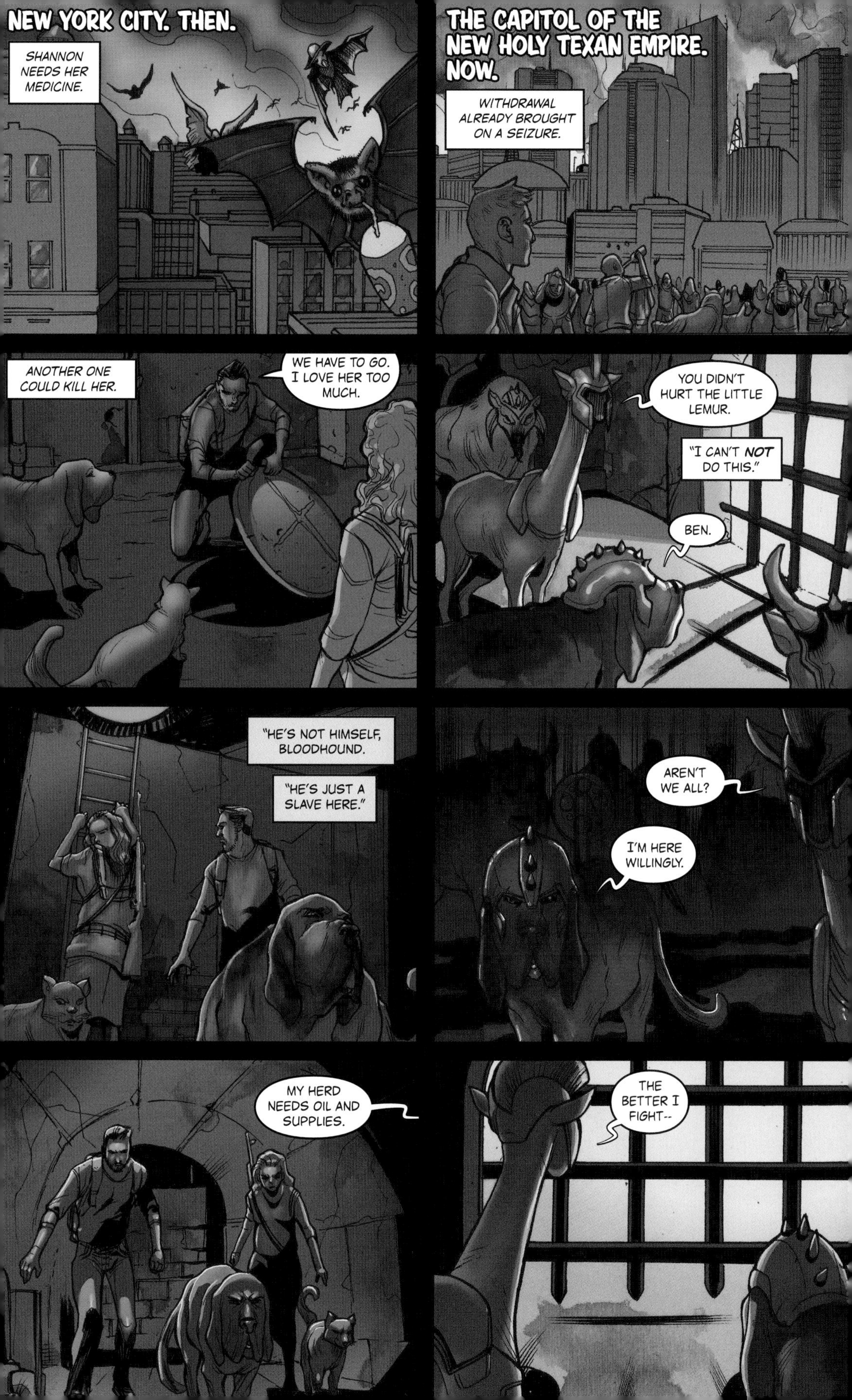
NEW YORK CITY. THEN.
SHANNON NEEDS HER MEDICINE.
THE CAPITOL OF THE NEW HOLY TEXAN EMPIRE. NOW.
WITHDRAWAL ALREADY BROUGHT ON A SEIZURE.
ANOTHER ONE COULD KILL HER.
WE HAVE TO GO. I LOVE HER TOO MUCH.
YOU DIDN'T HURT THE LITTLE LEMUR.
"I CAN'T NOT DO THIS."
BEN.
"HE'S NOT HIMSELF, BLOODHOUND.
"HE'S JUST A SLAVE HERE."
AREN'T WE ALL?
I'M HERE WILLINGLY.
MY HERD NEEDS OIL AND SUPPLIES.
THE BETTER I FIGHT--

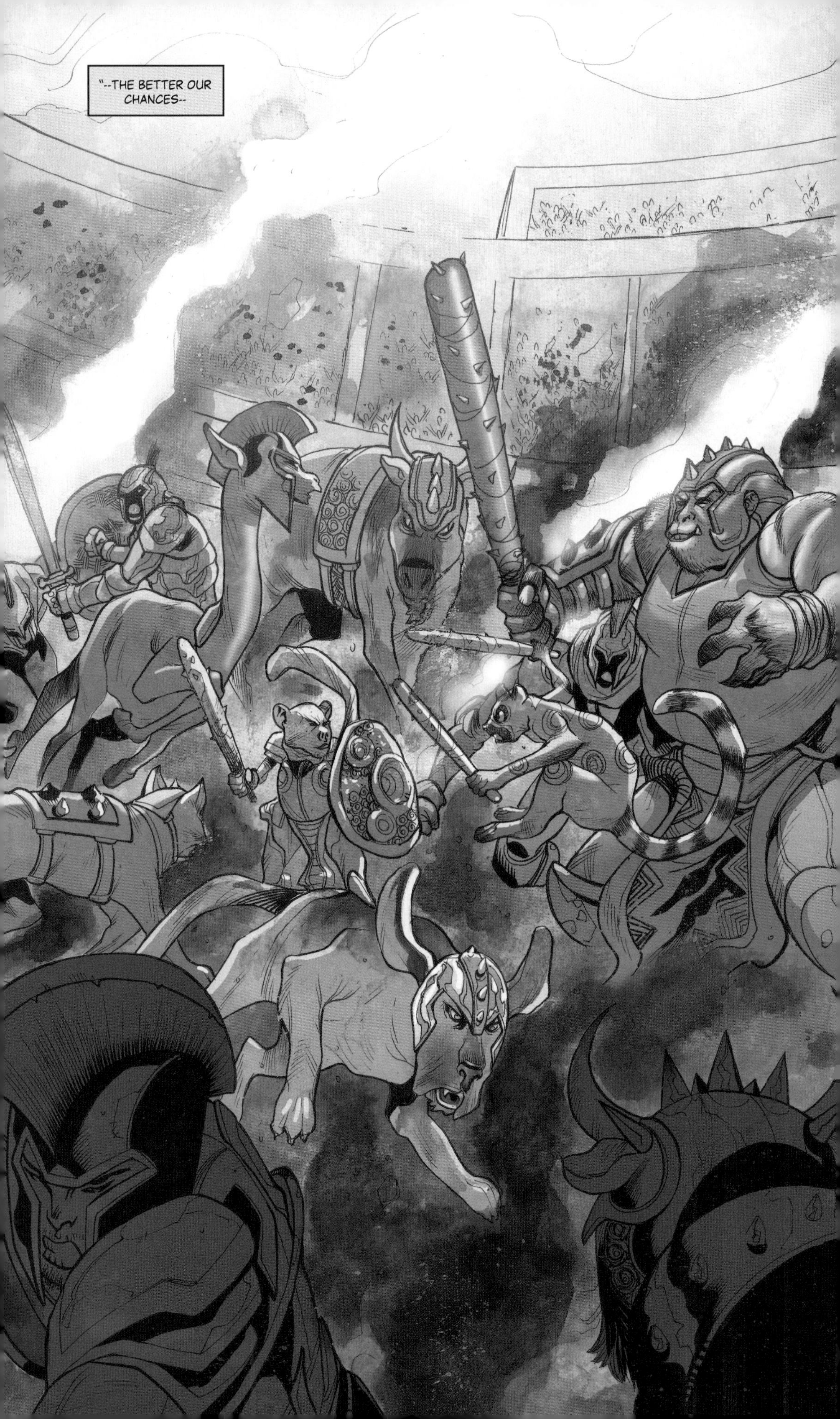
"--THE BETTER OUR CHANCES--

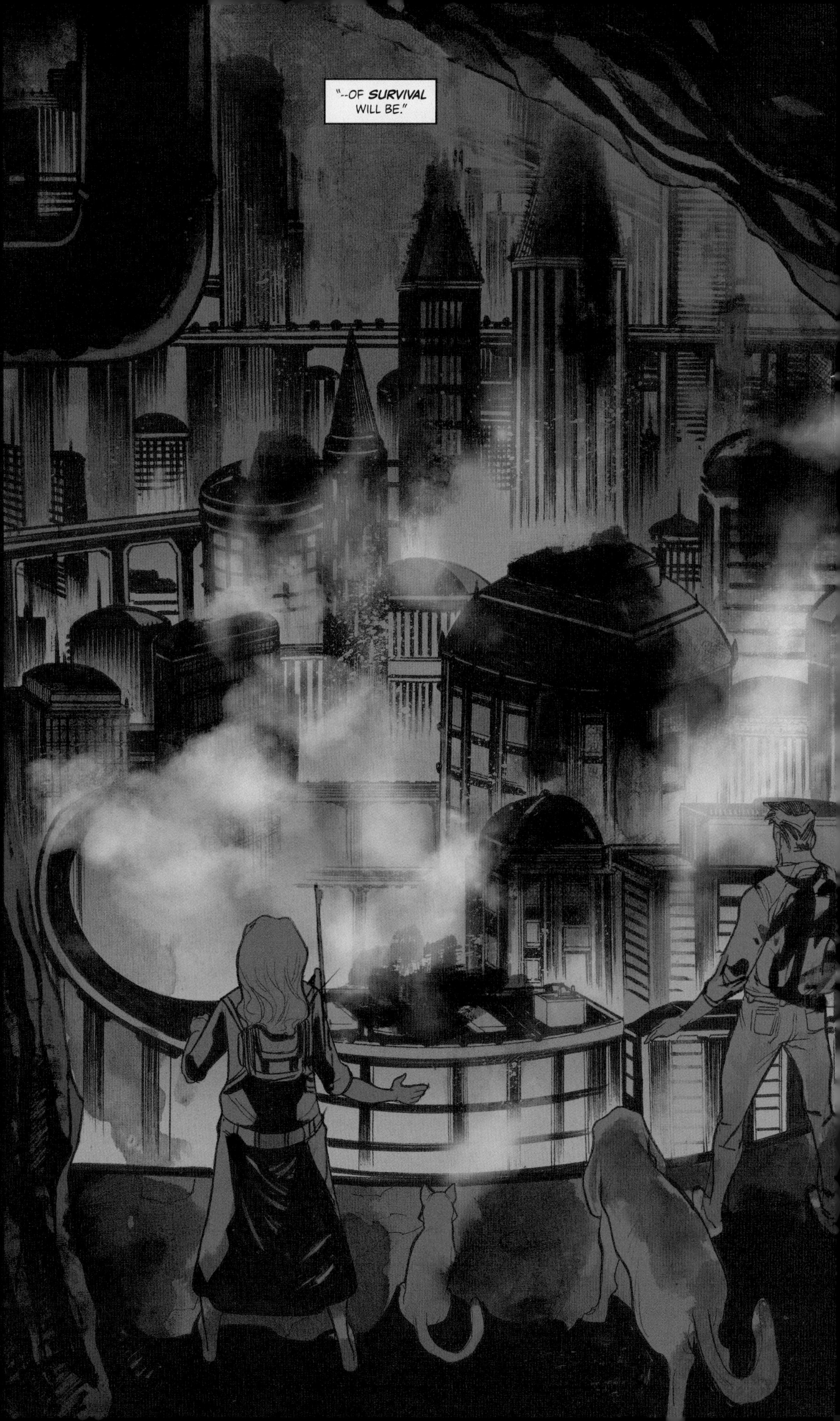
"--OF SURVIVAL
WILL BE."

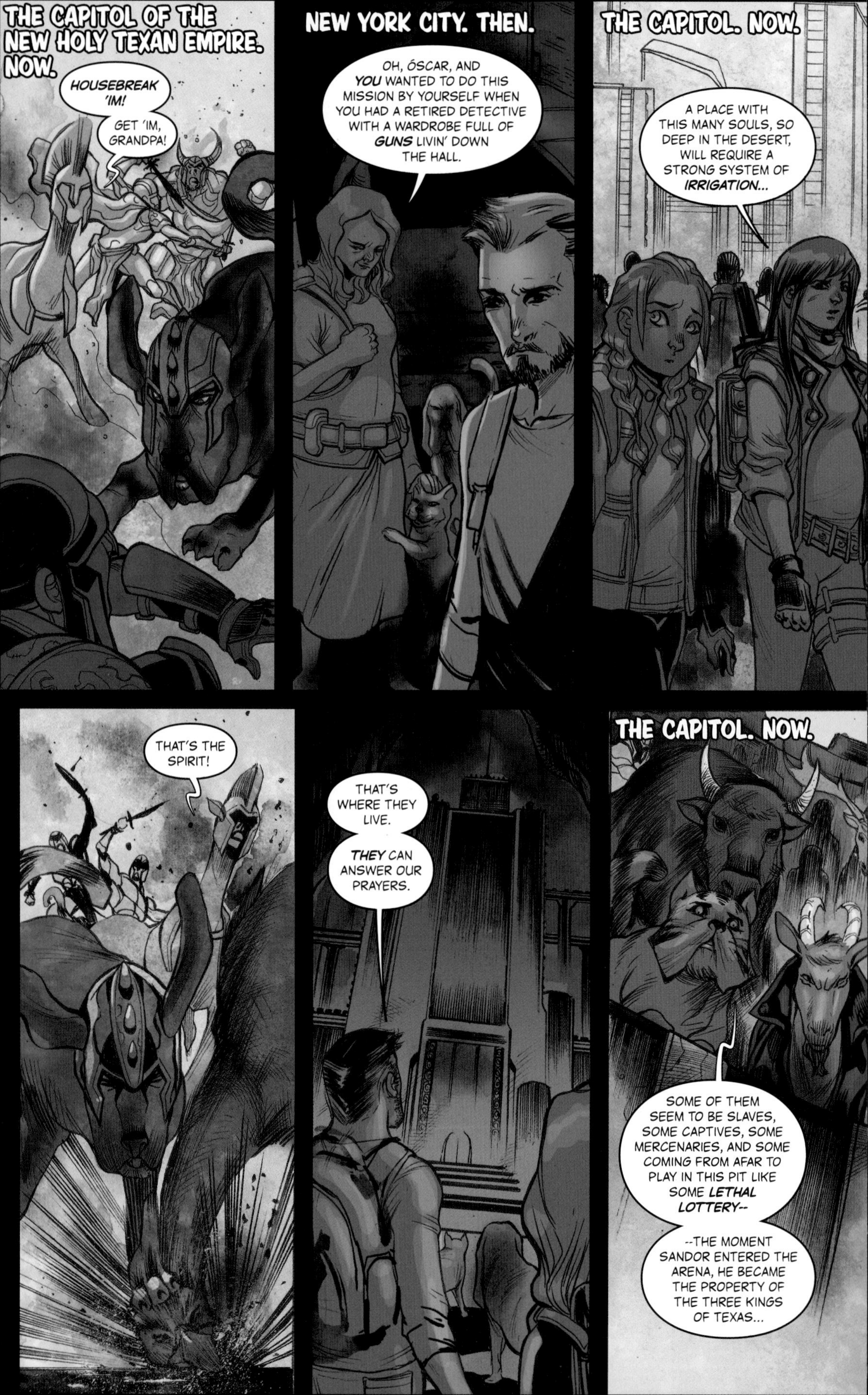
THE CAPITOL OF THE NEW HOLY TEXAN EMPIRE. NOW.
HOUSEBREAK 'IM!
GET 'IM, GRANDPA!
NEW YORK CITY. THEN.
OH, ÓSCAR, AND YOU WANTED TO DO THIS MISSION BY YOURSELF WHEN YOU HAD A RETIRED DETECTIVE WITH A WARDROBE FULL OF GUNS LIVIN' DOWN THE HALL.
THE CAPITOL. NOW.
A PLACE WITH THIS MANY SOULS, SO DEEP IN THE DESERT, WILL REQUIRE A STRONG SYSTEM OF IRRIGATION...
THAT'S THE SPIRIT!
THAT'S WHERE THEY LIVE.
THEY CAN ANSWER OUR PRAYERS.
THE CAPITOL. NOW.
SOME OF THEM SEEM TO BE SLAVES, SOME CAPTIVES, SOME MERCENARIES, AND SOME COMING FROM AFAR TO PLAY IN THIS PIT LIKE SOME LETHAL LOTTERY--
--THE MOMENT SANDOR ENTERED THE ARENA, HE BECAME THE PROPERTY OF THE THREE KINGS OF TEXAS...

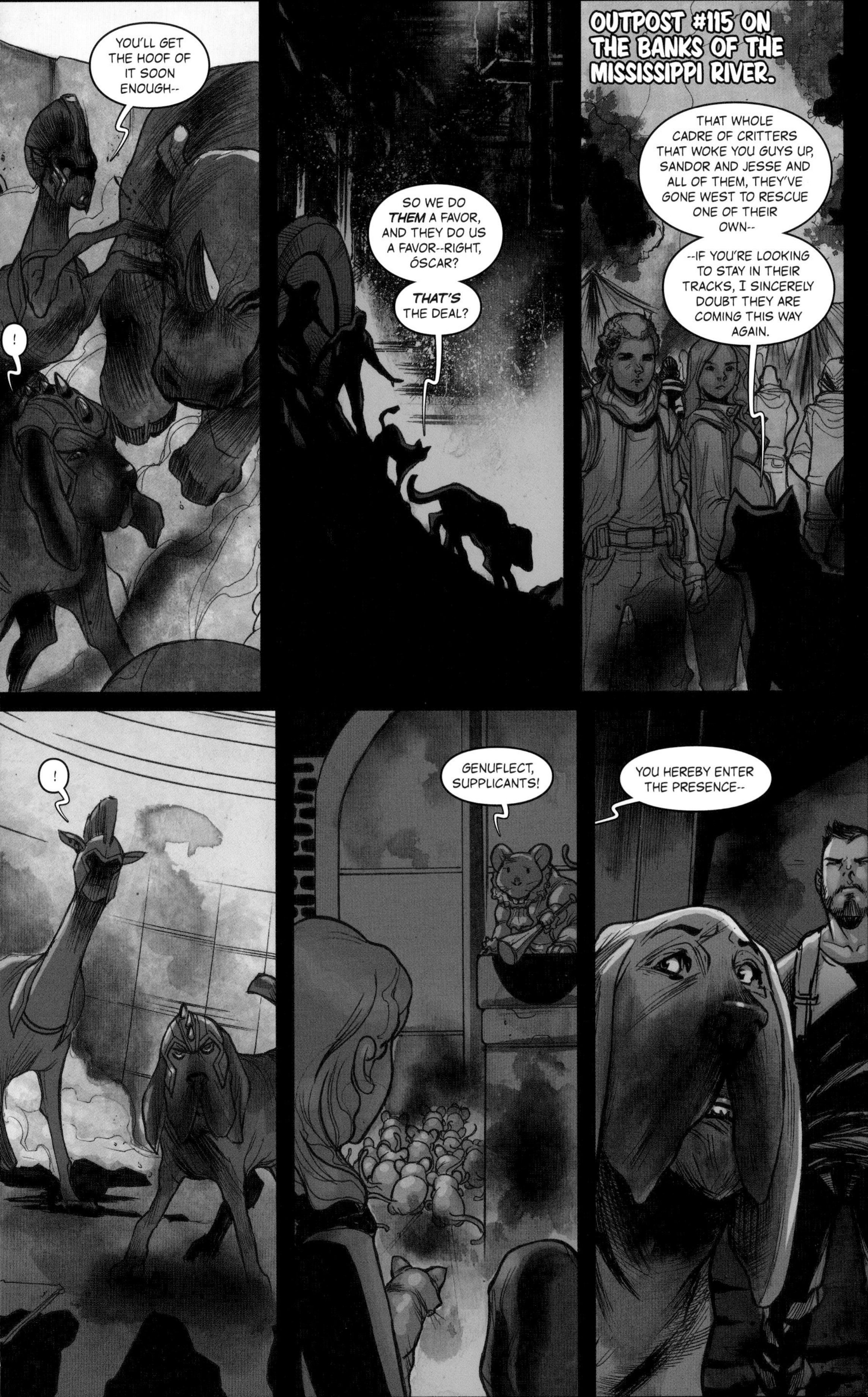
YOU'LL GET THE HOOF OF IT SOON ENOUGH--
!
SO WE DO THEM A FAVOR, AND THEY DO US A FAVOR--RIGHT, ÓSCAR?
THAT'S THE DEAL?
OUTPOST #115 ON THE BANKS OF THE MISSISSIPPI RIVER.
THAT WHOLE CADRE OF CRITTERS THAT WOKE YOU GUYS UP, SANDOR AND JESSE AND ALL OF THEM, THEY'VE GONE WEST TO RESCUE ONE OF THEIR OWN--
--IF YOU'RE LOOKING TO STAY IN THEIR TRACKS, I SINCERELY DOUBT THEY ARE COMING THIS WAY AGAIN.
!
GENUFLECT, SUPPLICANTS!
YOU HEREBY ENTER THE PRESENCE--

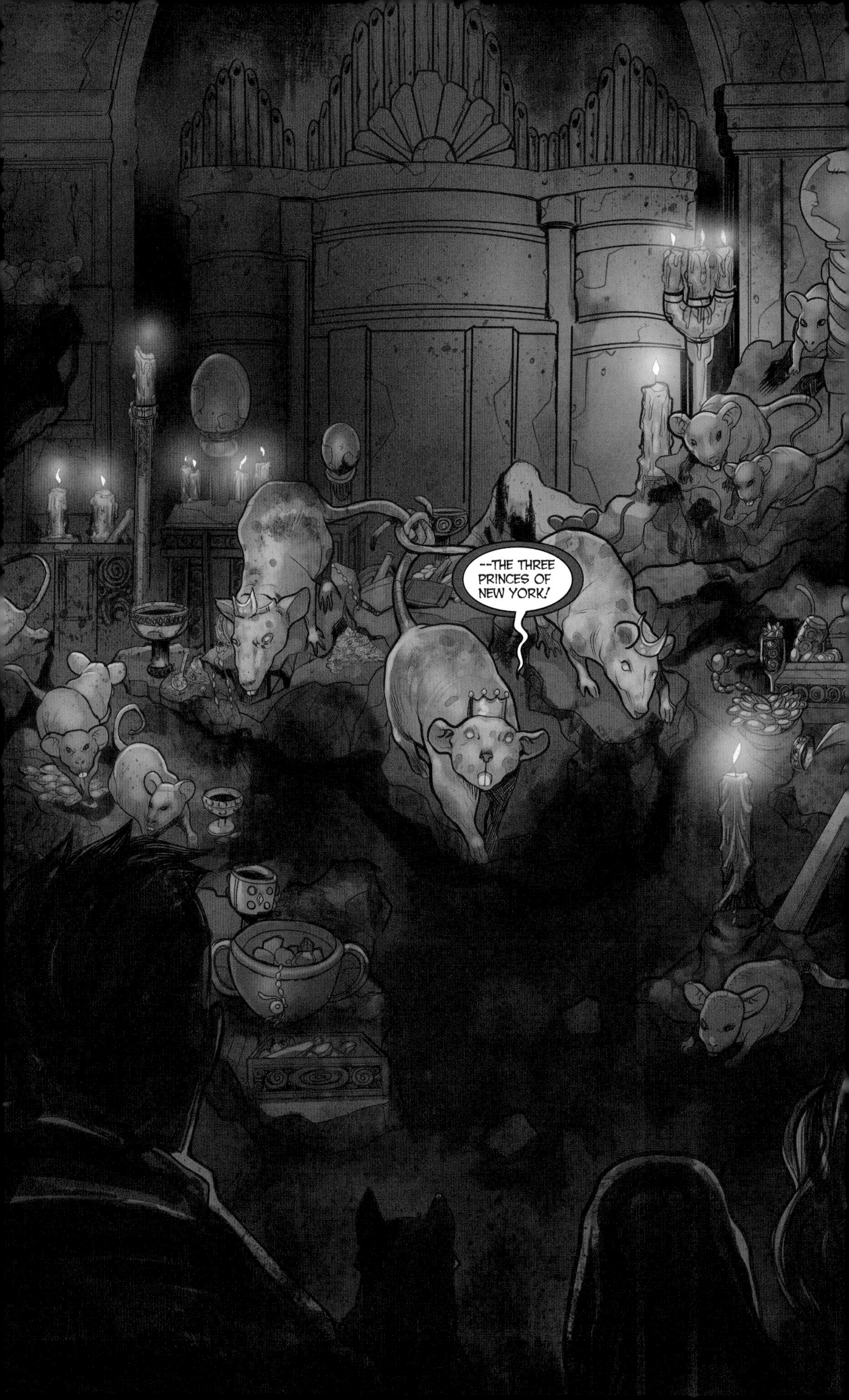
--THE THREE PRINCES OF NEW YORK!

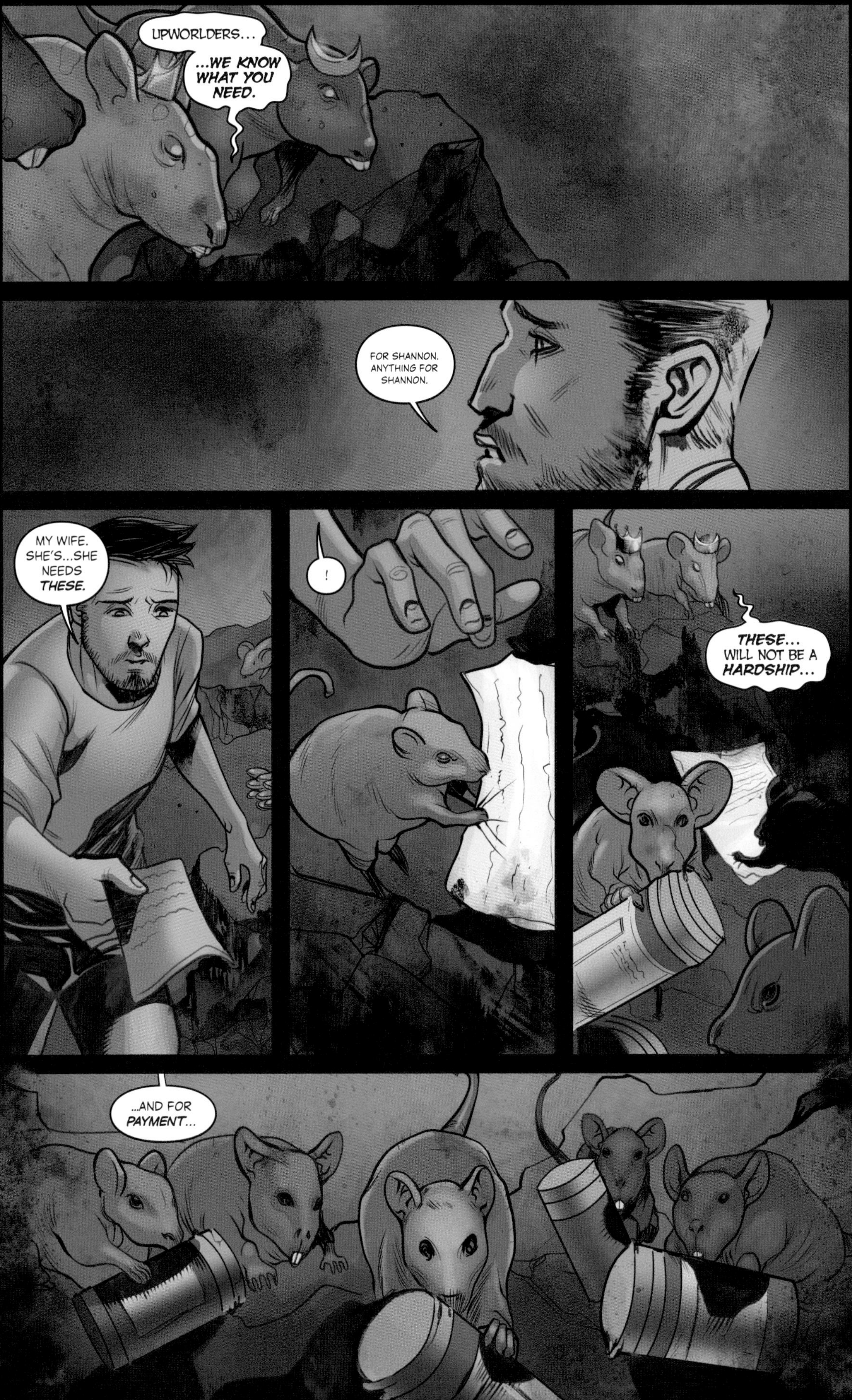
UPWORLDERS...
...WE KNOW WHAT YOU NEED.
FOR SHANNON. ANYTHING FOR SHANNON.
MY WIFE. SHE'S...SHE NEEDS THESE.
!
THESE... WILL NOT BE A HARDSHIP...
...AND FOR PAYMENT...

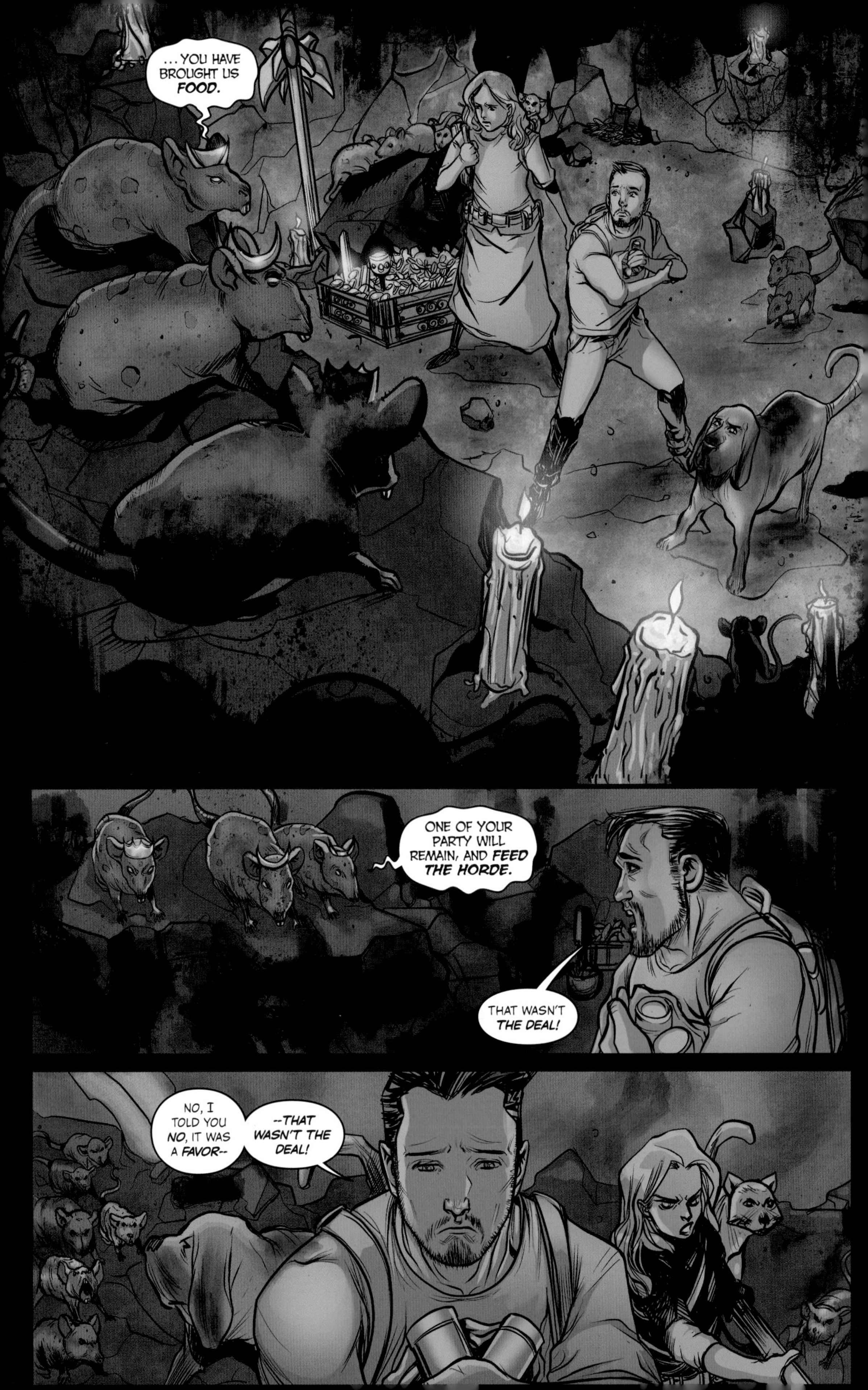
...YOU HAVE BROUGHT US FOOD.
ONE OF YOUR PARTY WILL REMAIN, AND FEED THE HORDE.
THAT WASN'T THE DEAL!
NO, I TOLD YOU NO, IT WAS A FAVOR--
--THAT WASN'T THE DEAL!

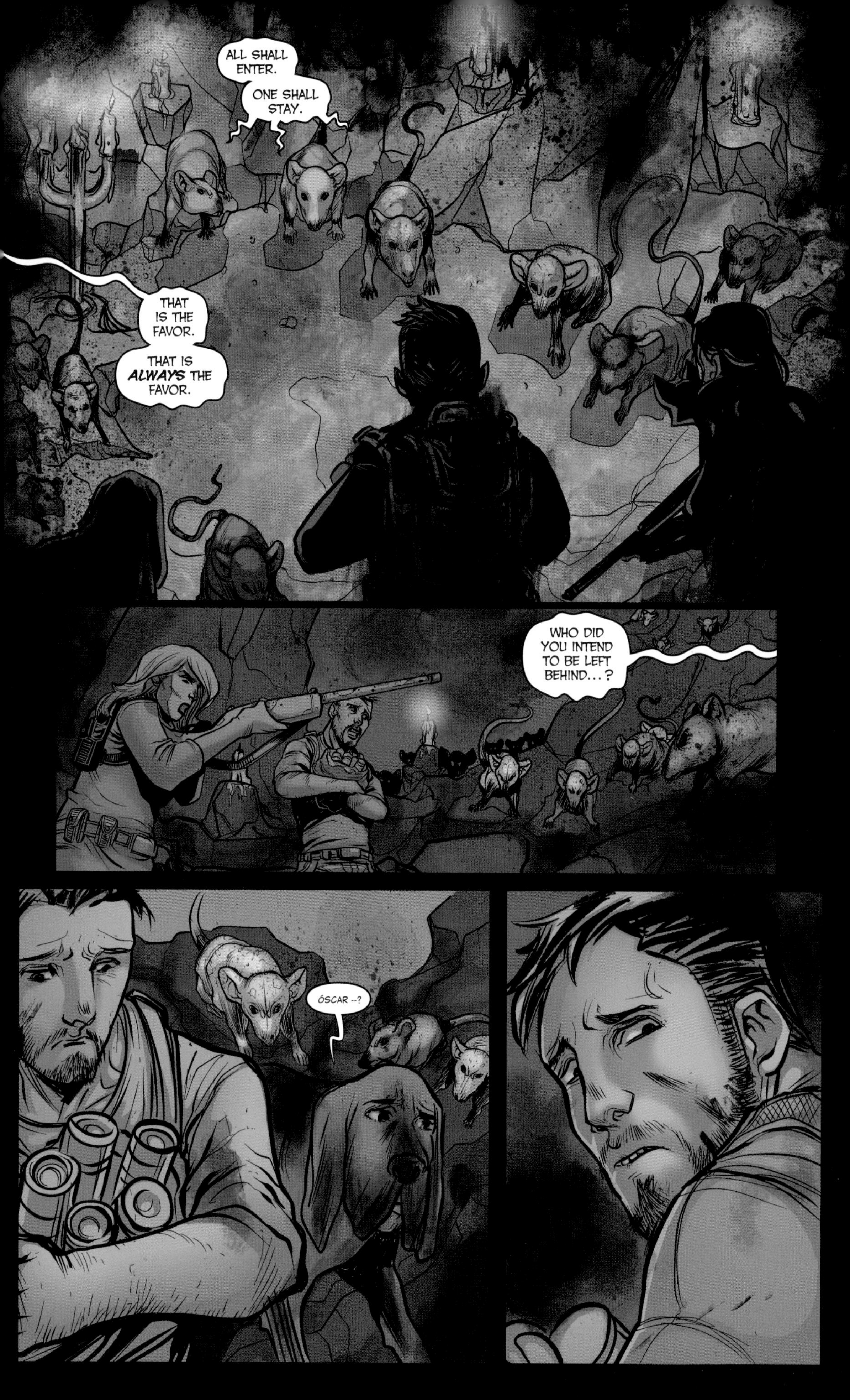
ALL SHALL ENTER.
ONE SHALL STAY.
THAT IS THE FAVOR.
THAT IS *ALWAYS* THE FAVOR.
WHO DID YOU INTEND TO BE LEFT BEHIND...?
ÓSCAR --?

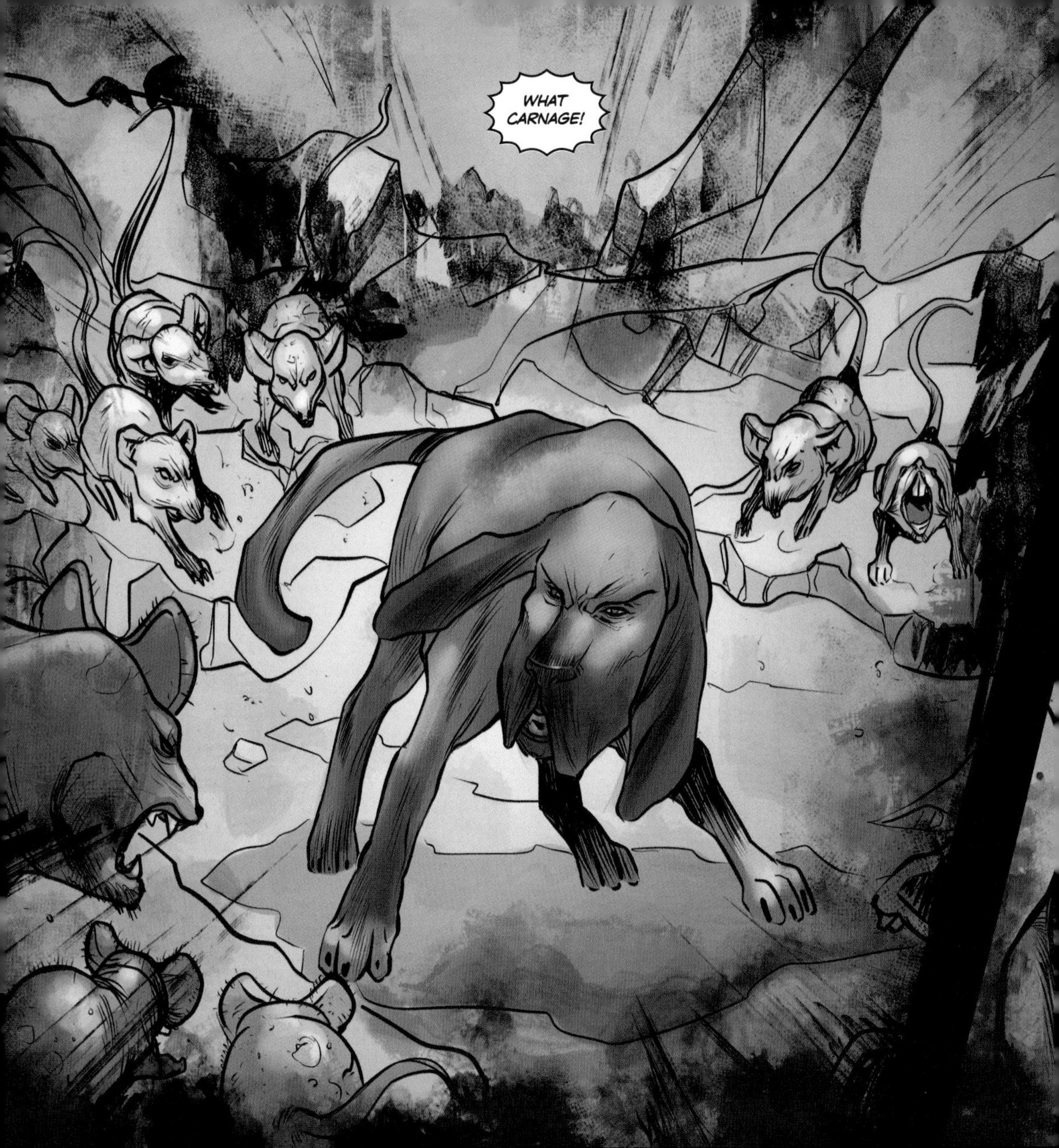
WHAT CARNAGE!

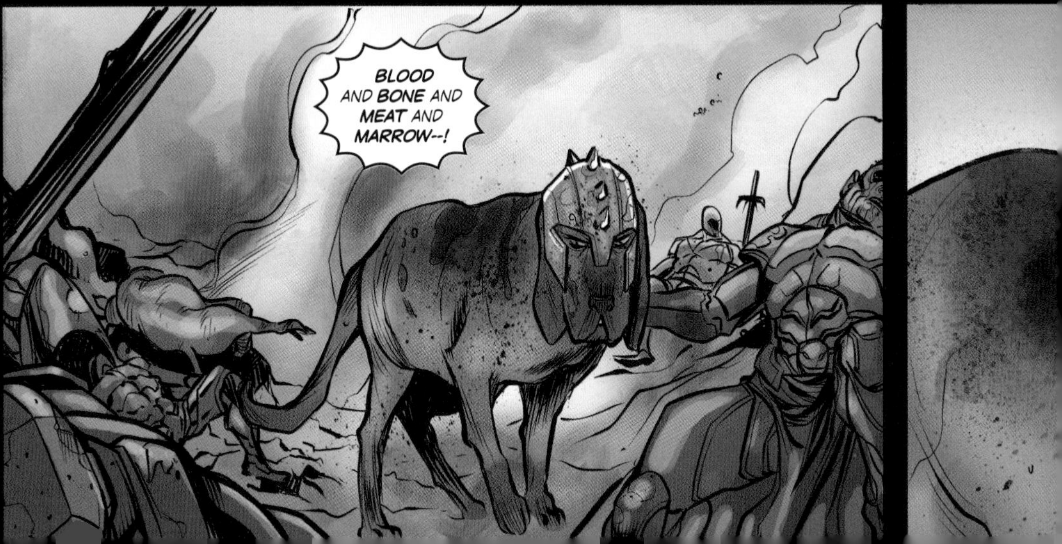
BLOOD AND BONE AND MEAT AND MARROW--!

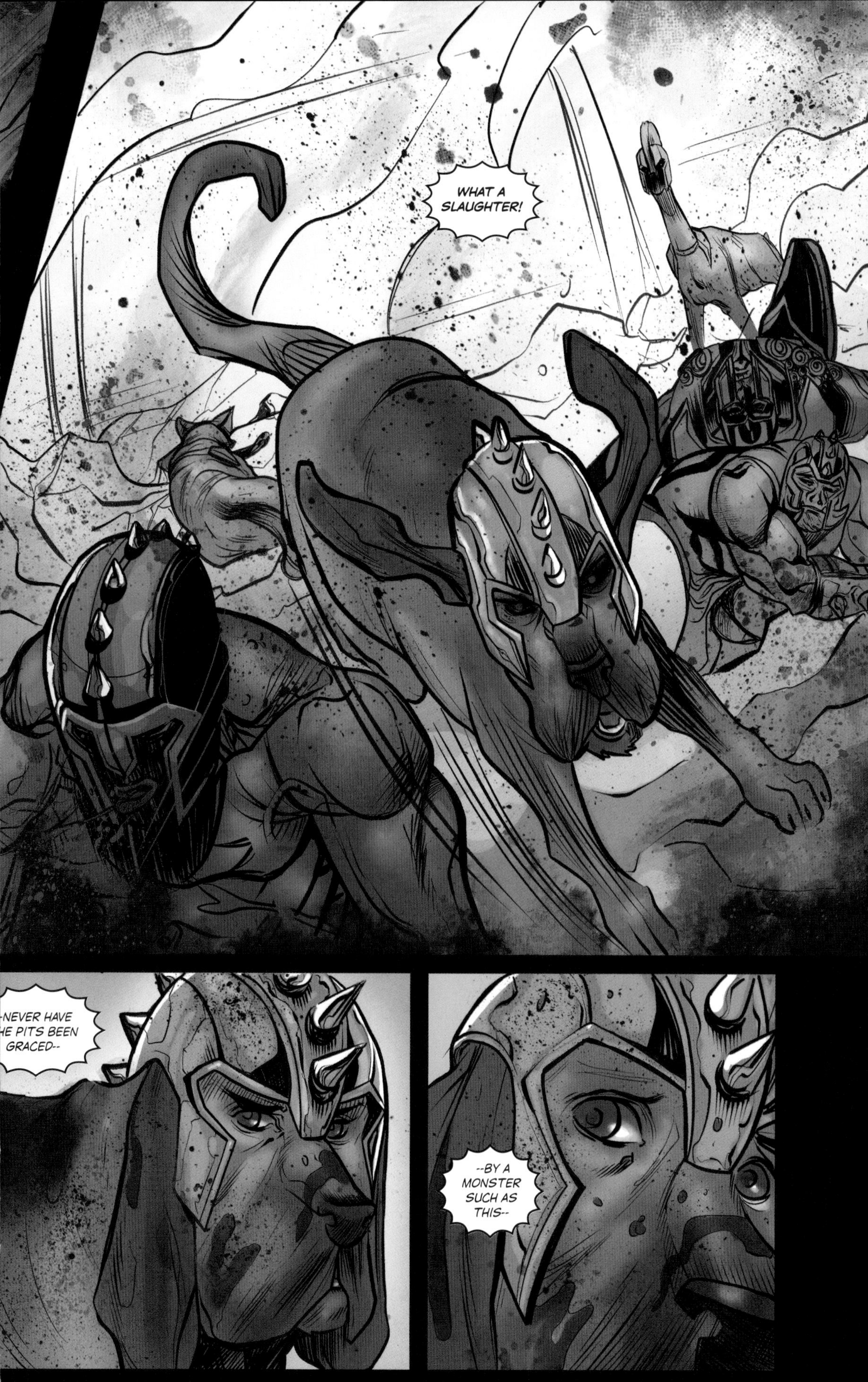
WHAT A SLAUGHTER!
-NEVER HAVE HE PITS BEEN GRACED--
--BY A MONSTER SUCH AS THIS--

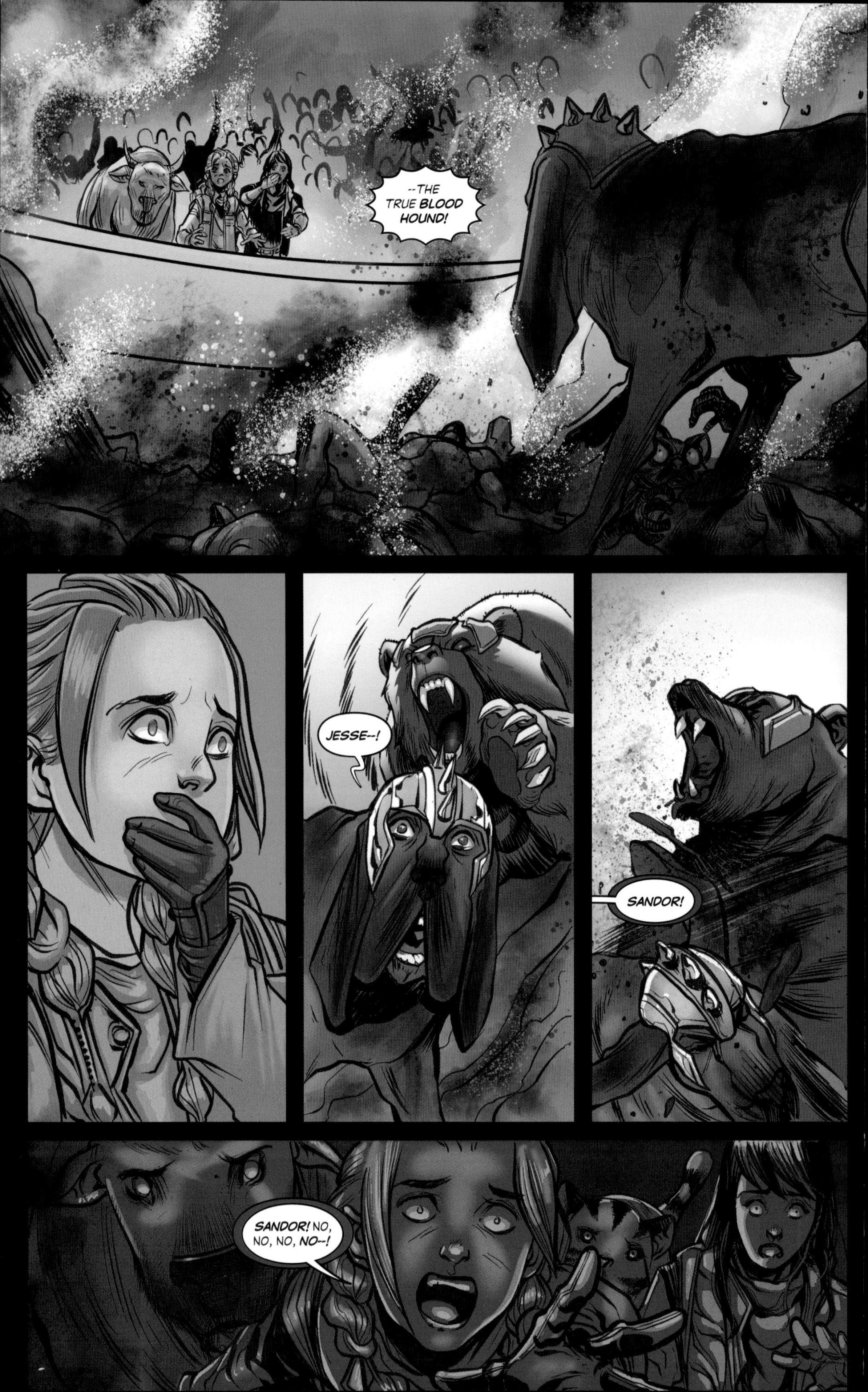
--THE TRUE BLOOD HOUND!
JESSE--!
SANDOR!
SANDOR! NO, NO, NO, NO--!

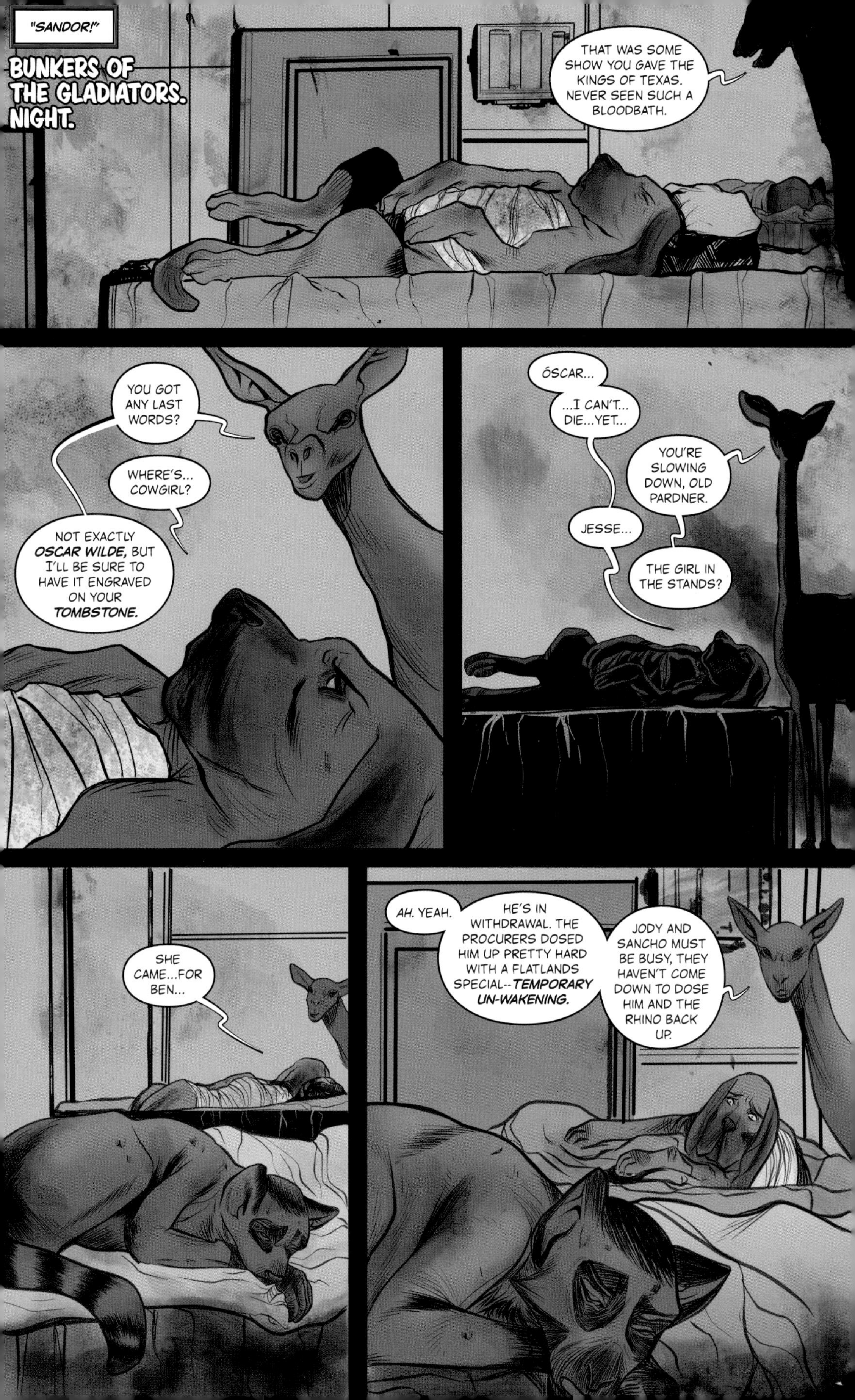
"SANDOR!"
BUNKERS OF THE GLADIATORS. NIGHT.
THAT WAS SOME SHOW YOU GAVE THE KINGS OF TEXAS. NEVER SEEN SUCH A BLOODBATH.
YOU GOT ANY LAST WORDS?
WHERE'S... COWGIRL?
NOT EXACTLY *OSCAR WILDE,* BUT I'LL BE SURE TO HAVE IT ENGRAVED ON YOUR *TOMBSTONE.*
ÓSCAR...
...I CAN'T... DIE...YET...
YOU'RE SLOWING DOWN, OLD PARDNER.
JESSE...
THE GIRL IN THE STANDS?
SHE CAME...FOR BEN...
AH. YEAH.
HE'S IN WITHDRAWAL. THE PROCURERS DOSED HIM UP PRETTY HARD WITH A FLATLANDS SPECIAL--*TEMPORARY UN-WAKENING.*
JODY AND SANCHO MUST BE BUSY, THEY HAVEN'T COME DOWN TO DOSE HIM AND THE RHINO BACK UP.

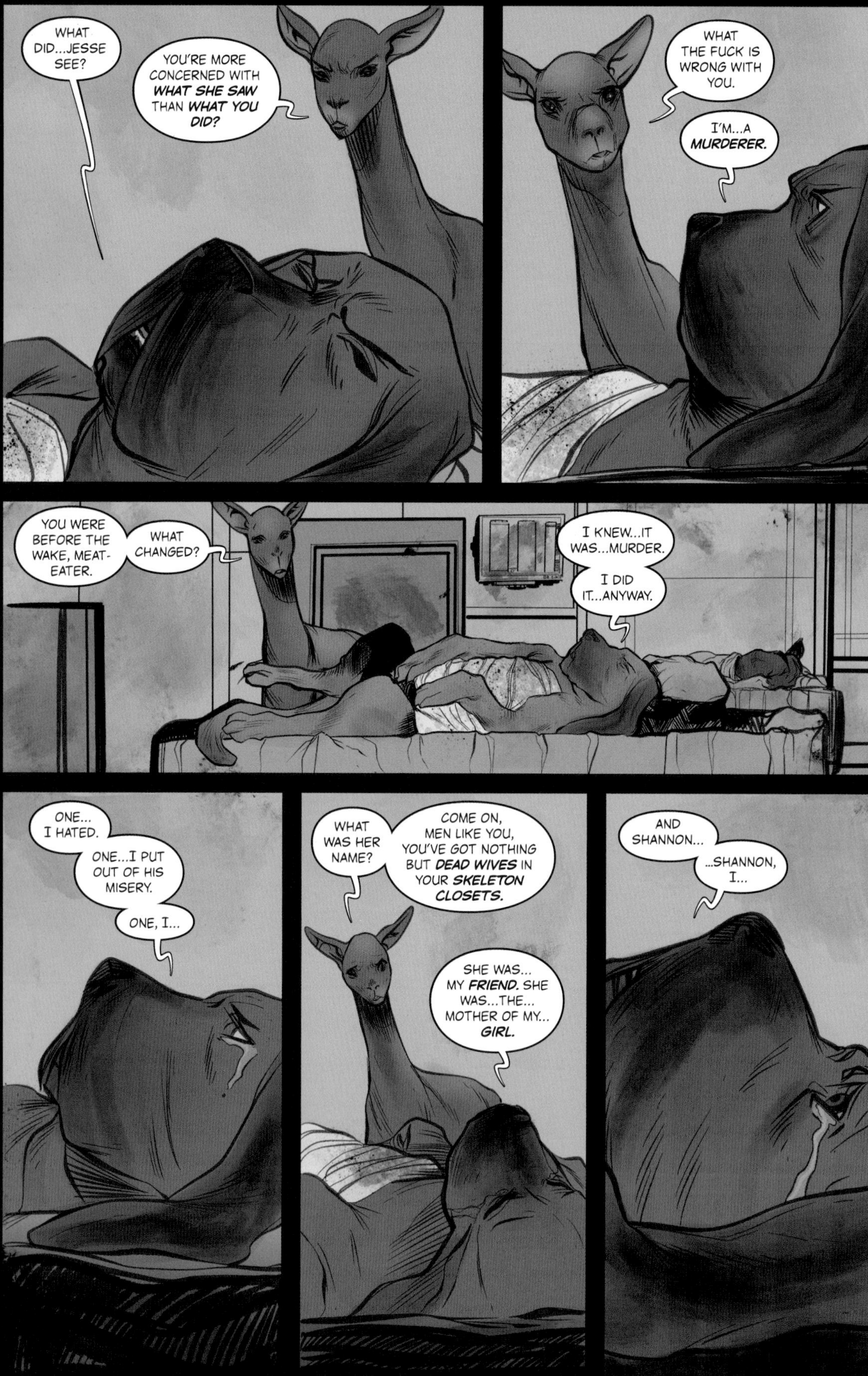
WHAT DID...JESSE SEE?
YOU'RE MORE CONCERNED WITH WHAT SHE SAW THAN WHAT YOU DID?
WHAT THE FUCK IS WRONG WITH YOU.
I'M...A MURDERER.
YOU WERE BEFORE THE WAKE, MEAT-EATER.
WHAT CHANGED?
I KNEW...IT WAS...MURDER.
I DID IT...ANYWAY.
ONE... I HATED.
ONE...I PUT OUT OF HIS MISERY.
ONE, I...
WHAT WAS HER NAME?
COME ON, MEN LIKE YOU, YOU'VE GOT NOTHING BUT DEAD WIVES IN YOUR SKELETON CLOSETS.
SHE WAS... MY FRIEND. SHE WAS...THE... MOTHER OF MY... GIRL.
AND SHANNON...
...SHANNON, I...

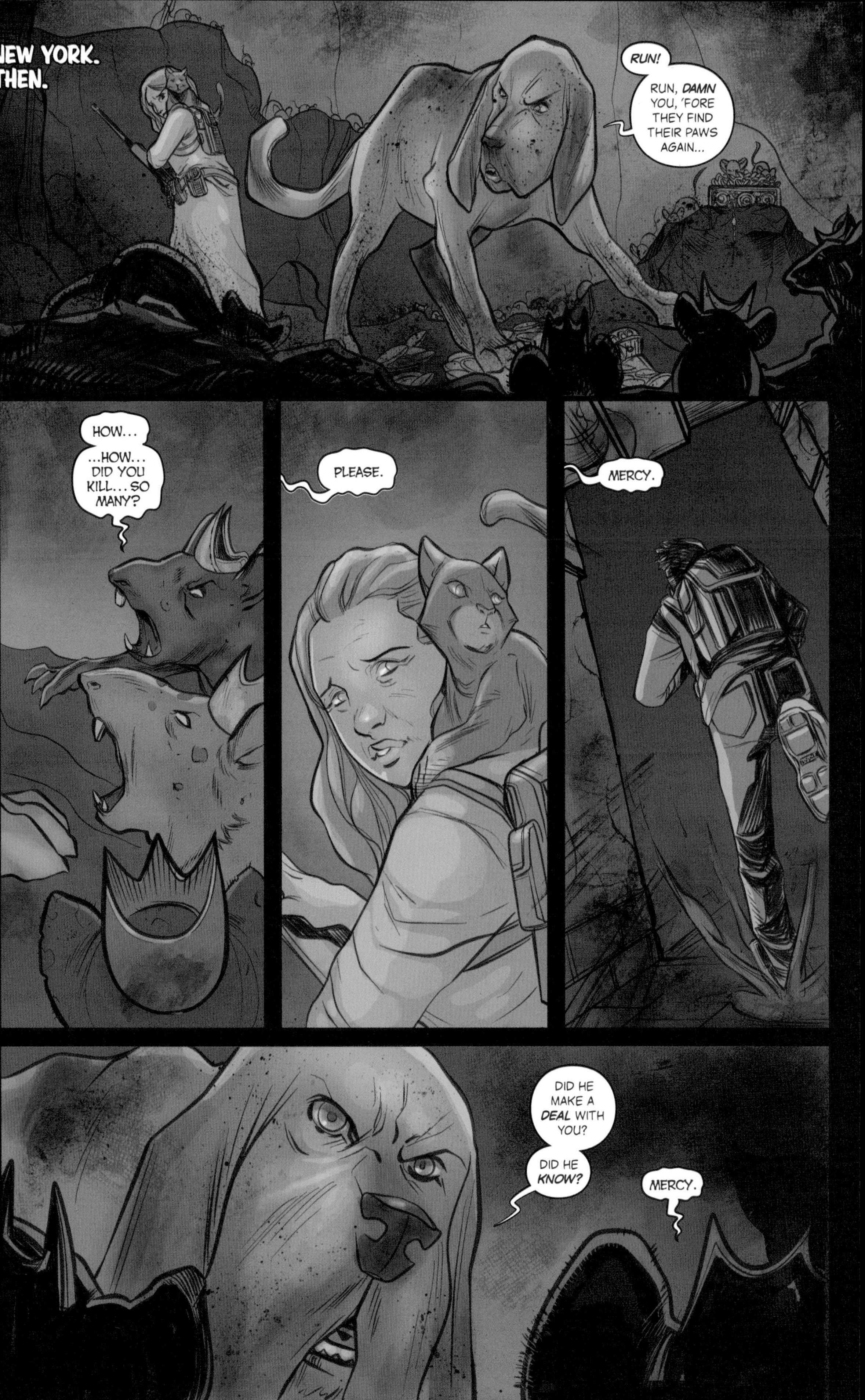
NEW YORK.
THEN.
RUN!
RUN, DAMN YOU, 'FORE THEY FIND THEIR PAWS AGAIN...
HOW...
...HOW... DID YOU KILL... SO MANY?
PLEASE.
MERCY.
DID HE MAKE A DEAL WITH YOU?
DID HE KNOW?
MERCY.

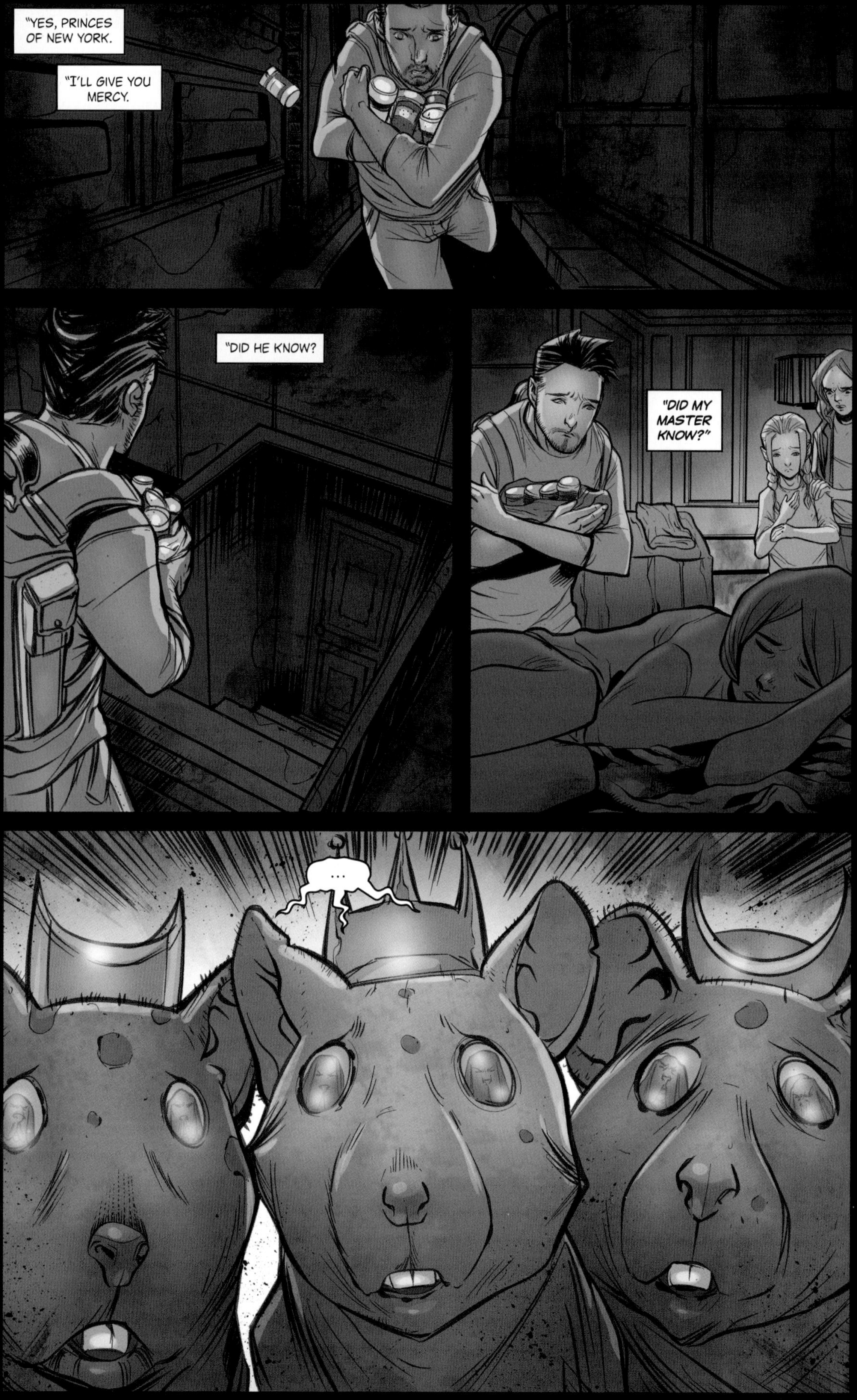
"YES, PRINCES OF NEW YORK.
"I'LL GIVE YOU MERCY.
"DID HE KNOW?
"DID MY MASTER KNOW?"
...

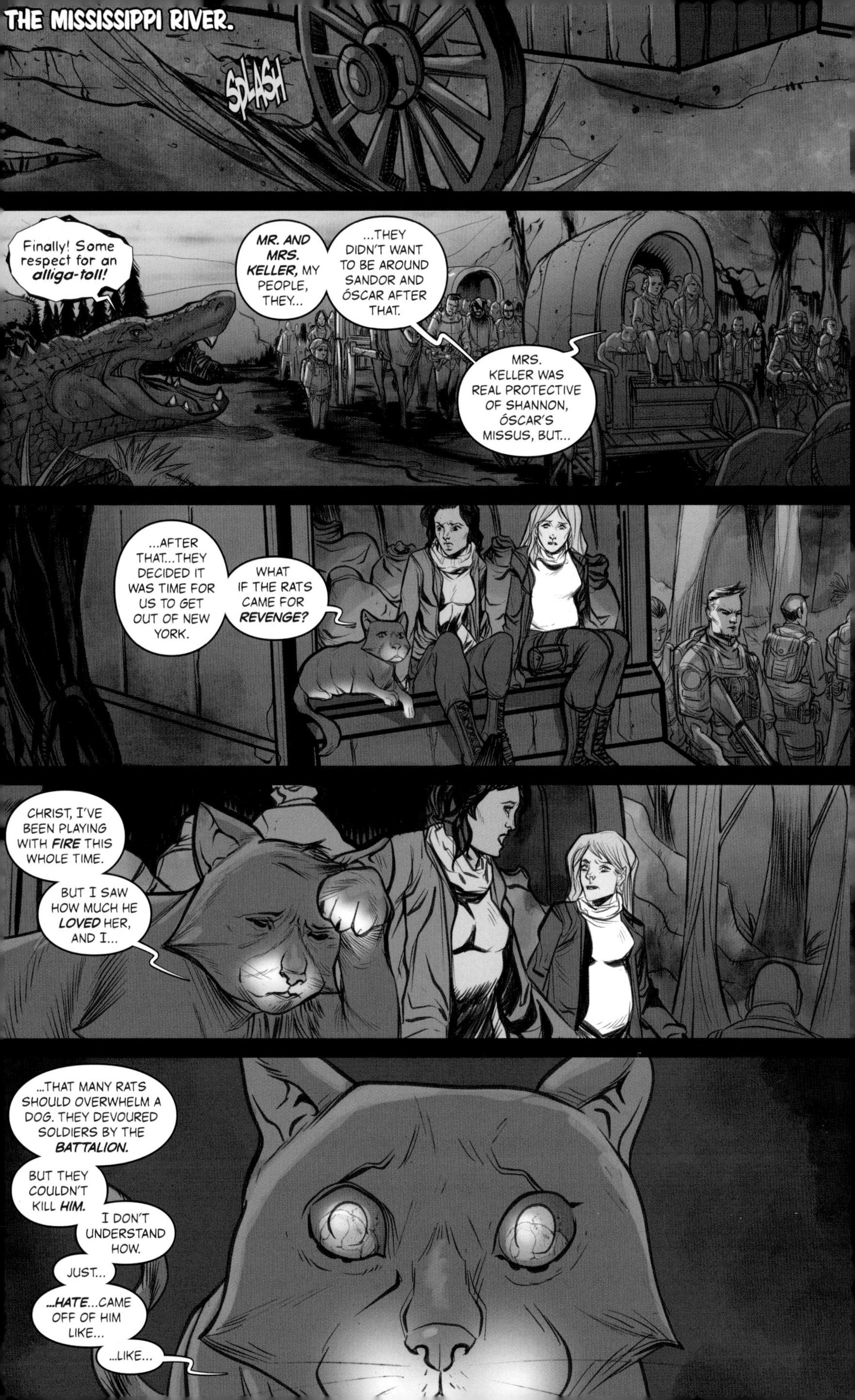
THE MISSISSIPPI RIVER.
SPLASH
Finally! Some respect for an alliga-toll!
MR. AND MRS. KELLER, MY PEOPLE, THEY...
...THEY DIDN'T WANT TO BE AROUND SANDOR AND ÓSCAR AFTER THAT.
MRS. KELLER WAS REAL PROTECTIVE OF SHANNON, ÓSCAR'S MISSUS, BUT...
...AFTER THAT...THEY DECIDED IT WAS TIME FOR US TO GET OUT OF NEW YORK.
WHAT IF THE RATS CAME FOR REVENGE?
CHRIST, I'VE BEEN PLAYING WITH FIRE THIS WHOLE TIME.
BUT I SAW HOW MUCH HE LOVED HER, AND I...
...THAT MANY RATS SHOULD OVERWHELM A DOG. THEY DEVOURED SOLDIERS BY THE BATTALION.
BUT THEY COULDN'T KILL HIM.
I DON'T UNDERSTAND HOW.
JUST...
...HATE...CAME OFF OF HIM LIKE...
...LIKE...

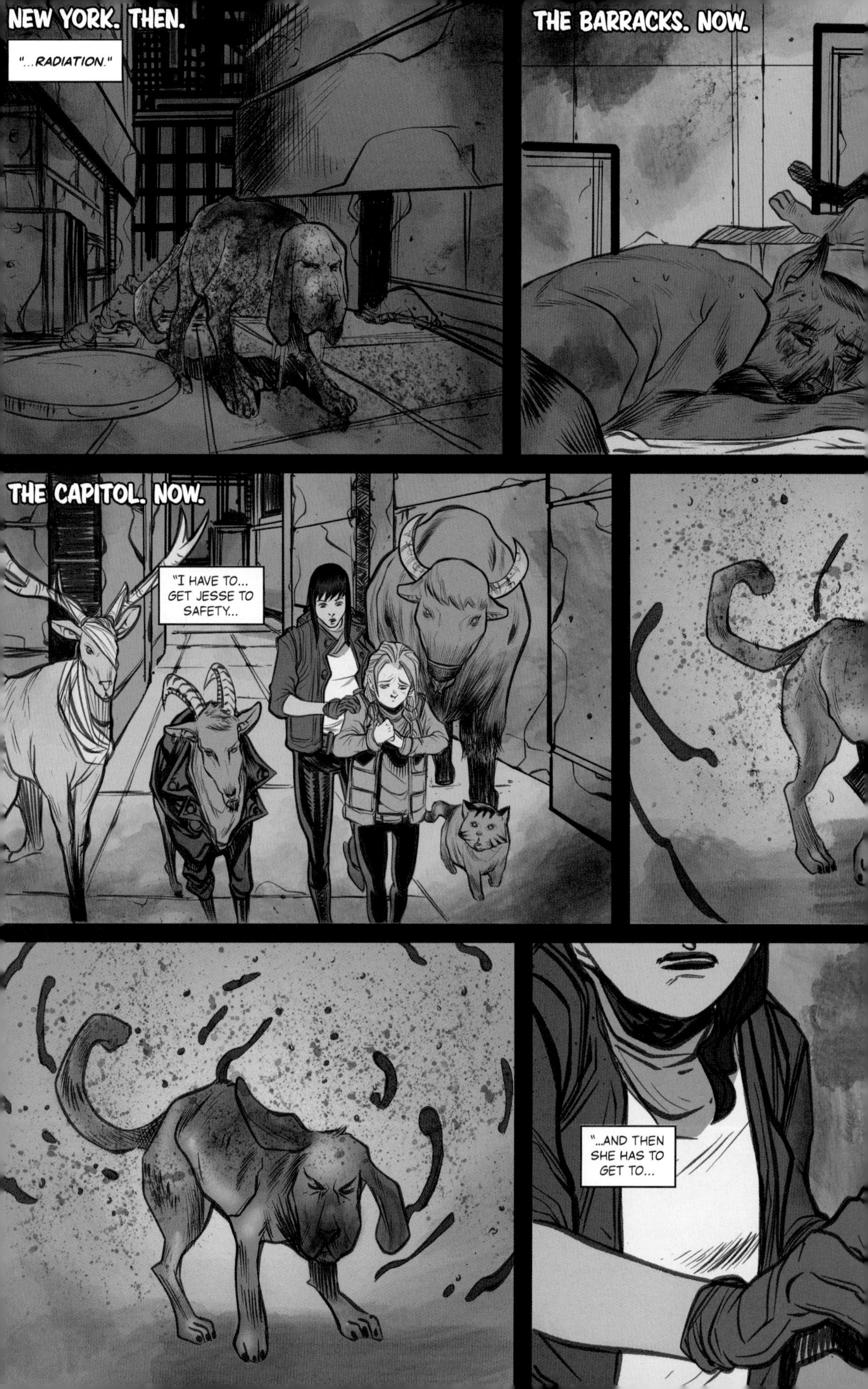
NEW YORK. THEN.
"...RADIATION."
THE BARRACKS. NOW.
THE CAPITOL. NOW.
"I HAVE TO... GET JESSE TO SAFETY...
"...AND THEN SHE HAS TO GET TO...

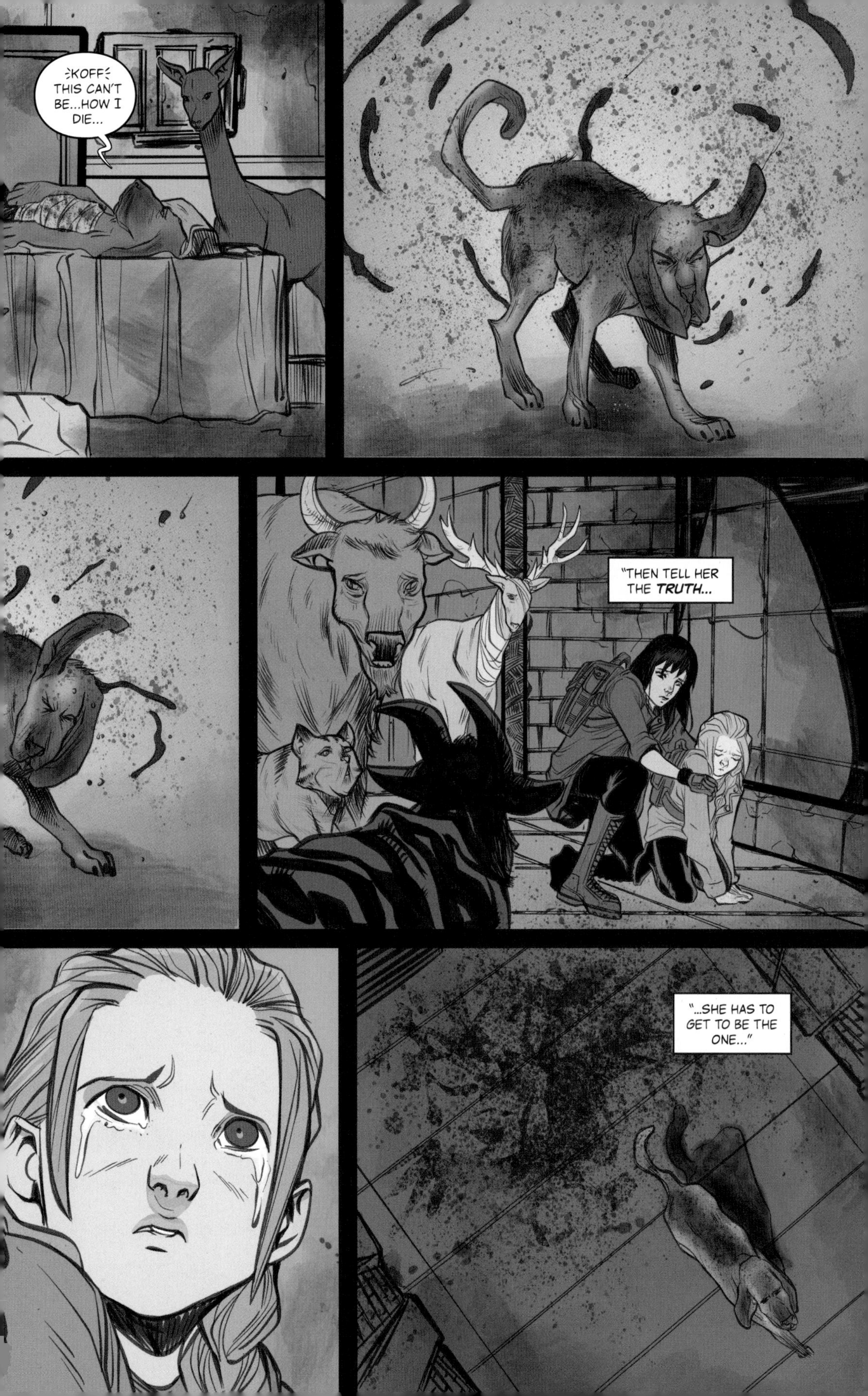
KOFF THIS CAN'T BE...HOW I DIE...
"THEN TELL HER THE *TRUTH*...
"...SHE HAS TO GET TO BE THE ONE..."

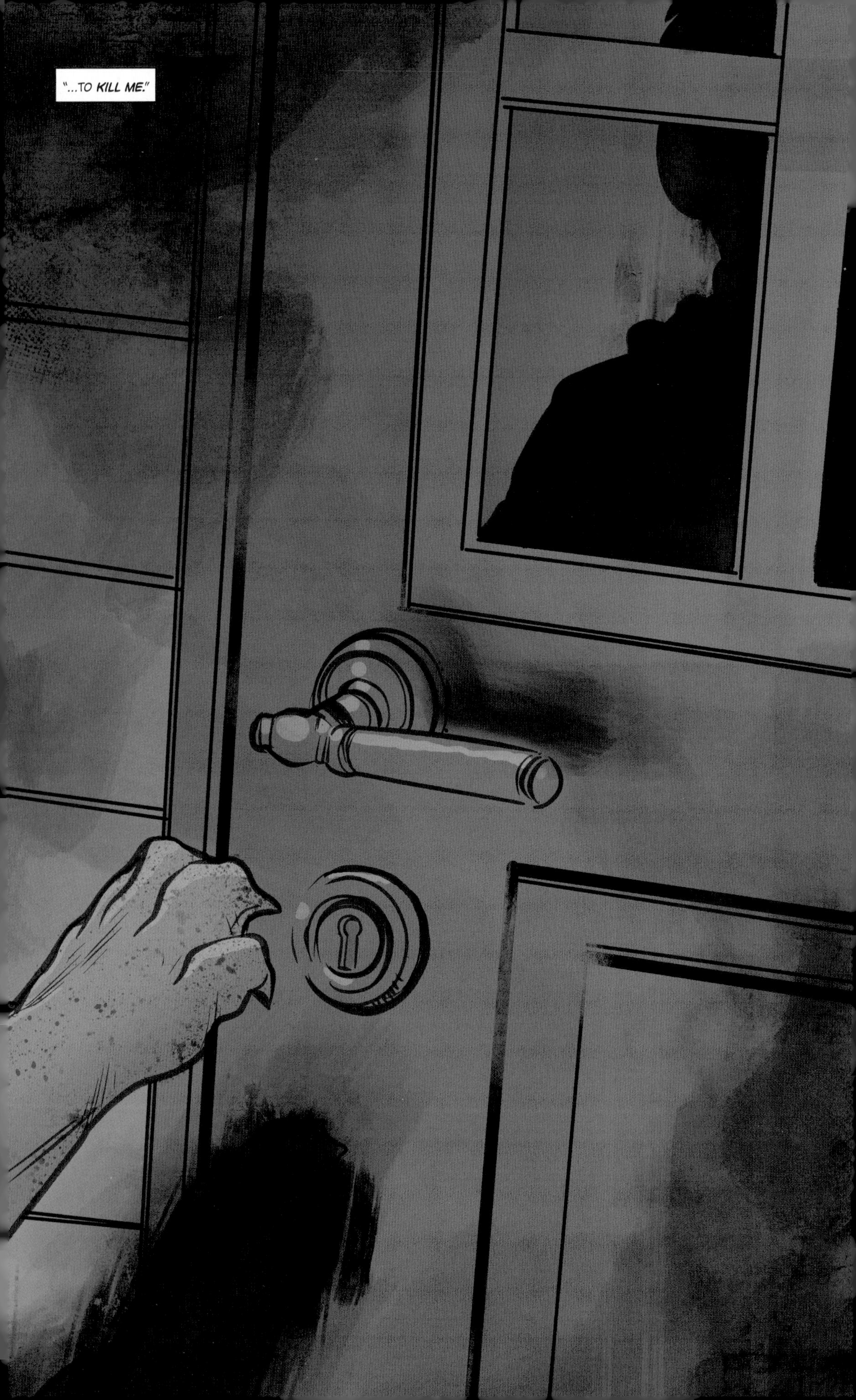
"...TO KILL ME."

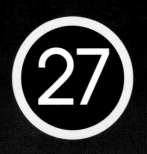

27

KING OF TEXAS, PART THREE

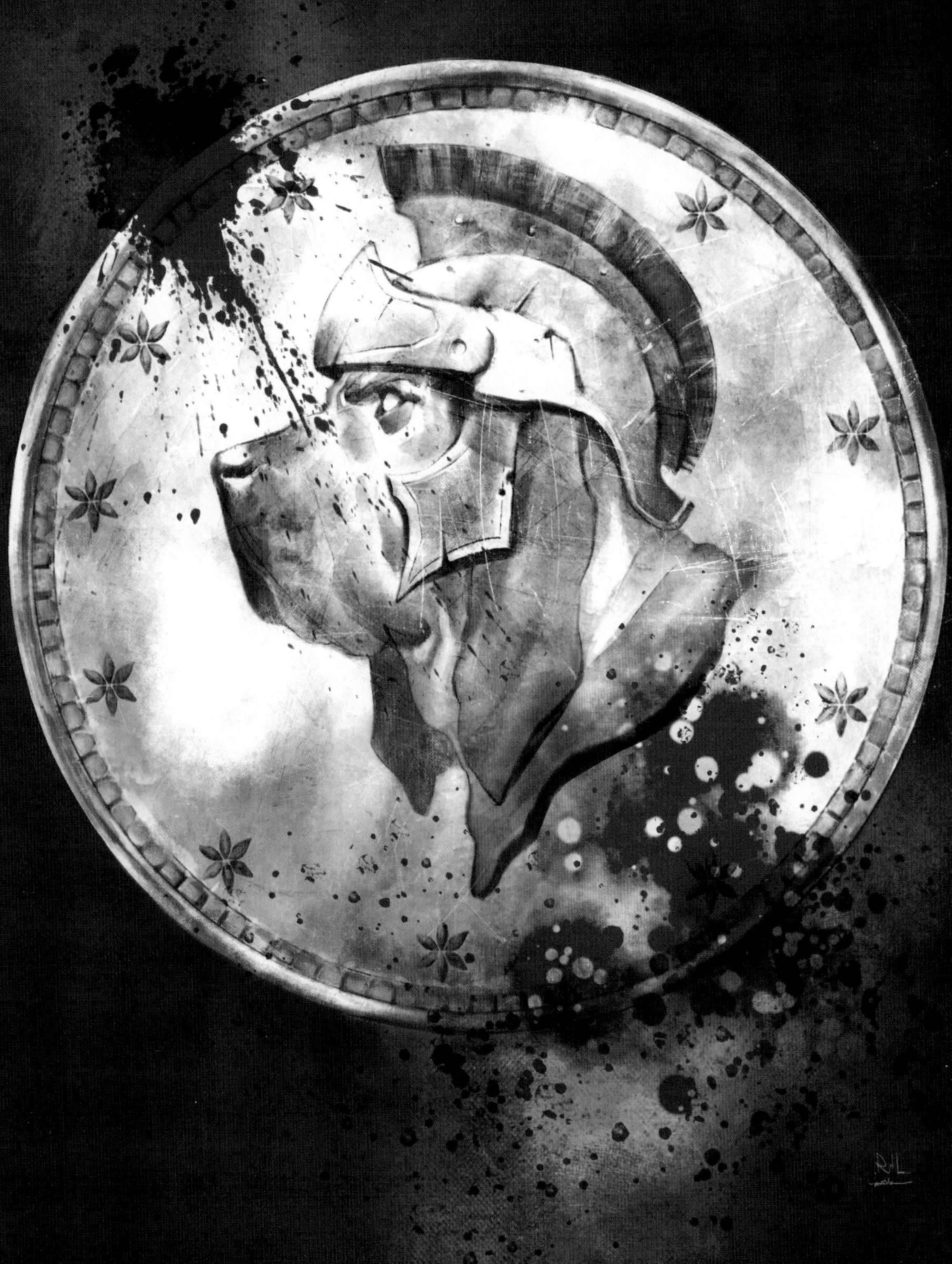

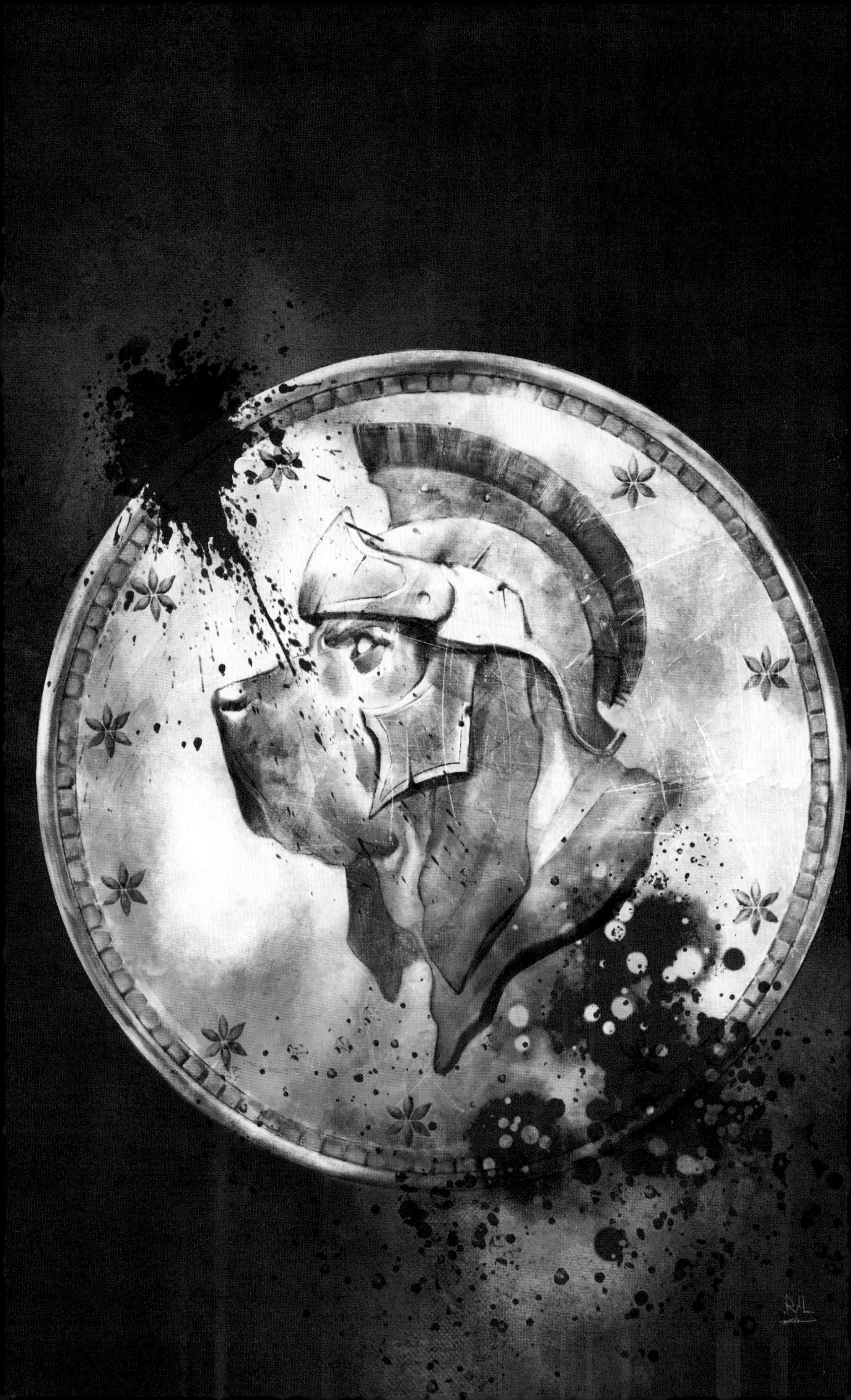

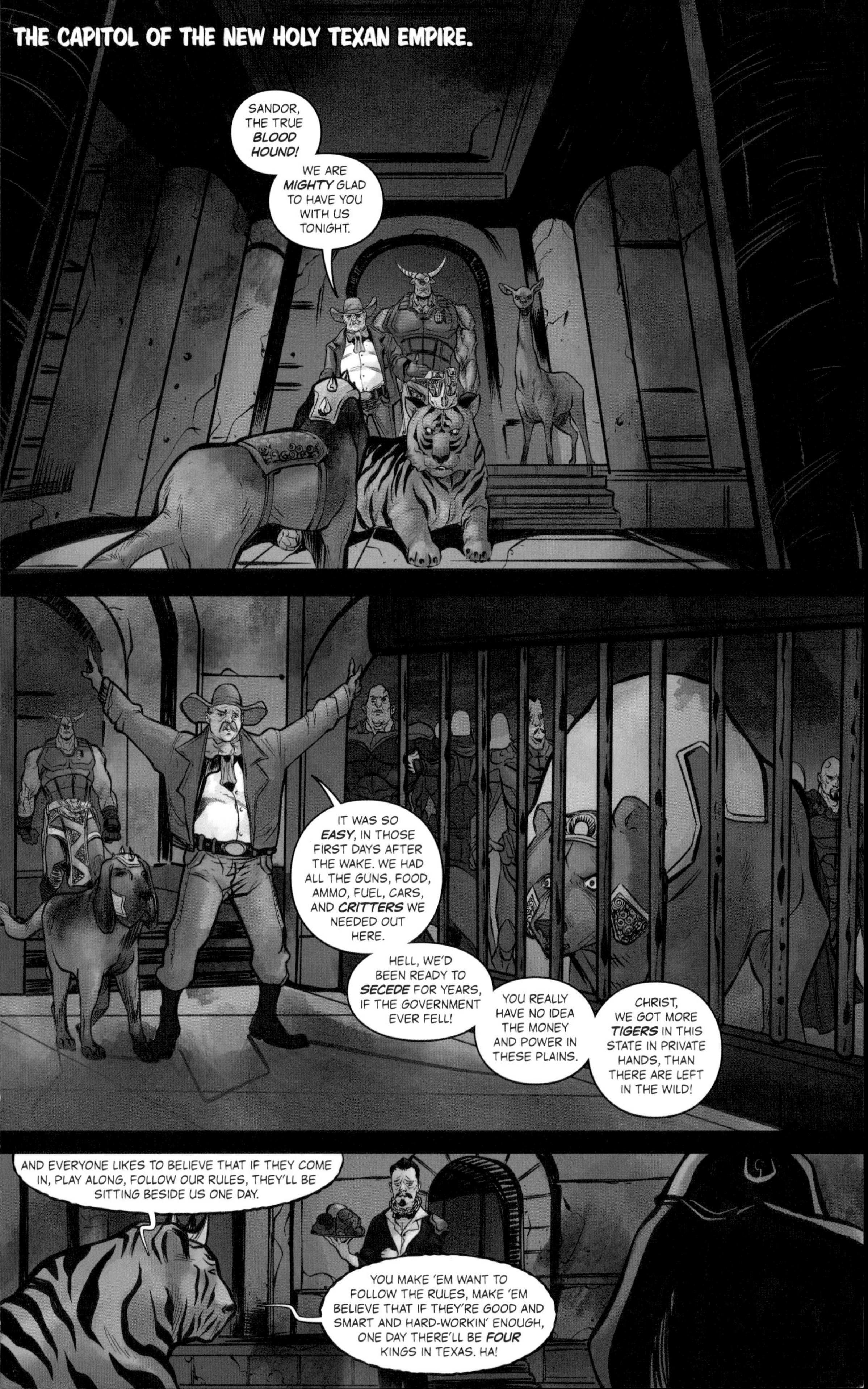
THE CAPITOL OF THE NEW HOLY TEXAN EMPIRE.
SANDOR, THE TRUE BLOOD HOUND!
WE ARE MIGHTY GLAD TO HAVE YOU WITH US TONIGHT.
IT WAS SO EASY, IN THOSE FIRST DAYS AFTER THE WAKE. WE HAD ALL THE GUNS, FOOD, AMMO, FUEL, CARS, AND CRITTERS WE NEEDED OUT HERE.
HELL, WE'D BEEN READY TO SECEDE FOR YEARS, IF THE GOVERNMENT EVER FELL!
YOU REALLY HAVE NO IDEA THE MONEY AND POWER IN THESE PLAINS.
CHRIST, WE GOT MORE TIGERS IN THIS STATE IN PRIVATE HANDS, THAN THERE ARE LEFT IN THE WILD!
AND EVERYONE LIKES TO BELIEVE THAT IF THEY COME IN, PLAY ALONG, FOLLOW OUR RULES, THEY'LL BE SITTING BESIDE US ONE DAY.
YOU MAKE 'EM WANT TO FOLLOW THE RULES, MAKE 'EM BELIEVE THAT IF THEY'RE GOOD AND SMART AND HARD-WORKIN' ENOUGH, ONE DAY THERE'LL BE FOUR KINGS IN TEXAS. HA!

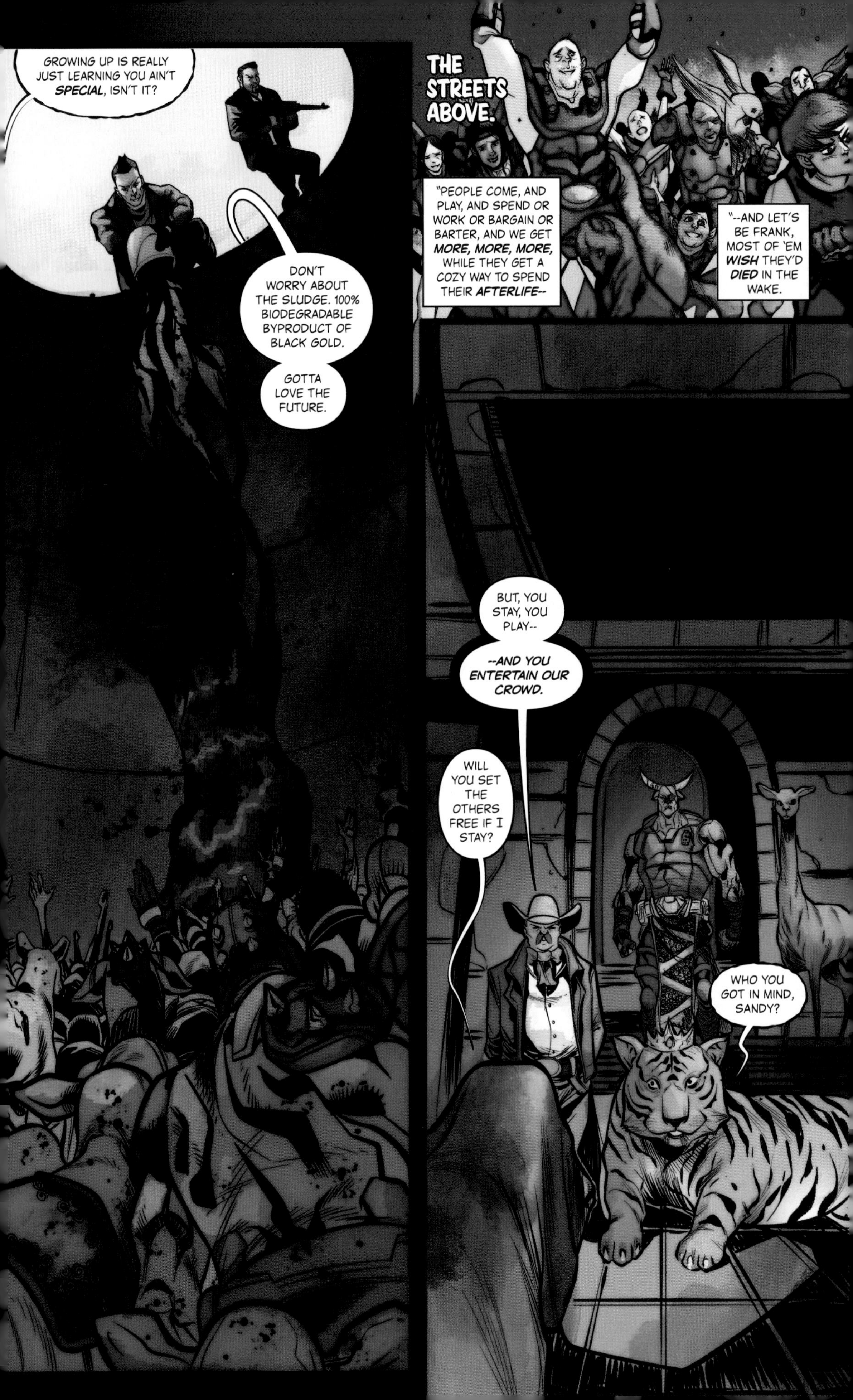
GROWING UP IS REALLY JUST LEARNING YOU AIN'T *SPECIAL*, ISN'T IT?
DON'T WORRY ABOUT THE SLUDGE. 100% BIODEGRADABLE BYPRODUCT OF BLACK GOLD.
GOTTA LOVE THE FUTURE.
THE STREETS ABOVE.
"PEOPLE COME, AND PLAY, AND SPEND OR WORK OR BARGAIN OR BARTER, AND WE GET *MORE, MORE, MORE,* WHILE THEY GET A COZY WAY TO SPEND THEIR *AFTERLIFE*--
"--AND LET'S BE FRANK, MOST OF 'EM *WISH* THEY'D *DIED* IN THE WAKE.
BUT, YOU STAY, YOU PLAY--
--AND YOU ENTERTAIN OUR CROWD.
WILL YOU SET THE OTHERS FREE IF I STAY?
WHO YOU GOT IN MIND, SANDY?

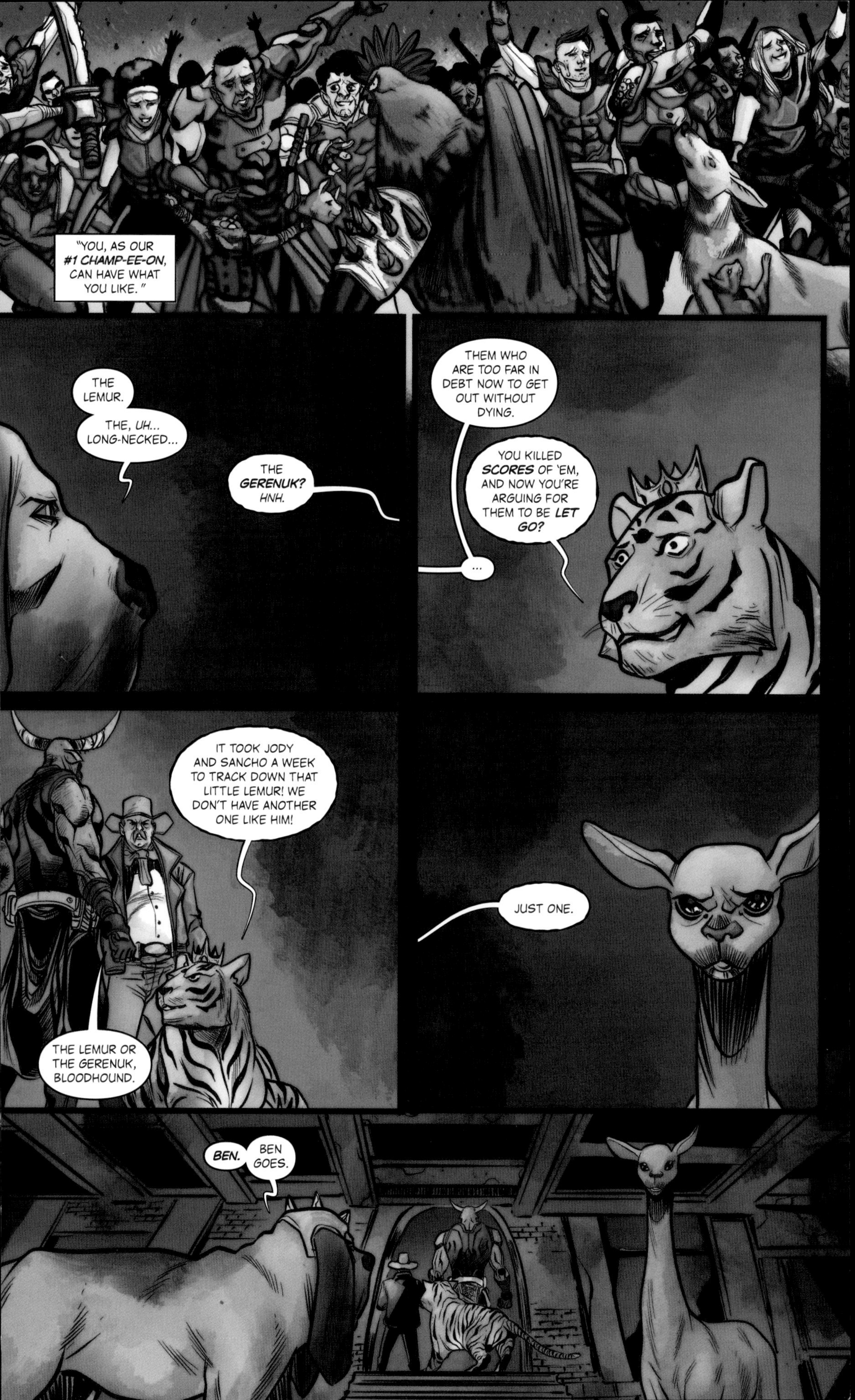
"YOU, AS OUR #1 CHAMP-EE-ON, CAN HAVE WHAT YOU LIKE."
THE LEMUR.
THE, UH... LONG-NECKED...
THE GERENUK? HNH.
THEM WHO ARE TOO FAR IN DEBT NOW TO GET OUT WITHOUT DYING.
...
YOU KILLED SCORES OF 'EM, AND NOW YOU'RE ARGUING FOR THEM TO BE LET GO?
IT TOOK JODY AND SANCHO A WEEK TO TRACK DOWN THAT LITTLE LEMUR! WE DON'T HAVE ANOTHER ONE LIKE HIM!
THE LEMUR OR THE GERENUK, BLOODHOUND.
JUST ONE.
BEN.
BEN GOES.

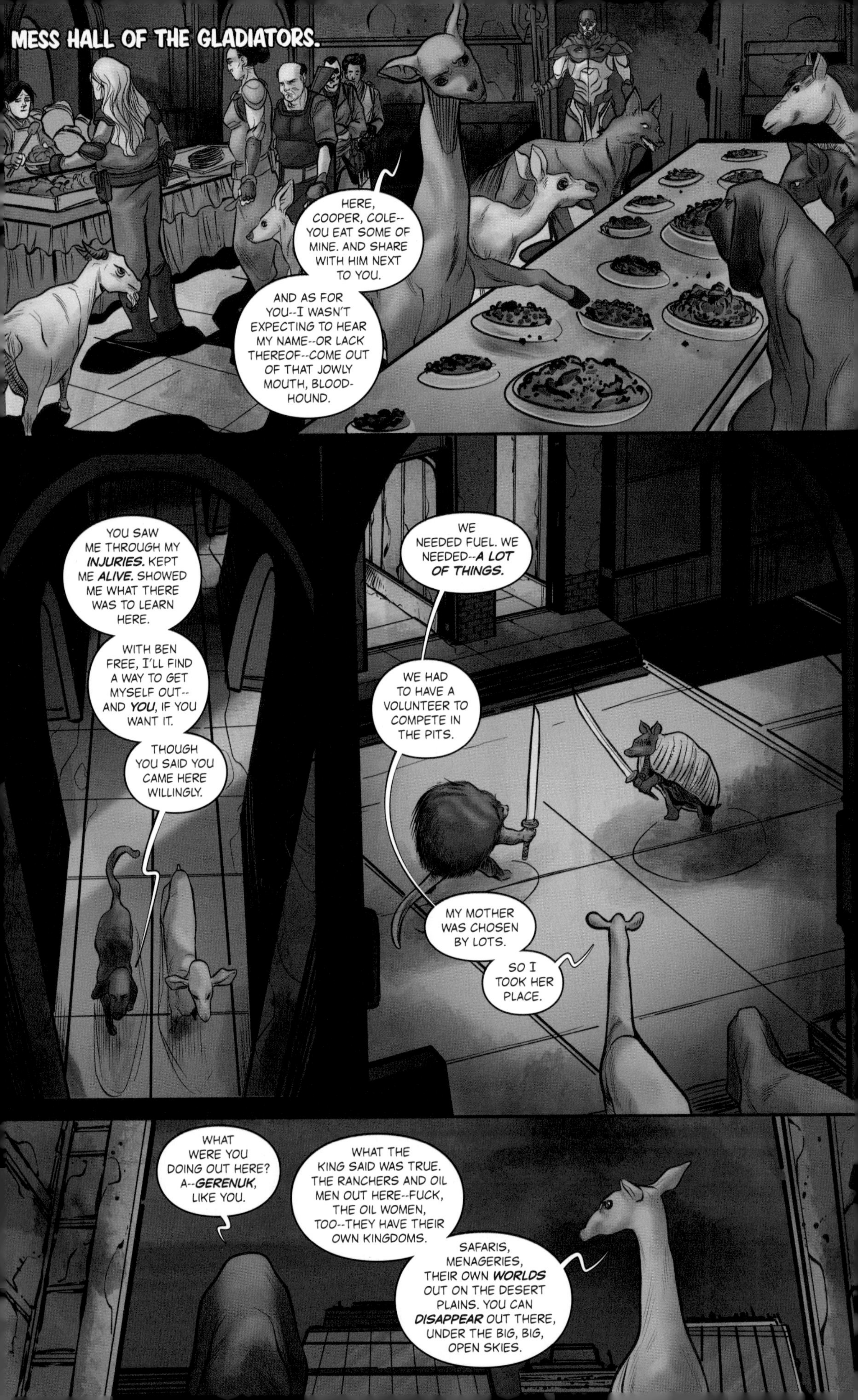
MESS HALL OF THE GLADIATORS.
HERE, COOPER, COLE-- YOU EAT SOME OF MINE. AND SHARE WITH HIM NEXT TO YOU.
AND AS FOR YOU--I WASN'T EXPECTING TO HEAR MY NAME--OR LACK THEREOF--COME OUT OF THAT JOWLY MOUTH, BLOOD-HOUND.
YOU SAW ME THROUGH MY INJURIES. KEPT ME ALIVE. SHOWED ME WHAT THERE WAS TO LEARN HERE.
WITH BEN FREE, I'LL FIND A WAY TO GET MYSELF OUT-- AND YOU, IF YOU WANT IT.
THOUGH YOU SAID YOU CAME HERE WILLINGLY.
WE NEEDED FUEL. WE NEEDED--A LOT OF THINGS.
WE HAD TO HAVE A VOLUNTEER TO COMPETE IN THE PITS.
MY MOTHER WAS CHOSEN BY LOTS.
SO I TOOK HER PLACE.
WHAT WERE YOU DOING OUT HERE? A--GERENUK, LIKE YOU.
WHAT THE KING SAID WAS TRUE. THE RANCHERS AND OIL MEN OUT HERE--FUCK, THE OIL WOMEN, TOO--THEY HAVE THEIR OWN KINGDOMS.
SAFARIS, MENAGERIES, THEIR OWN WORLDS OUT ON THE DESERT PLAINS. YOU CAN DISAPPEAR OUT THERE, UNDER THE BIG, BIG, OPEN SKIES.

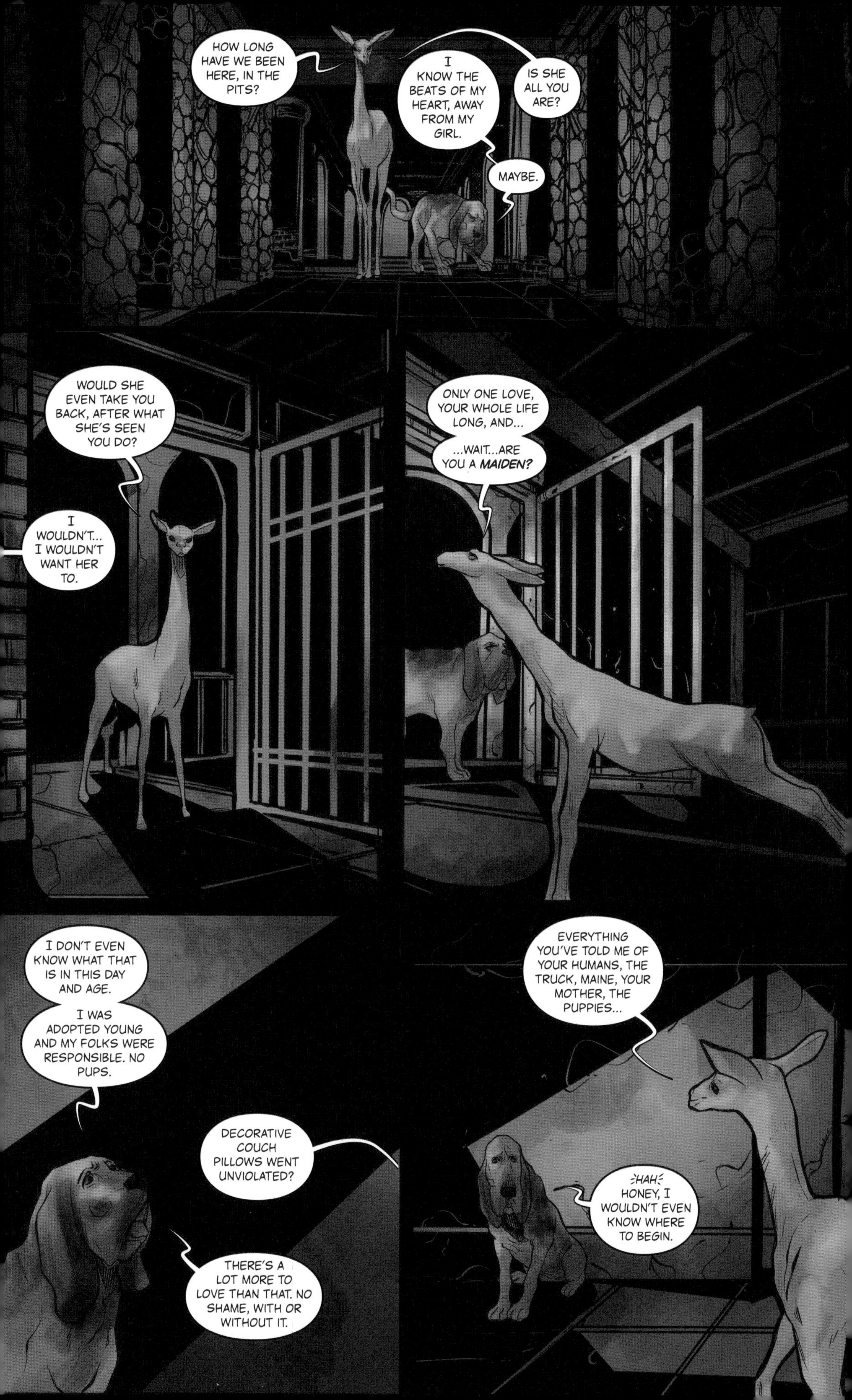
HOW LONG HAVE WE BEEN HERE, IN THE PITS?
I KNOW THE BEATS OF MY HEART, AWAY FROM MY GIRL.
IS SHE ALL YOU ARE?
MAYBE.
WOULD SHE EVEN TAKE YOU BACK, AFTER WHAT SHE'S SEEN YOU DO?
I WOULDN'T... I WOULDN'T WANT HER TO.
ONLY ONE LOVE, YOUR WHOLE LIFE LONG, AND...
...WAIT...ARE YOU A MAIDEN?
I DON'T EVEN KNOW WHAT THAT IS IN THIS DAY AND AGE.
I WAS ADOPTED YOUNG AND MY FOLKS WERE RESPONSIBLE. NO PUPS.
DECORATIVE COUCH PILLOWS WENT UNVIOLATED?
THERE'S A LOT MORE TO LOVE THAN THAT. NO SHAME, WITH OR WITHOUT IT.
EVERYTHING YOU'VE TOLD ME OF YOUR HUMANS, THE TRUCK, MAINE, YOUR MOTHER, THE PUPPIES...
HAH
HONEY, I WOULDN'T EVEN KNOW WHERE TO BEGIN.

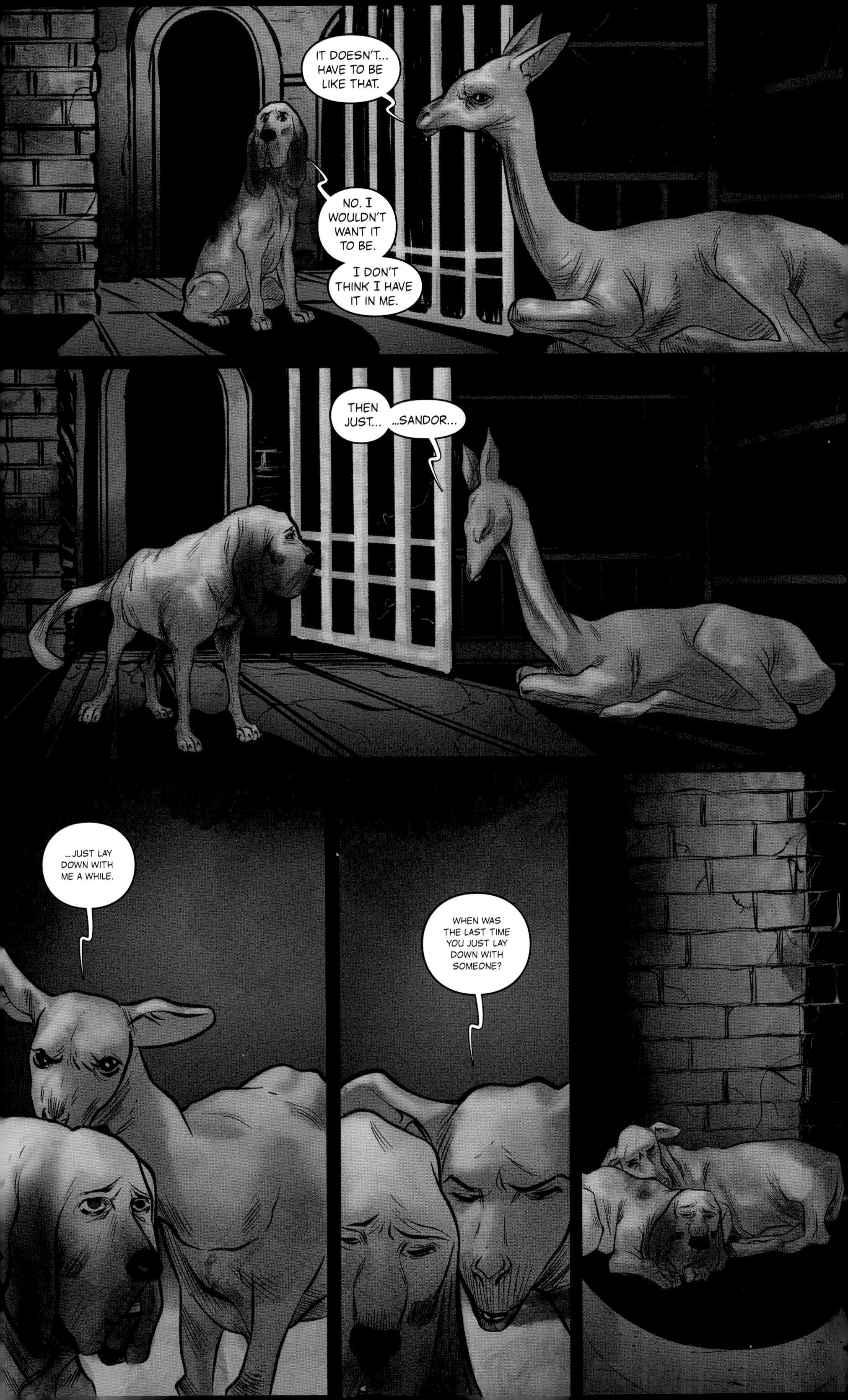
IT DOESN'T... HAVE TO BE LIKE THAT.
NO. I WOULDN'T WANT IT TO BE.
I DON'T THINK I HAVE IT IN ME.
THEN JUST...
...SANDOR...
...JUST LAY DOWN WITH ME A WHILE.
WHEN WAS THE LAST TIME YOU JUST LAY DOWN WITH SOMEONE?

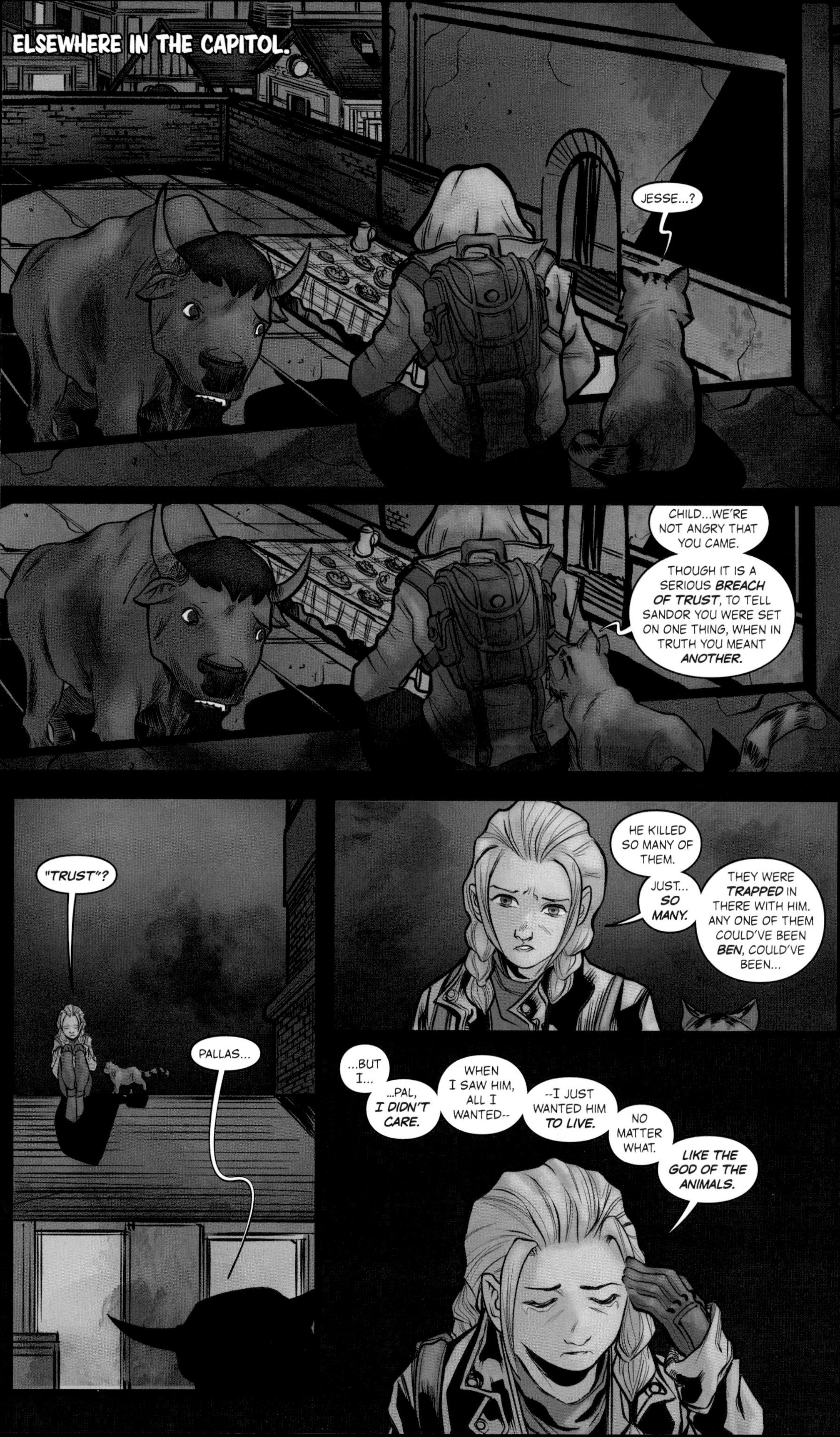
ELSEWHERE IN THE CAPITOL.
JESSE...?
CHILD...WE'RE NOT ANGRY THAT YOU CAME.
THOUGH IT IS A SERIOUS BREACH OF TRUST, TO TELL SANDOR YOU WERE SET ON ONE THING, WHEN IN TRUTH YOU MEANT ANOTHER.
"TRUST"?
HE KILLED SO MANY OF THEM.
JUST... SO MANY.
THEY WERE TRAPPED IN THERE WITH HIM. ANY ONE OF THEM COULD'VE BEEN BEN, COULD'VE BEEN...
PALLAS...
...BUT I...
...PAL, I DIDN'T CARE.
WHEN I SAW HIM, ALL I WANTED--
--I JUST WANTED HIM TO LIVE.
NO MATTER WHAT.
LIKE THE GOD OF THE ANIMALS.

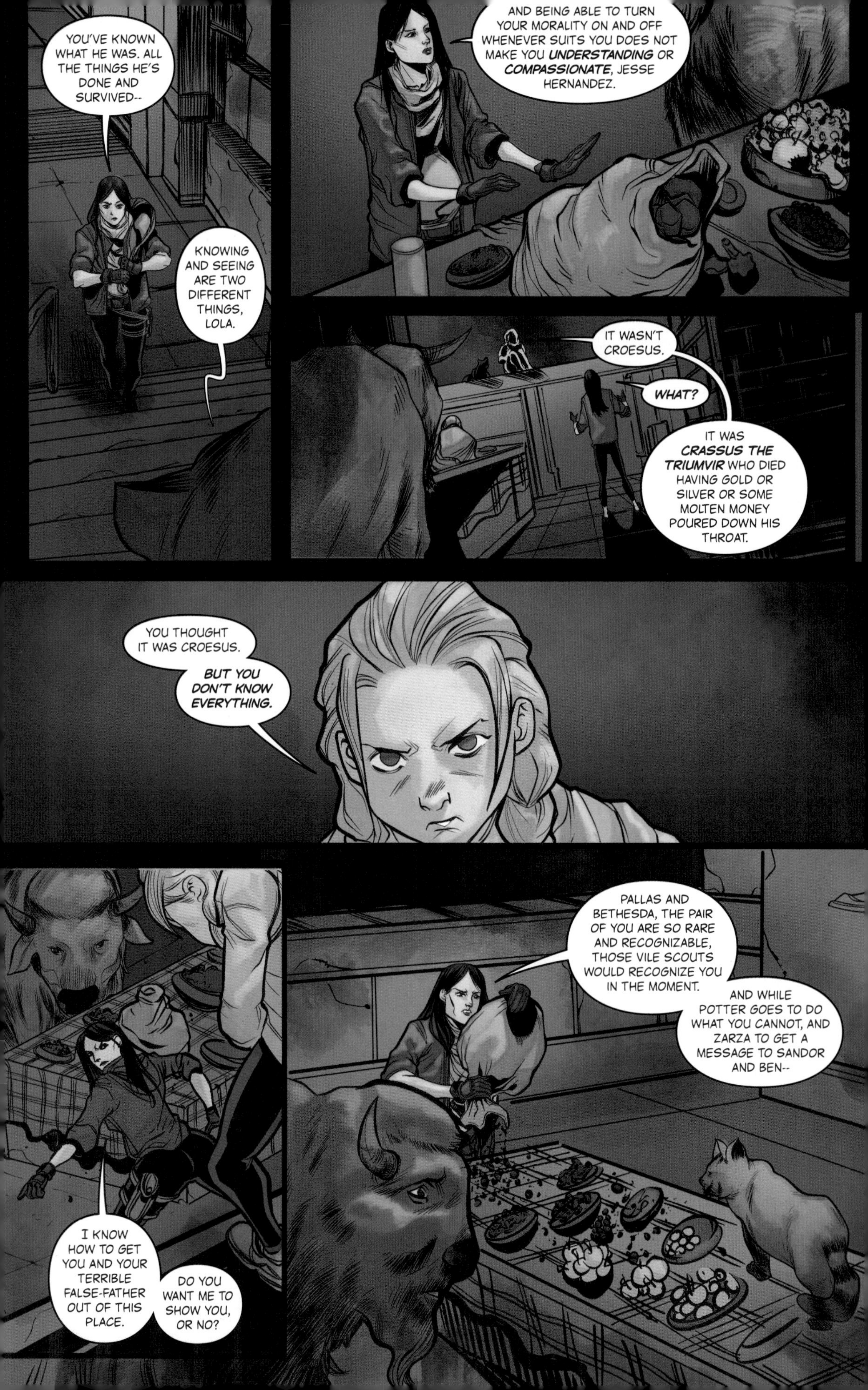
YOU'VE KNOWN WHAT HE WAS. ALL THE THINGS HE'S DONE AND SURVIVED--
KNOWING AND SEEING ARE TWO DIFFERENT THINGS, LOLA.
AND BEING ABLE TO TURN YOUR MORALITY ON AND OFF WHENEVER SUITS YOU DOES NOT MAKE YOU UNDERSTANDING OR COMPASSIONATE, JESSE HERNANDEZ.
IT WASN'T CROESUS.
WHAT?
IT WAS CRASSUS THE TRIUMVIR WHO DIED HAVING GOLD OR SILVER OR SOME MOLTEN MONEY POURED DOWN HIS THROAT.
YOU THOUGHT IT WAS CROESUS.
BUT YOU DON'T KNOW EVERYTHING.
I KNOW HOW TO GET YOU AND YOUR TERRIBLE FALSE-FATHER OUT OF THIS PLACE.
DO YOU WANT ME TO SHOW YOU, OR NO?
PALLAS AND BETHESDA, THE PAIR OF YOU ARE SO RARE AND RECOGNIZABLE, THOSE VILE SCOUTS WOULD RECOGNIZE YOU IN THE MOMENT.
AND WHILE POTTER GOES TO DO WHAT YOU CANNOT, AND ZARZA TO GET A MESSAGE TO SANDOR AND BEN--

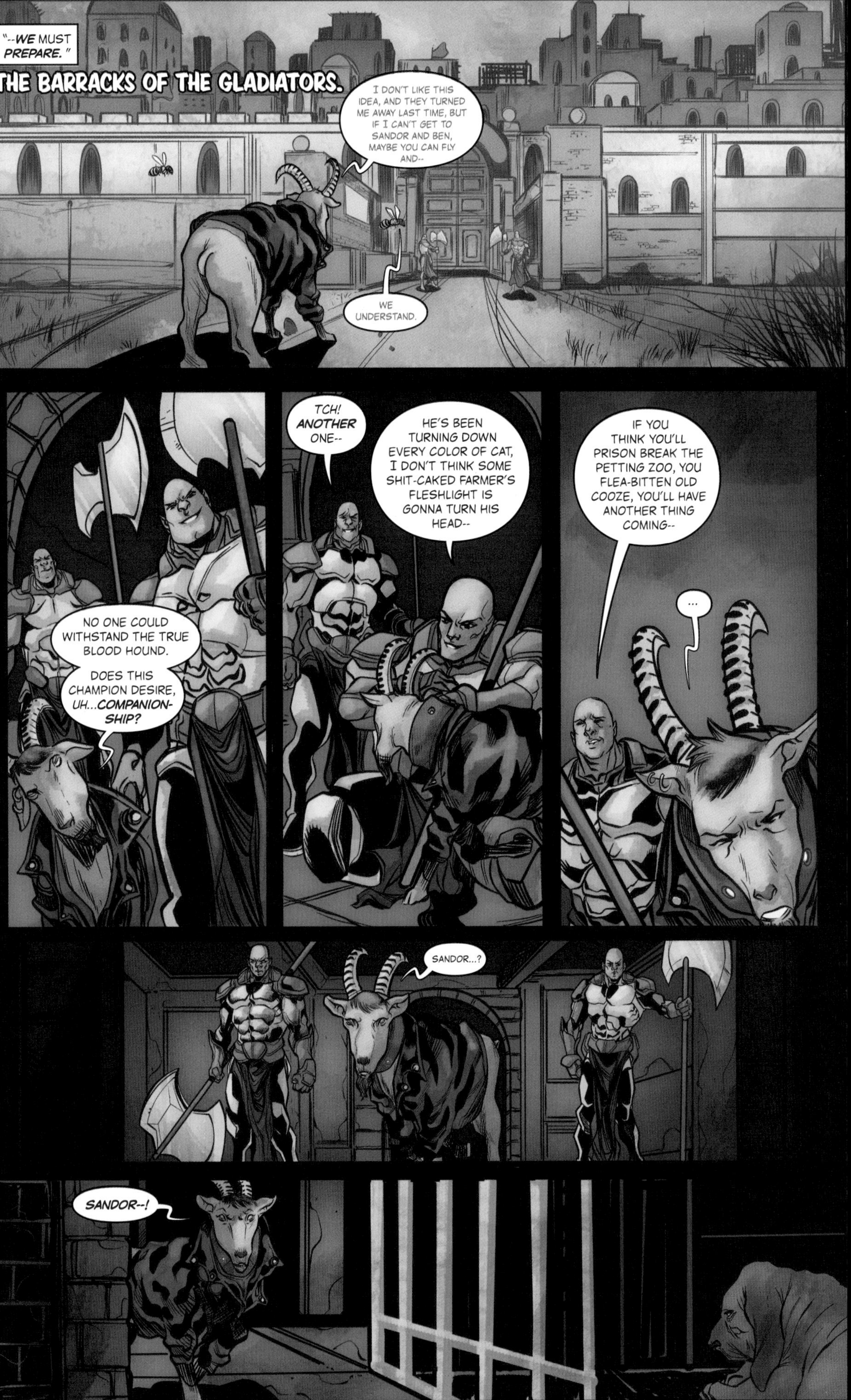
"--WE MUST PREPARE."
THE BARRACKS OF THE GLADIATORS.
I DON'T LIKE THIS IDEA, AND THEY TURNED ME AWAY LAST TIME, BUT IF I CAN'T GET TO SANDOR AND BEN, MAYBE YOU CAN FLY AND--
WE UNDERSTAND.
NO ONE COULD WITHSTAND THE TRUE BLOOD HOUND.
DOES THIS CHAMPION DESIRE, UH...COMPANIONSHIP?
TCH! ANOTHER ONE--
HE'S BEEN TURNING DOWN EVERY COLOR OF CAT, I DON'T THINK SOME SHIT-CAKED FARMER'S FLESHLIGHT IS GONNA TURN HIS HEAD--
IF YOU THINK YOU'LL PRISON BREAK THE PETTING ZOO, YOU FLEA-BITTEN OLD COOZE, YOU'LL HAVE ANOTHER THING COMING--
...
SANDOR...?
SANDOR--!

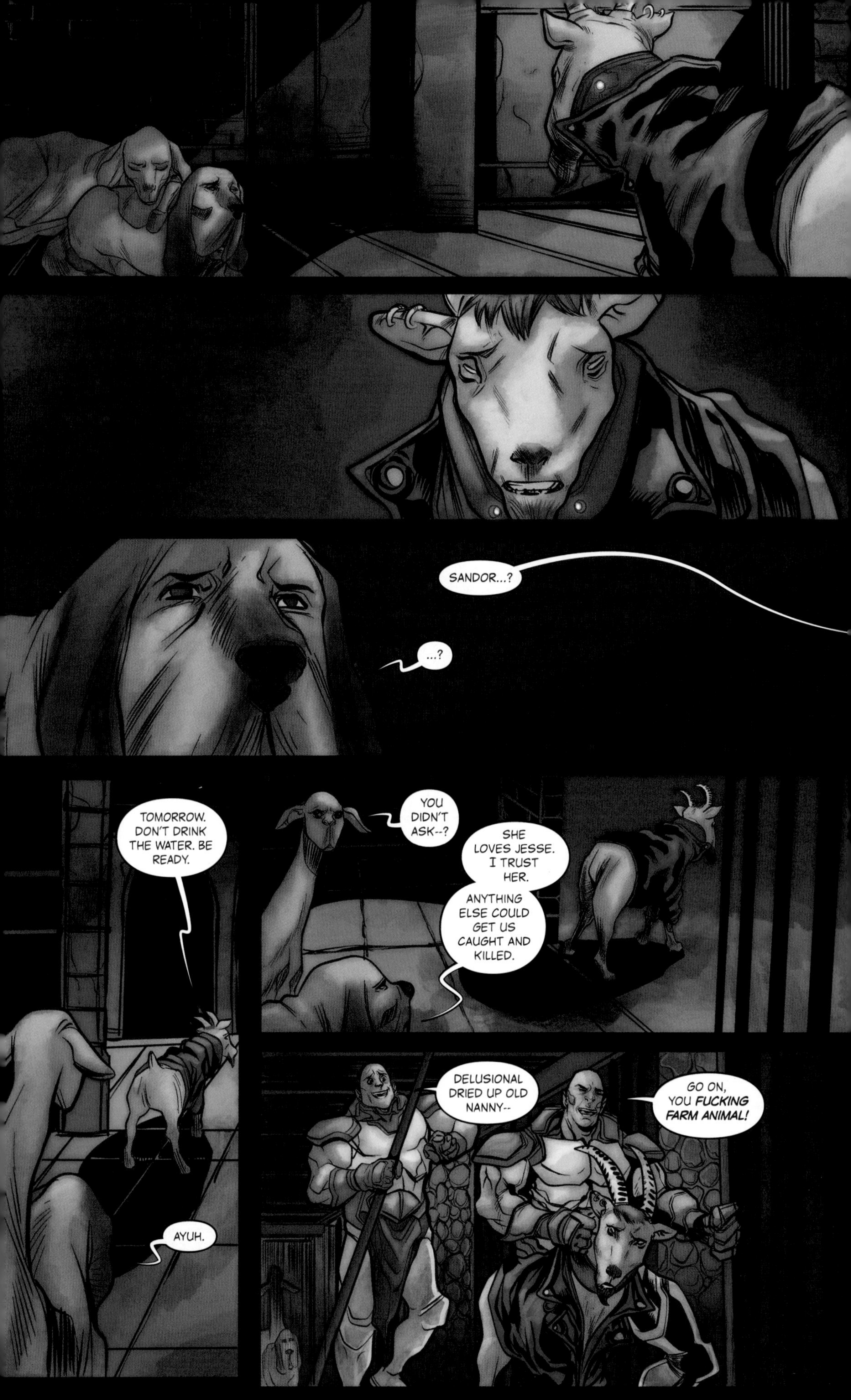
SANDOR...?
...?
TOMORROW. DON'T DRINK THE WATER. BE READY.
YOU DIDN'T ASK--?
SHE LOVES JESSE. I TRUST HER.
ANYTHING ELSE COULD GET US CAUGHT AND KILLED.
AYUH.
DELUSIONAL DRIED UP OLD NANNY--
GO ON, YOU **FUCKING FARM ANIMAL!**

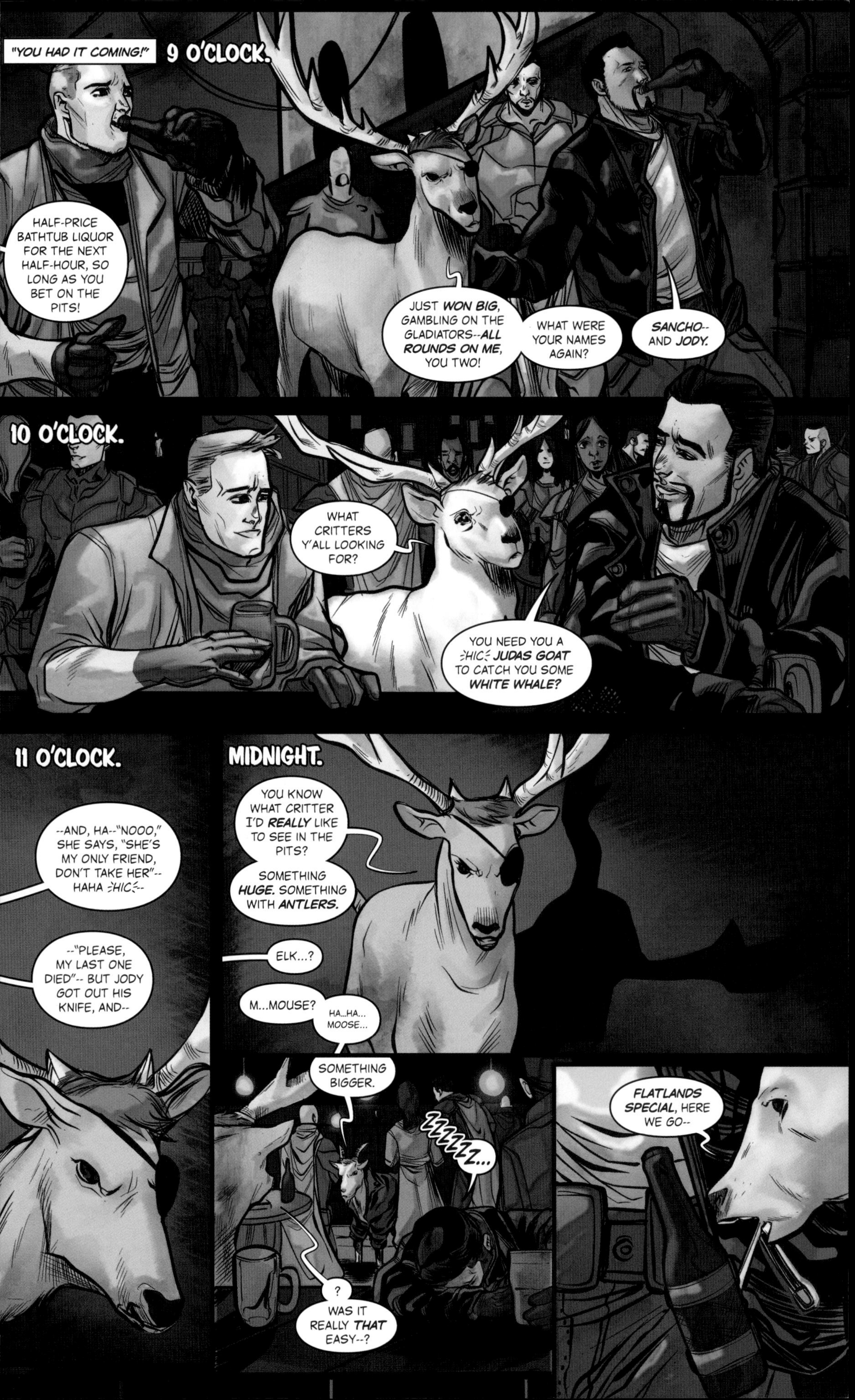
"YOU HAD IT COMING!"
9 O'CLOCK.
HALF-PRICE BATHTUB LIQUOR FOR THE NEXT HALF-HOUR, SO LONG AS YOU BET ON THE PITS!
JUST WON BIG, GAMBLING ON THE GLADIATORS--ALL ROUNDS ON ME, YOU TWO!
WHAT WERE YOUR NAMES AGAIN?
SANCHO--AND JODY.
10 O'CLOCK.
WHAT CRITTERS Y'ALL LOOKING FOR?
YOU NEED YOU A *HIC* JUDAS GOAT TO CATCH YOU SOME WHITE WHALE?
11 O'CLOCK.
--AND, HA--"NOOO," SHE SAYS, "SHE'S MY ONLY FRIEND, DON'T TAKE HER"--HAHA *HIC*--
--"PLEASE, MY LAST ONE DIED"-- BUT JODY GOT OUT HIS KNIFE, AND--
MIDNIGHT.
YOU KNOW WHAT CRITTER I'D REALLY LIKE TO SEE IN THE PITS?
SOMETHING HUGE. SOMETHING WITH ANTLERS.
ELK...?
M...MOUSE?
HA...HA... MOOSE...
SOMETHING BIGGER.
ZZZZZZ...
?
WAS IT REALLY THAT EASY--?
FLATLANDS SPECIAL, HERE WE GO--

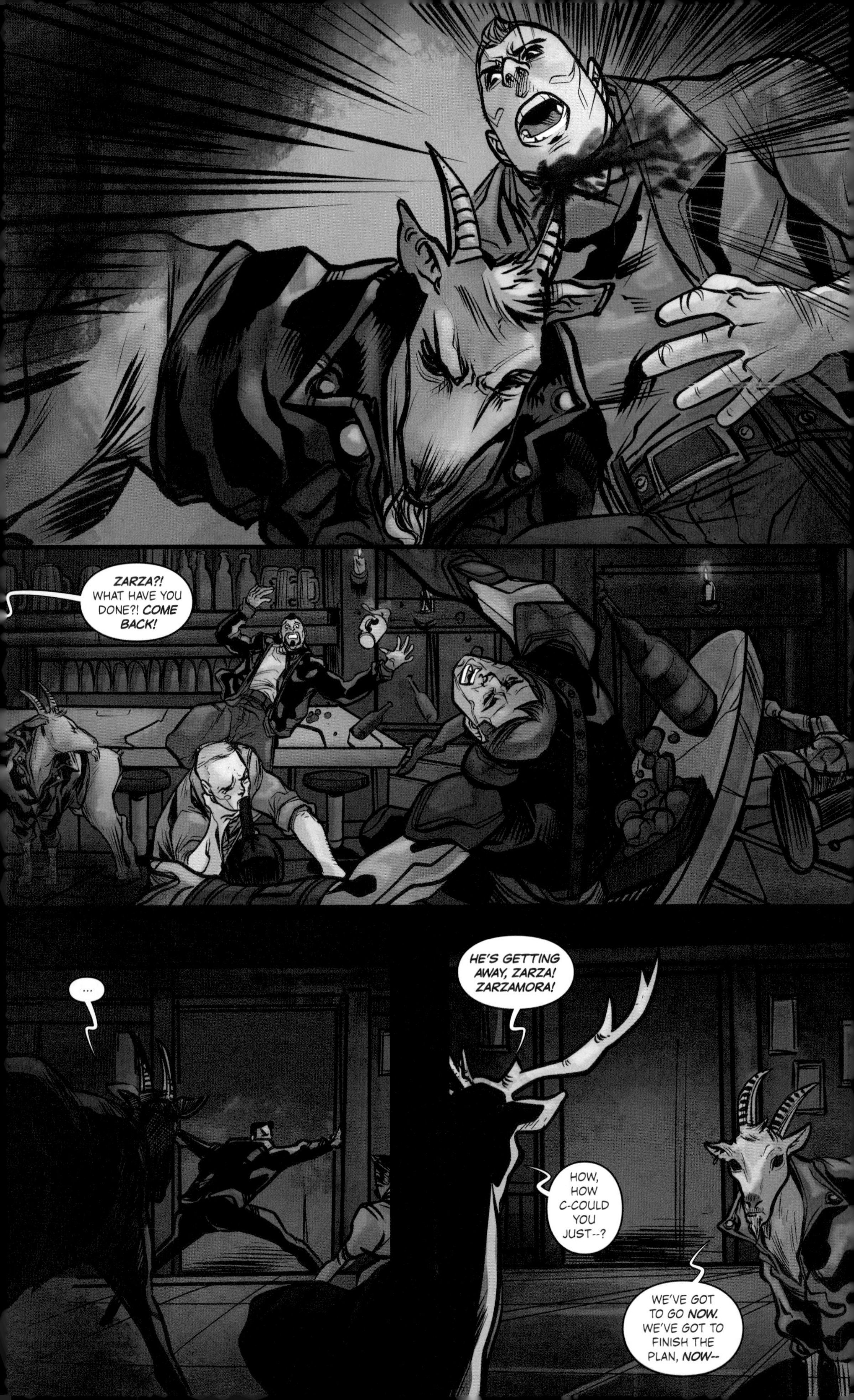
ZARZA?! WHAT HAVE YOU DONE?! COME BACK!
...
HE'S GETTING AWAY, ZARZA! ZARZAMORA!
HOW, HOW C-COULD YOU JUST--?
WE'VE GOT TO GO NOW. WE'VE GOT TO FINISH THE PLAN, NOW--

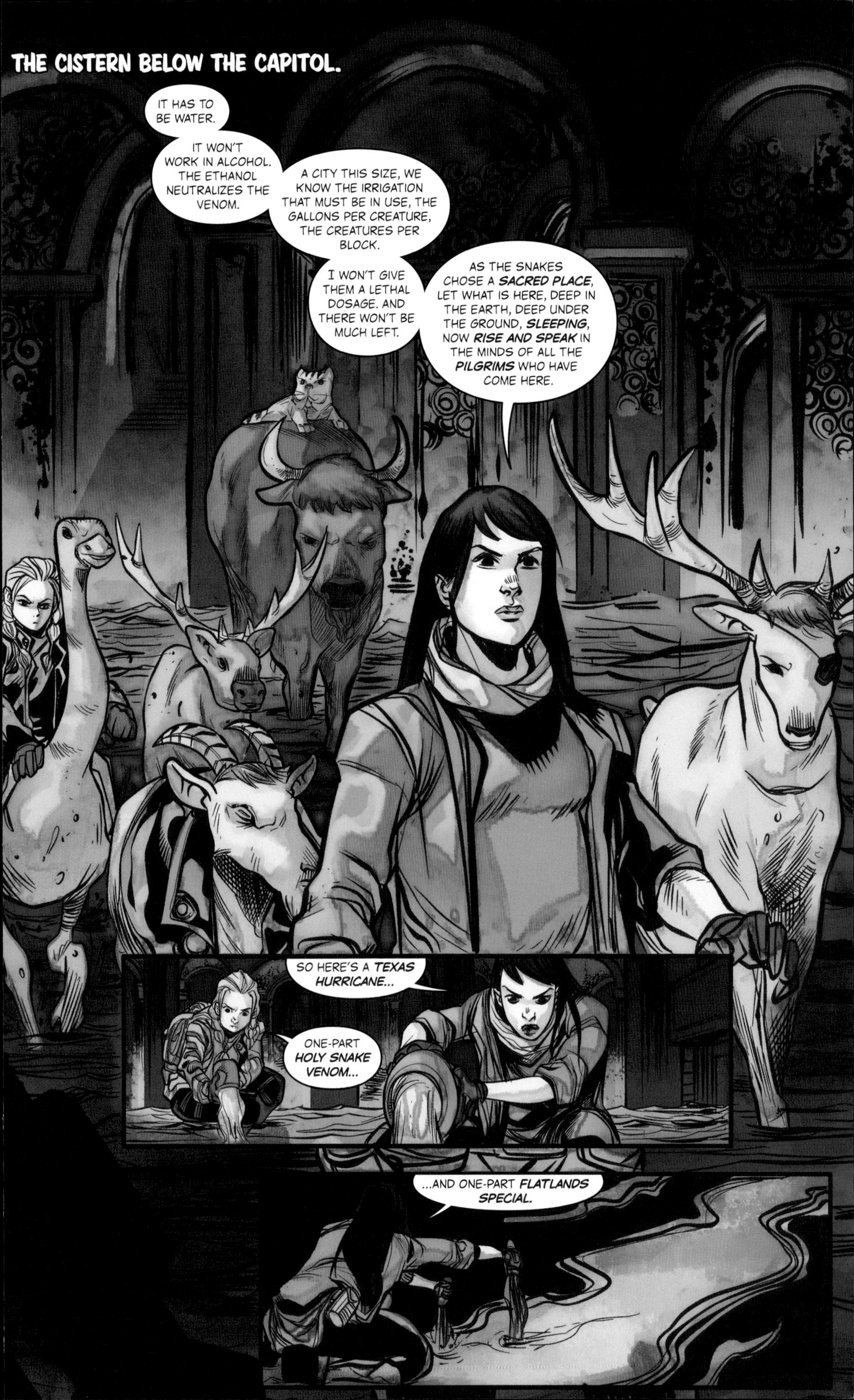
THE CISTERN BELOW THE CAPITOL.
IT HAS TO BE WATER.
IT WON'T WORK IN ALCOHOL. THE ETHANOL NEUTRALIZES THE VENOM.
A CITY THIS SIZE, WE KNOW THE IRRIGATION THAT MUST BE IN USE, THE GALLONS PER CREATURE, THE CREATURES PER BLOCK.
I WON'T GIVE THEM A LETHAL DOSAGE. AND THERE WON'T BE MUCH LEFT.
AS THE SNAKES CHOSE A SACRED PLACE, LET WHAT IS HERE, DEEP IN THE EARTH, DEEP UNDER THE GROUND, SLEEPING, NOW RISE AND SPEAK IN THE MINDS OF ALL THE PILGRIMS WHO HAVE COME HERE.
SO HERE'S A TEXAS HURRICANE...
ONE-PART HOLY SNAKE VENOM...
...AND ONE-PART FLATLANDS SPECIAL.

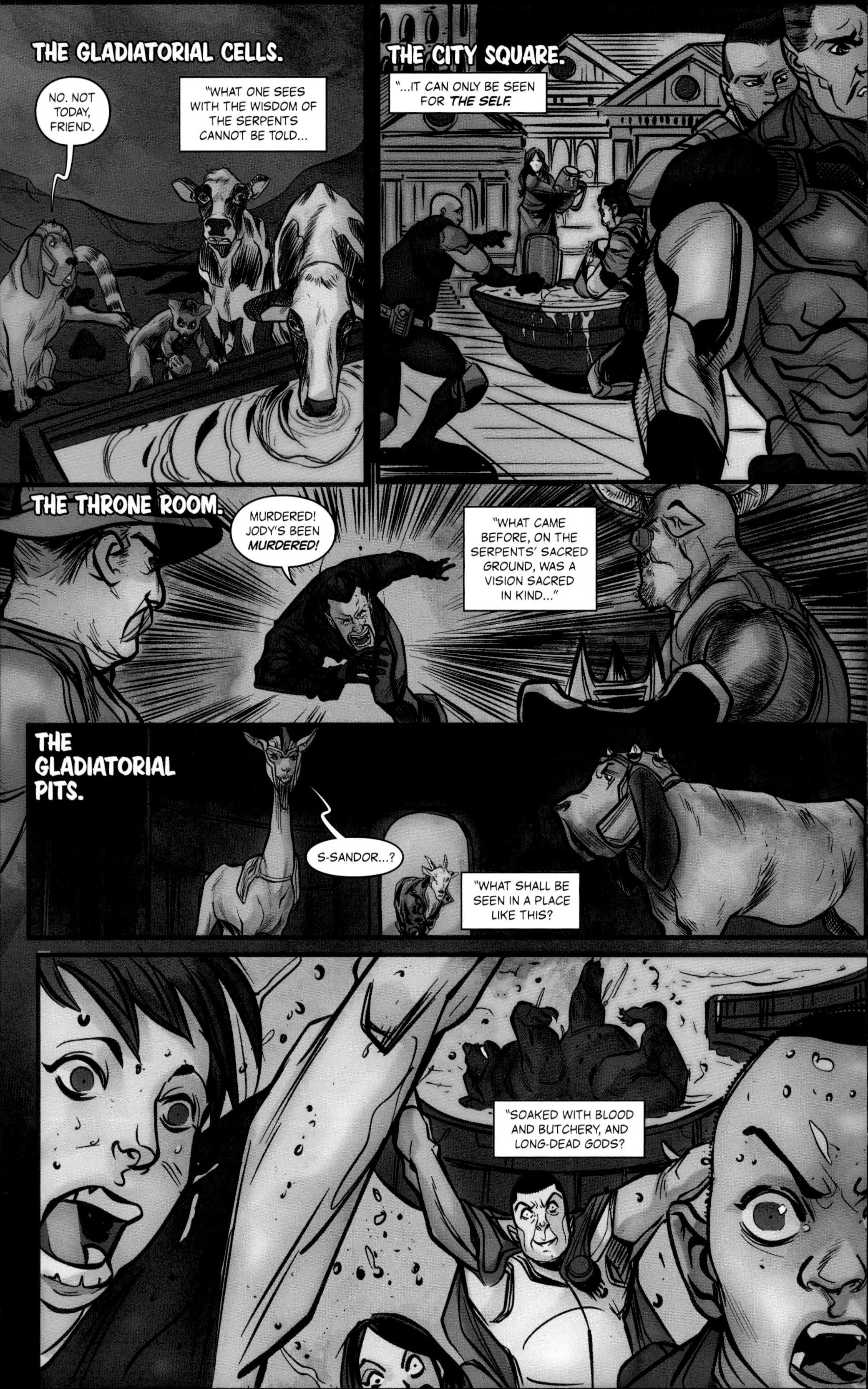
THE GLADIATORIAL CELLS.
NO. NOT TODAY, FRIEND.
"WHAT ONE SEES WITH THE WISDOM OF THE SERPENTS CANNOT BE TOLD...
THE CITY SQUARE.
"...IT CAN ONLY BE SEEN FOR THE SELF.
THE THRONE ROOM.
MURDERED! JODY'S BEEN MURDERED!
"WHAT CAME BEFORE, ON THE SERPENTS' SACRED GROUND, WAS A VISION SACRED IN KIND..."
THE GLADIATORIAL PITS.
S-SANDOR...?
"WHAT SHALL BE SEEN IN A PLACE LIKE THIS?
"SOAKED WITH BLOOD AND BUTCHERY, AND LONG-DEAD GODS?

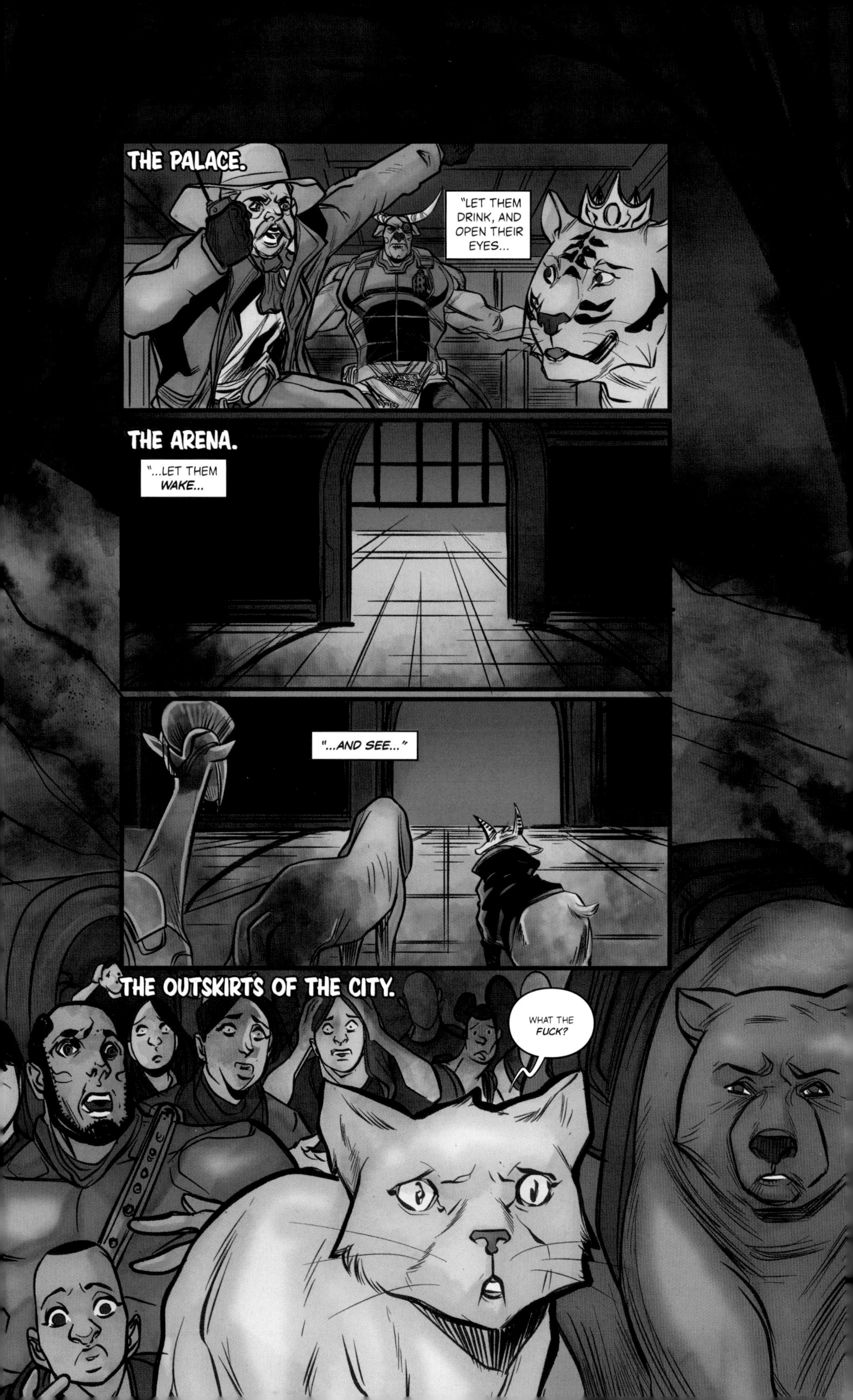
THE PALACE.
"LET THEM DRINK, AND OPEN THEIR EYES...
THE ARENA.
"...LET THEM WAKE...
"...AND SEE..."
THE OUTSKIRTS OF THE CITY.
WHAT THE FUCK?

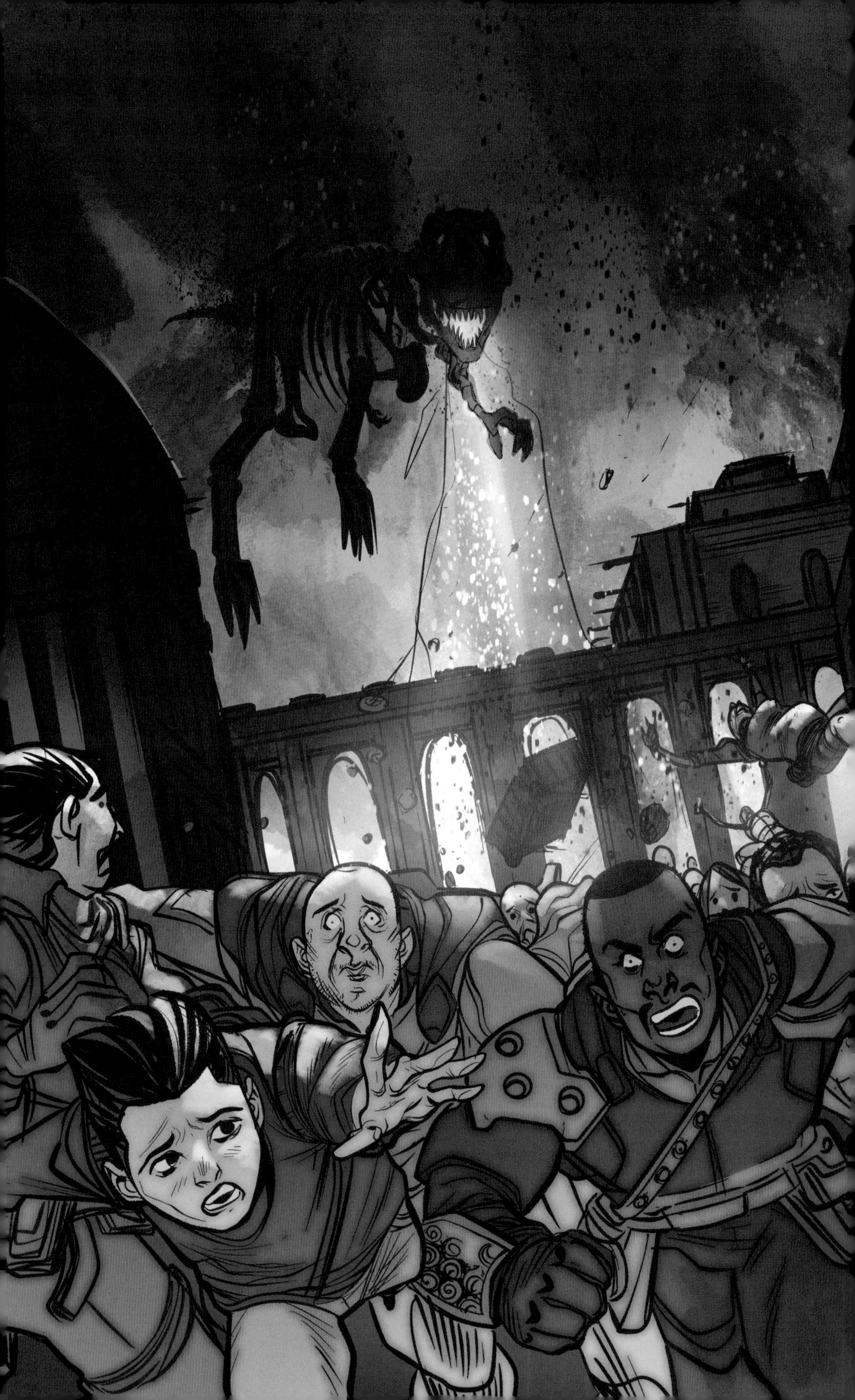

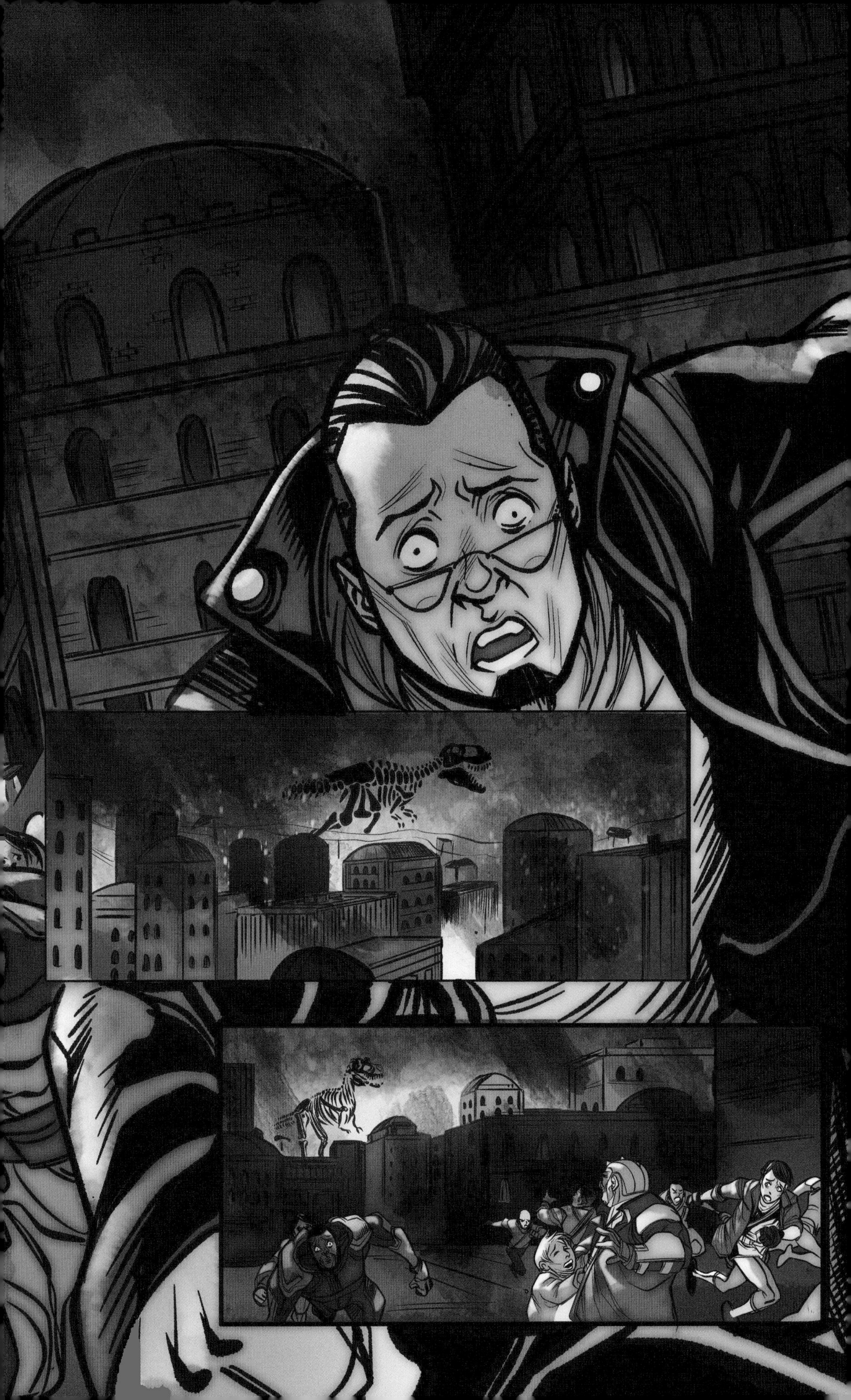

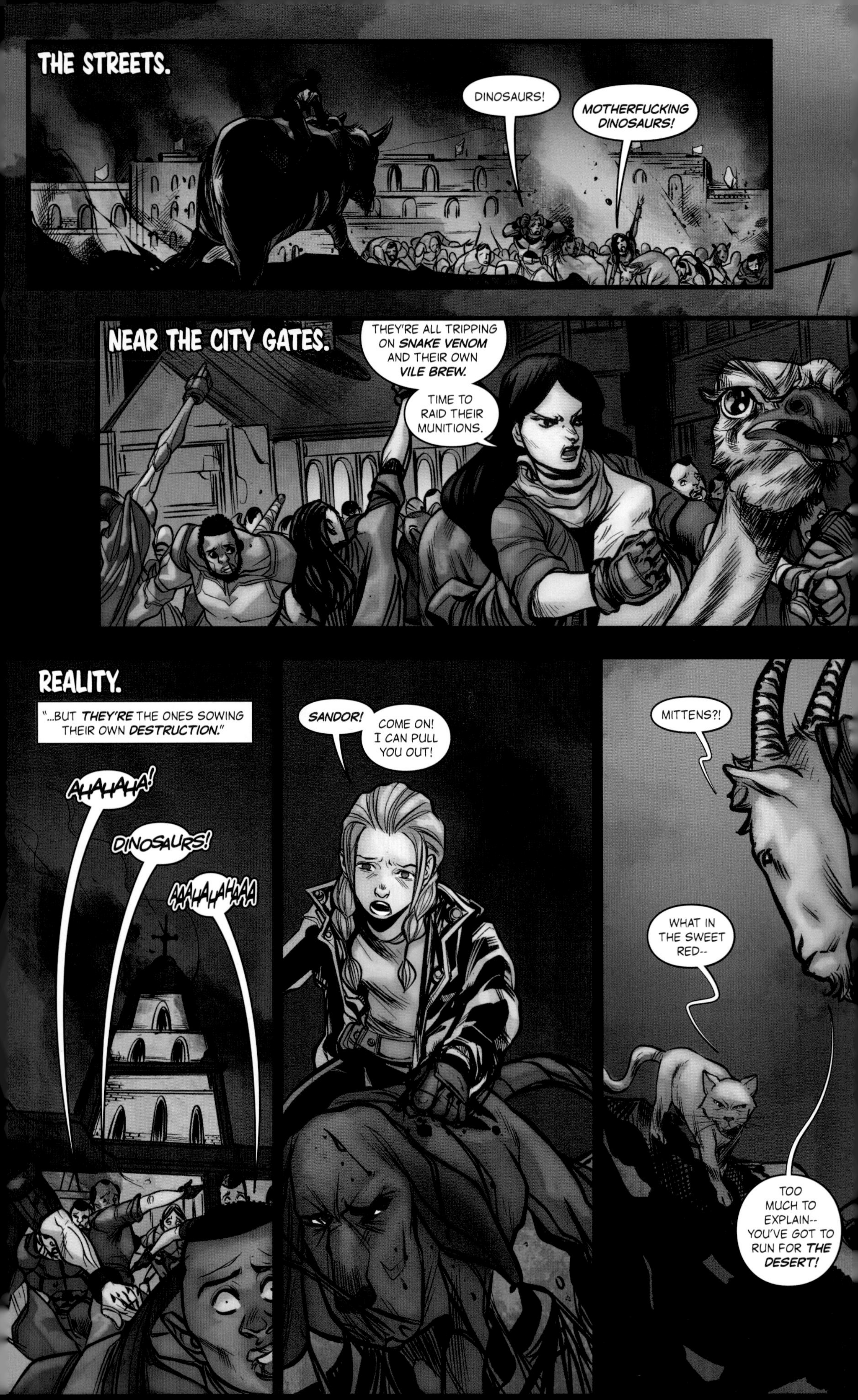
THE STREETS.
DINOSAURS!
MOTHERFUCKING DINOSAURS!
NEAR THE CITY GATES.
THEY'RE ALL TRIPPING ON SNAKE VENOM AND THEIR OWN VILE BREW.
TIME TO RAID THEIR MUNITIONS.
REALITY.
"...BUT THEY'RE THE ONES SOWING THEIR OWN DESTRUCTION."
AHAHAHA!
DINOSAURS!
AAAHAHAHAA
SANDOR!
COME ON! I CAN PULL YOU OUT!
MITTENS?!
WHAT IN THE SWEET RED--
TOO MUCH TO EXPLAIN-- YOU'VE GOT TO RUN FOR THE DESERT!

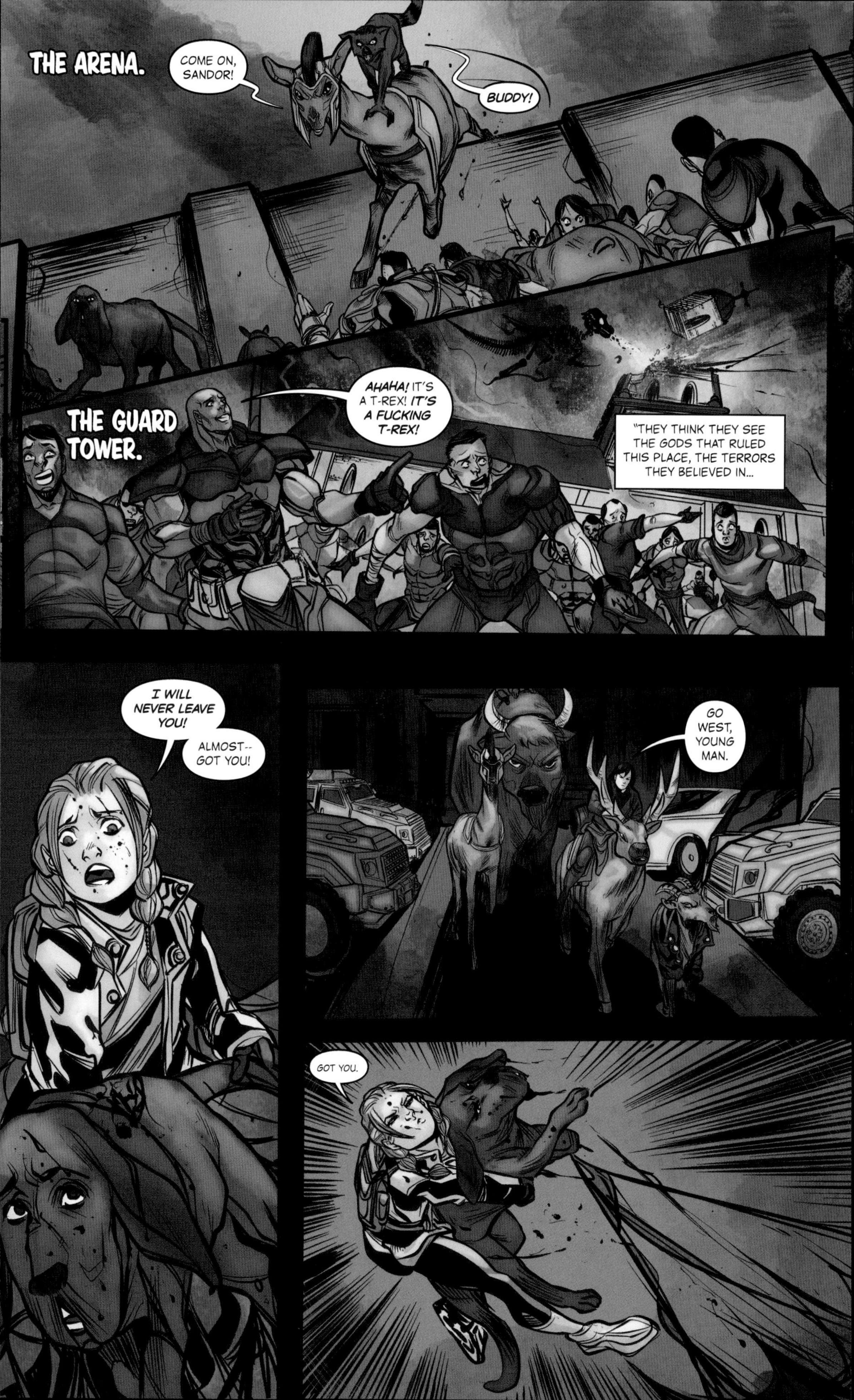
THE ARENA.
COME ON, SANDOR!
BUDDY!
THE GUARD TOWER.
AHAHA! IT'S A T-REX! IT'S A FUCKING T-REX!
"THEY THINK THEY SEE THE GODS THAT RULED THIS PLACE, THE TERRORS THEY BELIEVED IN...
I WILL NEVER LEAVE YOU!
ALMOST--GOT YOU!
GO WEST, YOUNG MAN.
GOT YOU.

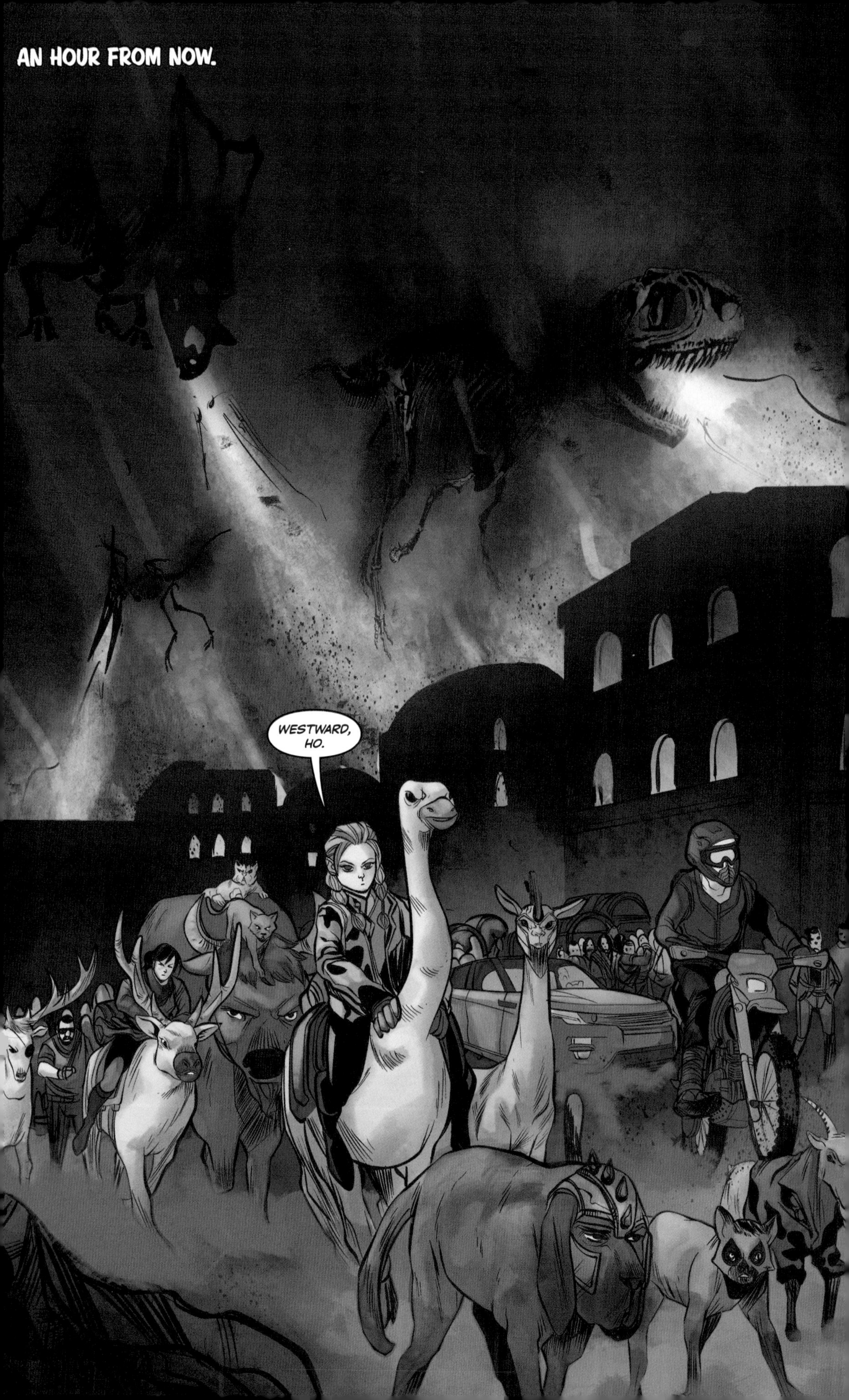
AN HOUR FROM NOW.
WESTWARD, HO.

28

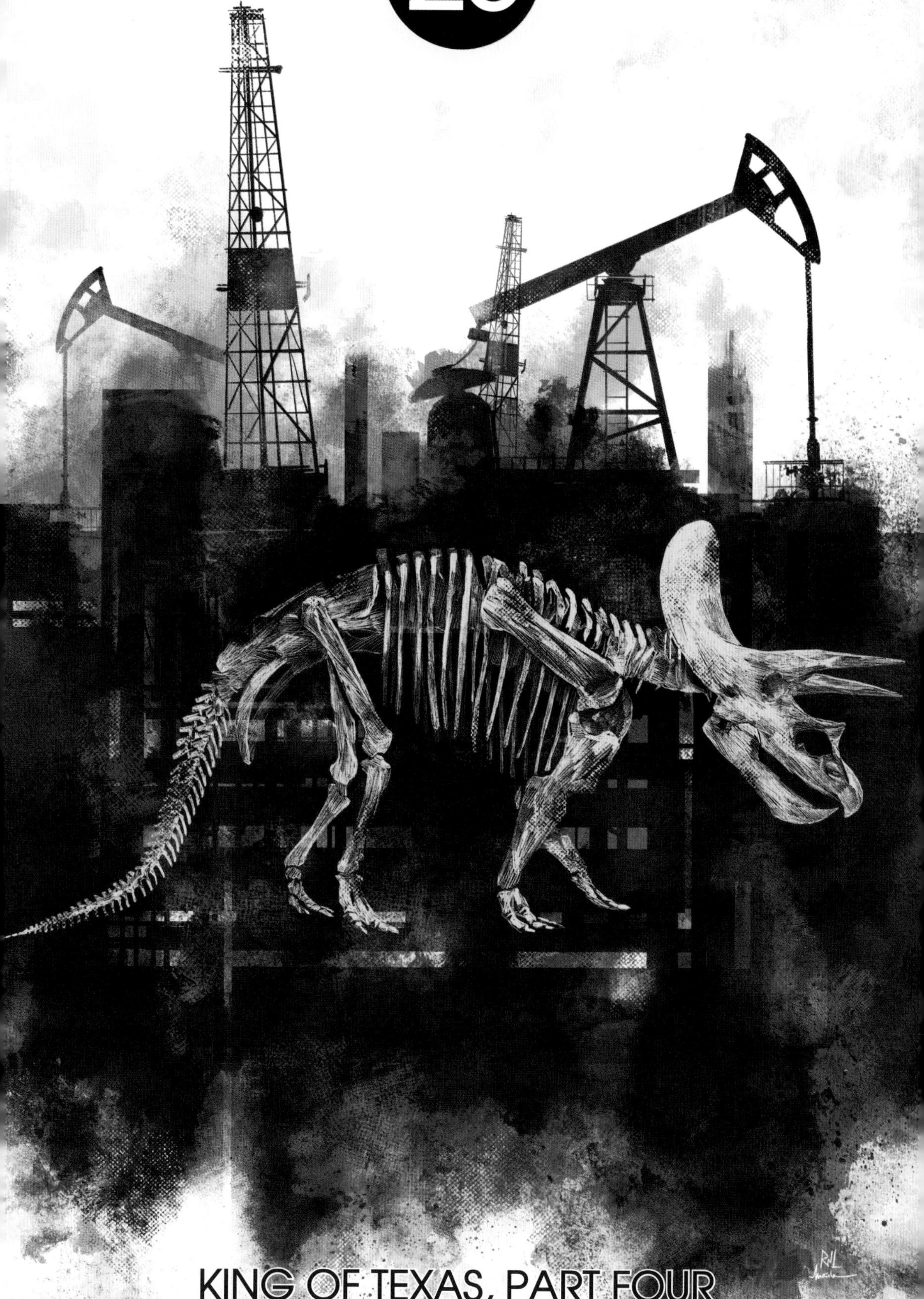

KING OF TEXAS, PART FOUR

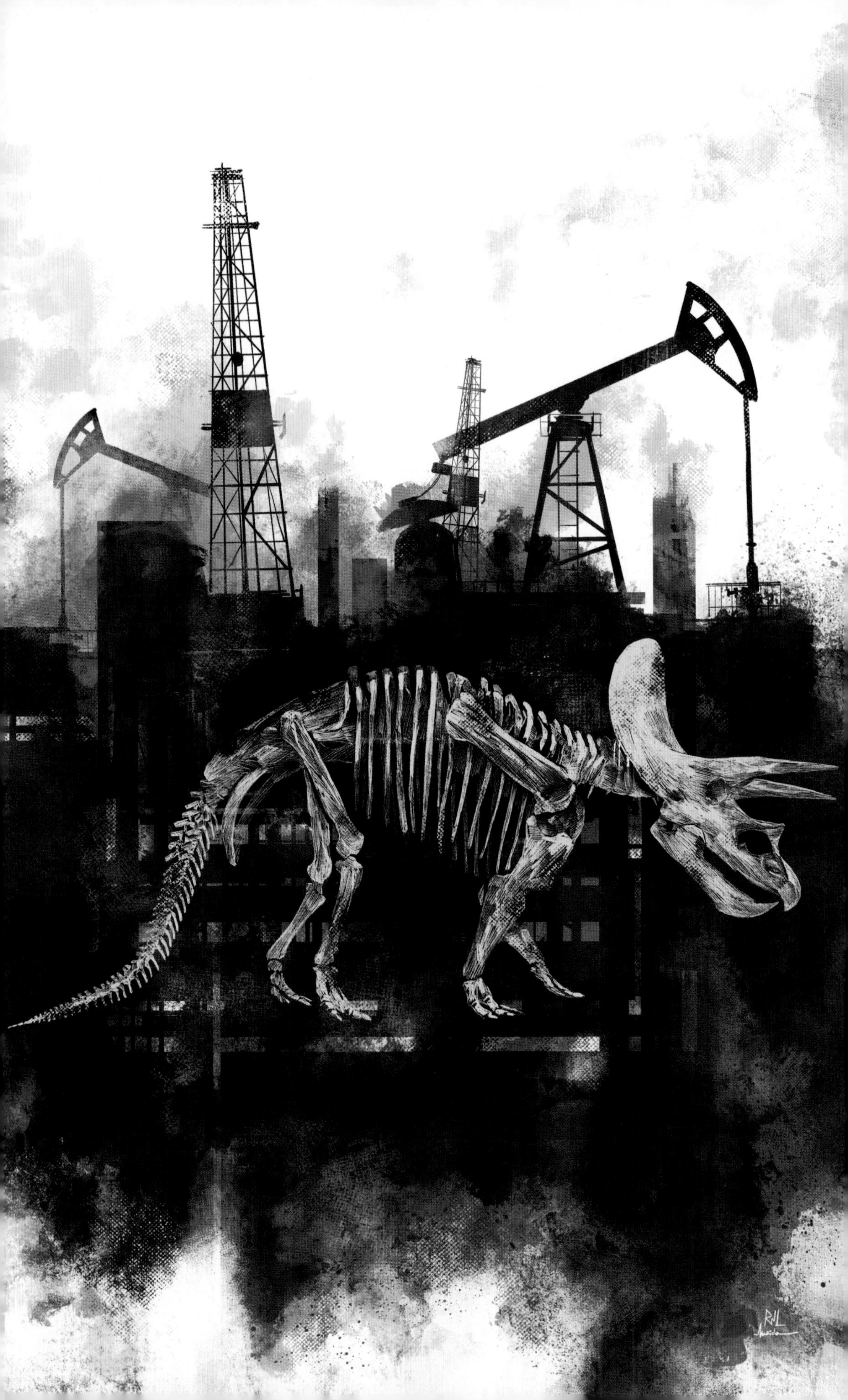

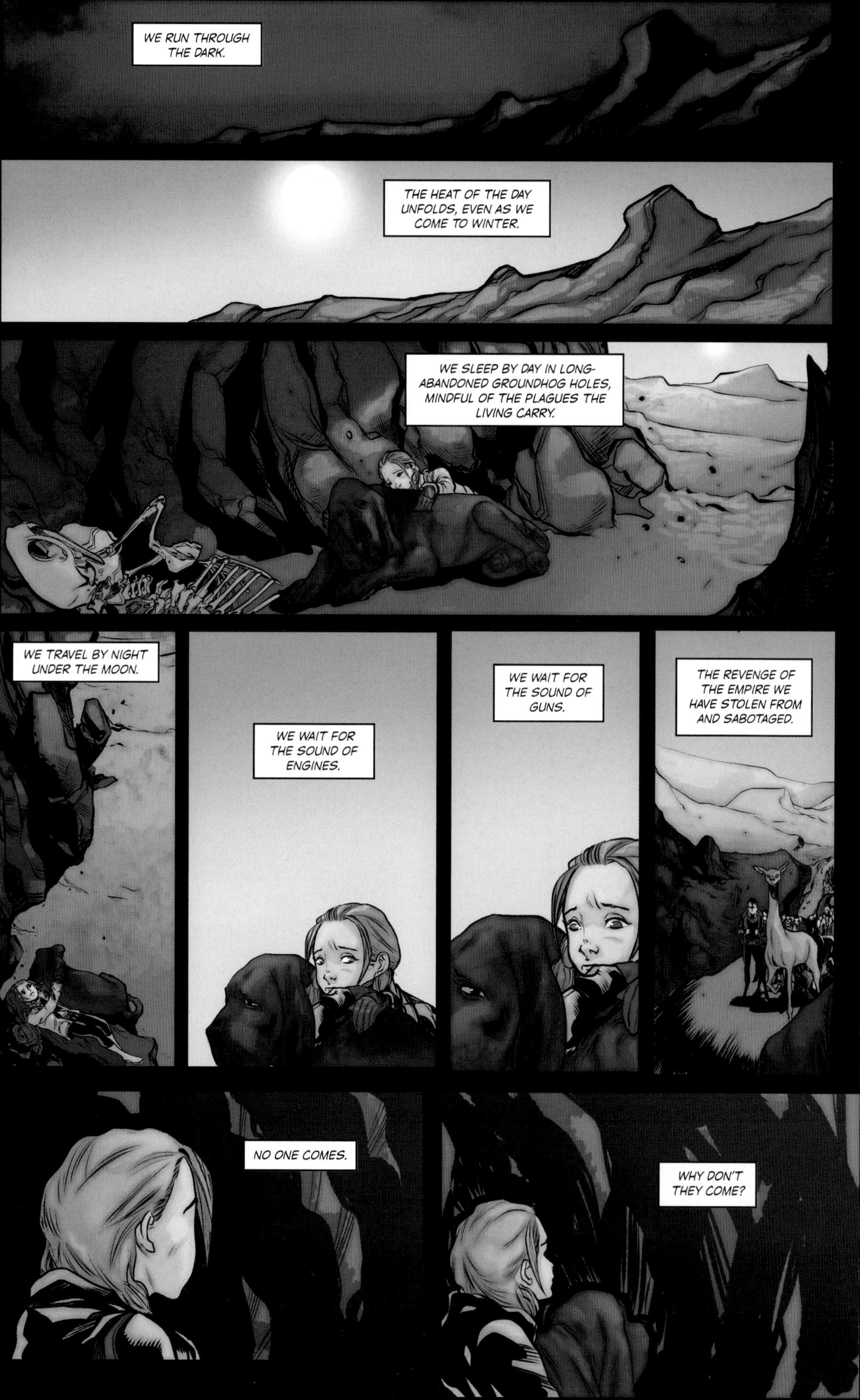
WE RUN THROUGH THE DARK.
THE HEAT OF THE DAY UNFOLDS, EVEN AS WE COME TO WINTER.
WE SLEEP BY DAY IN LONG-ABANDONED GROUNDHOG HOLES, MINDFUL OF THE PLAGUES THE LIVING CARRY.
WE TRAVEL BY NIGHT UNDER THE MOON.
WE WAIT FOR THE SOUND OF ENGINES.
WE WAIT FOR THE SOUND OF GUNS.
THE REVENGE OF THE EMPIRE WE HAVE STOLEN FROM AND SABOTAGED.
NO ONE COMES.
WHY DON'T THEY COME?

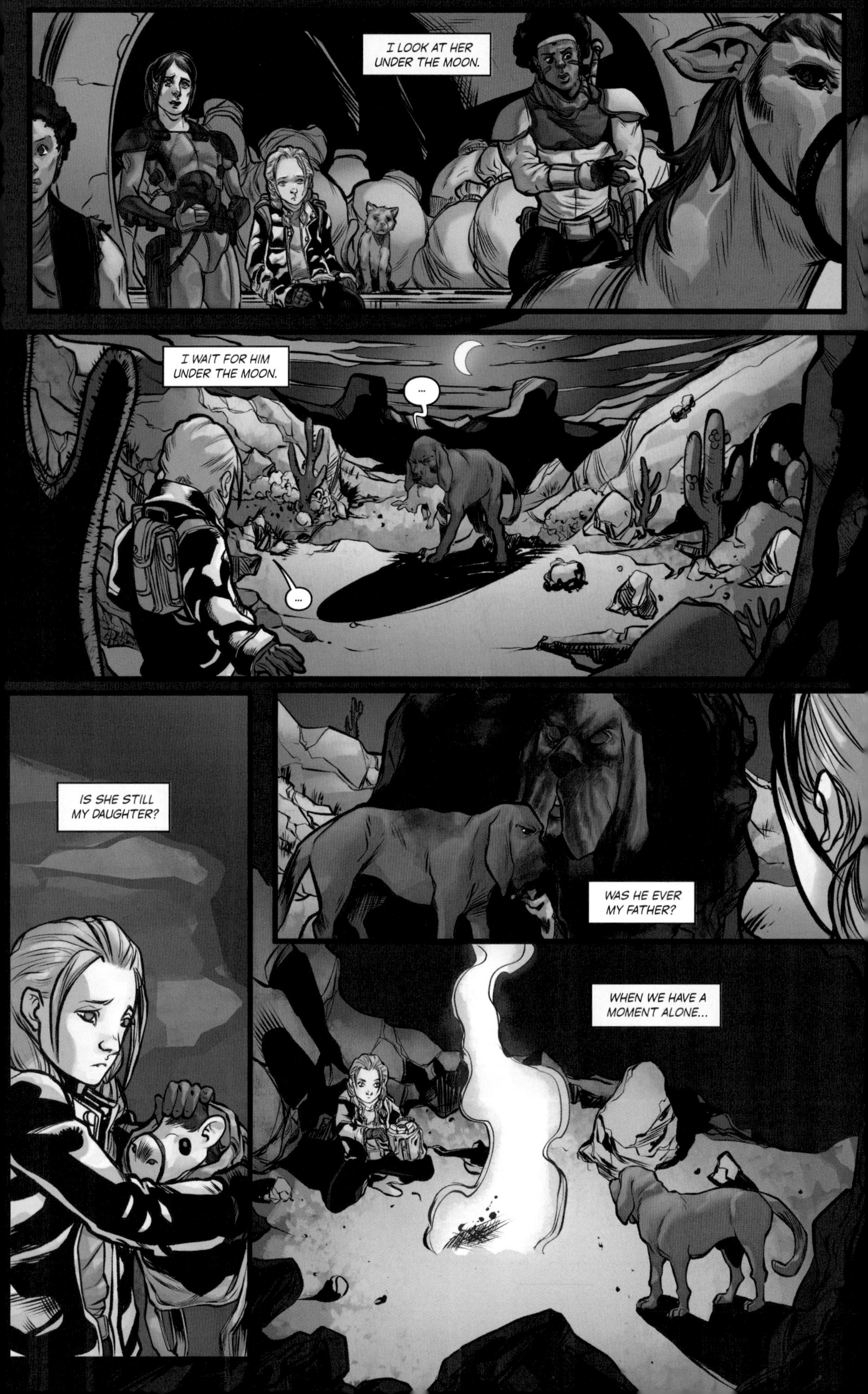
I LOOK AT HER UNDER THE MOON.
I WAIT FOR HIM UNDER THE MOON.
...
...
IS SHE STILL MY DAUGHTER?
WAS HE EVER MY FATHER?
WHEN WE HAVE A MOMENT ALONE...

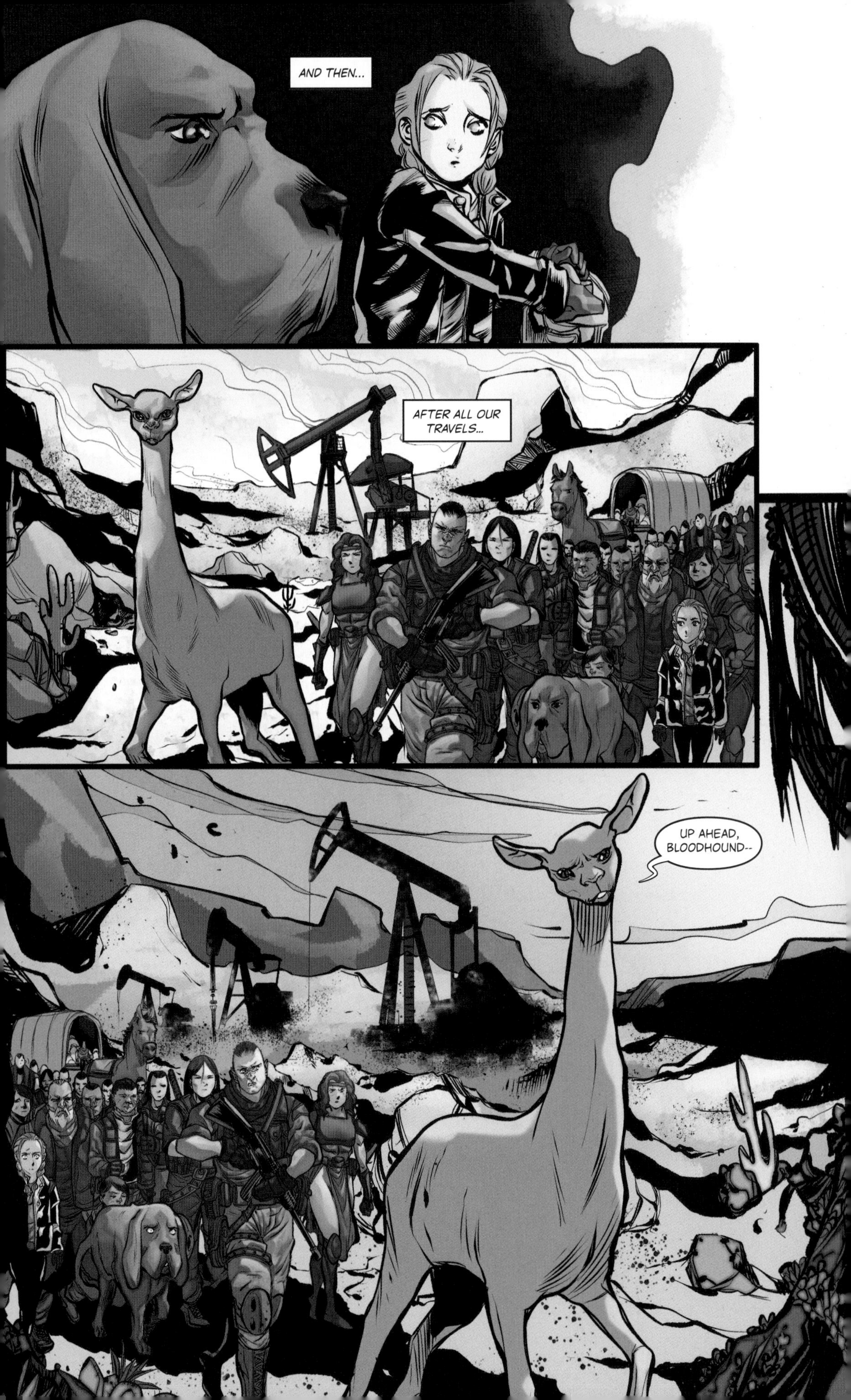
AND THEN...
AFTER ALL OUR TRAVELS...
UP AHEAD, BLOODHOUND--

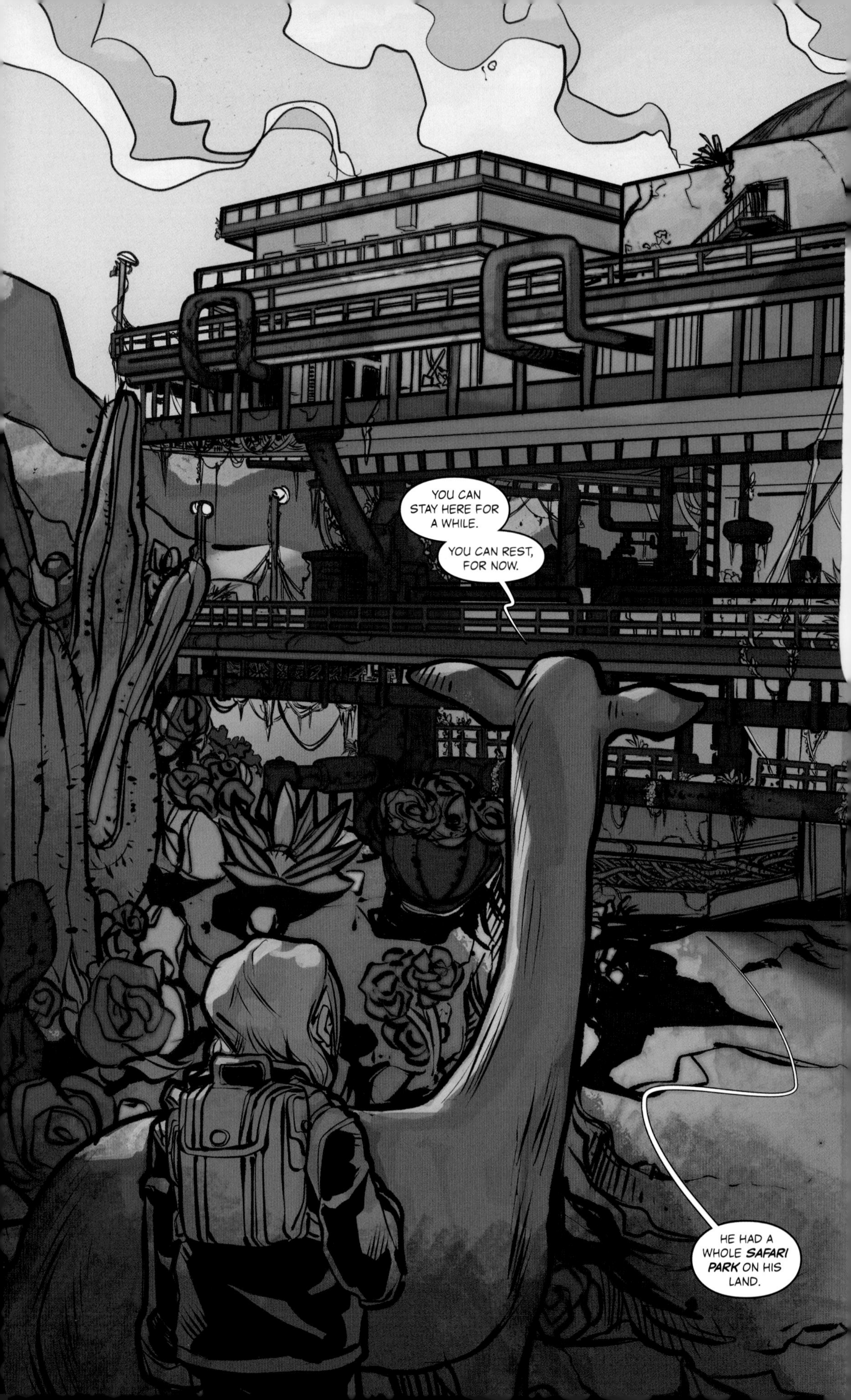
YOU CAN STAY HERE FOR A WHILE.
YOU CAN REST, FOR NOW.
HE HAD A WHOLE **SAFARI PARK** ON HIS LAND.

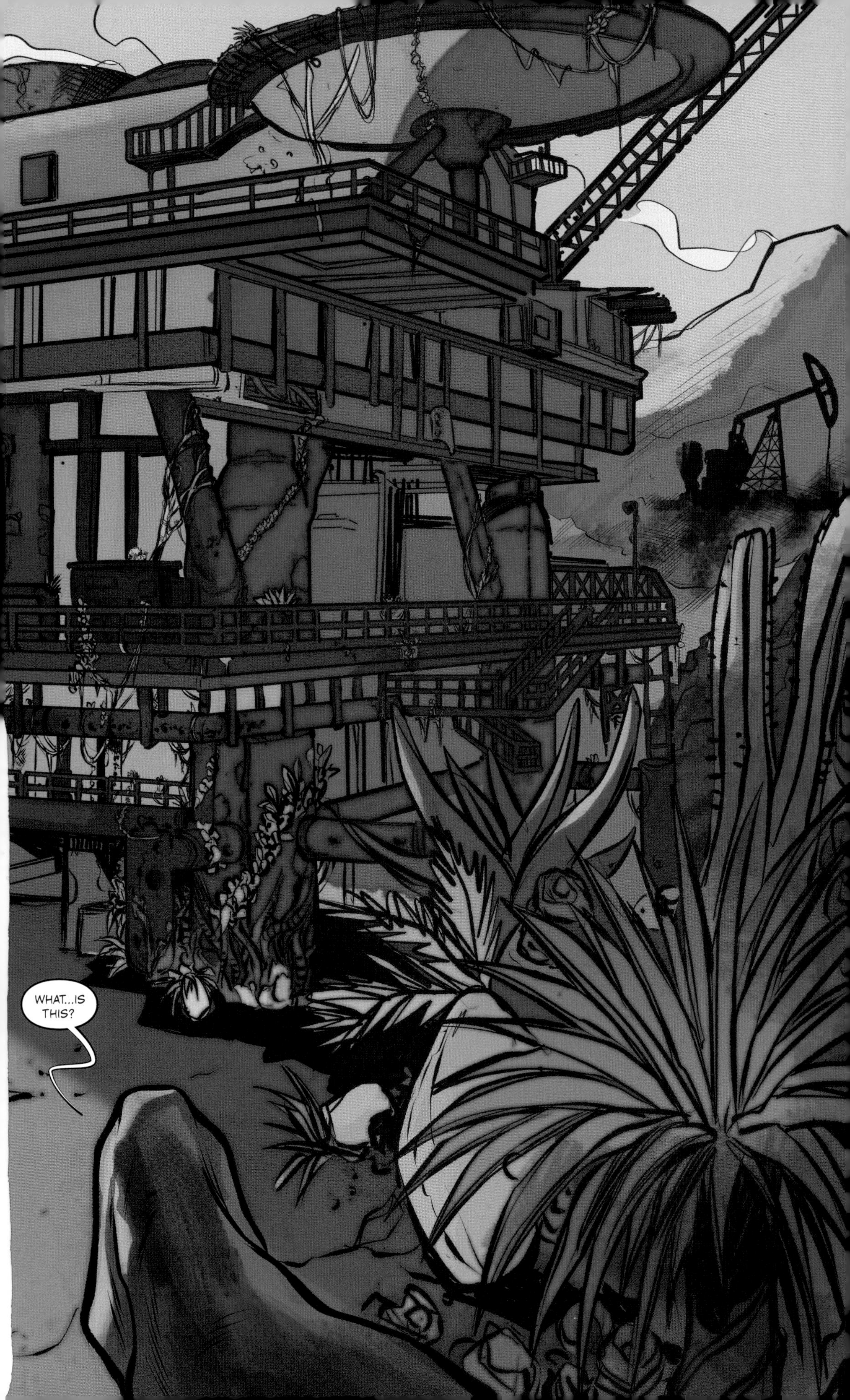
WHAT...IS THIS?

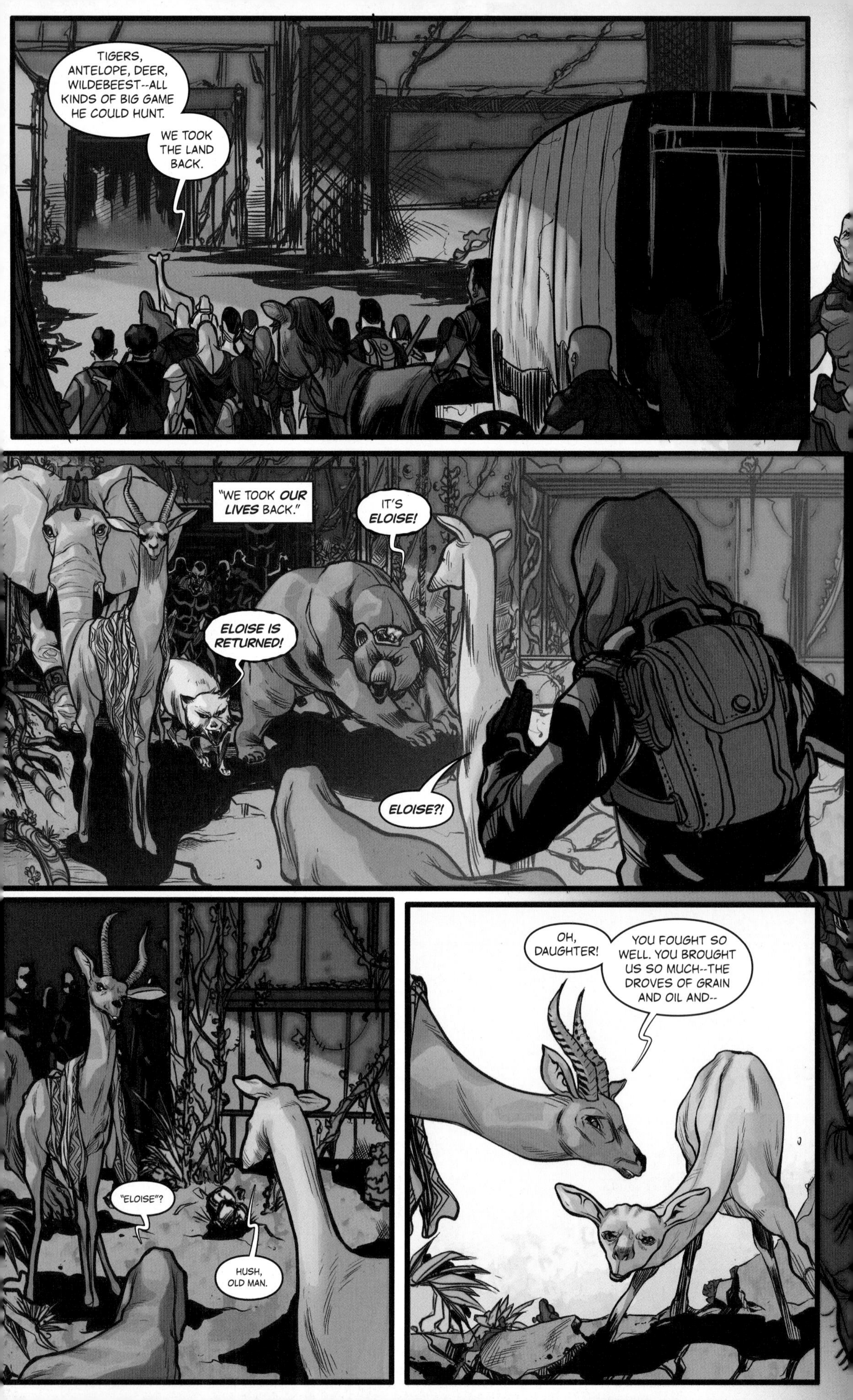
TIGERS, ANTELOPE, DEER, WILDEBEEST--ALL KINDS OF BIG GAME HE COULD HUNT.
WE TOOK THE LAND BACK.
"WE TOOK OUR LIVES BACK."
IT'S ELOISE!
ELOISE IS RETURNED!
ELOISE?!
"ELOISE"?
HUSH, OLD MAN.
OH, DAUGHTER!
YOU FOUGHT SO WELL. YOU BROUGHT US SO MUCH--THE DROVES OF GRAIN AND OIL AND--

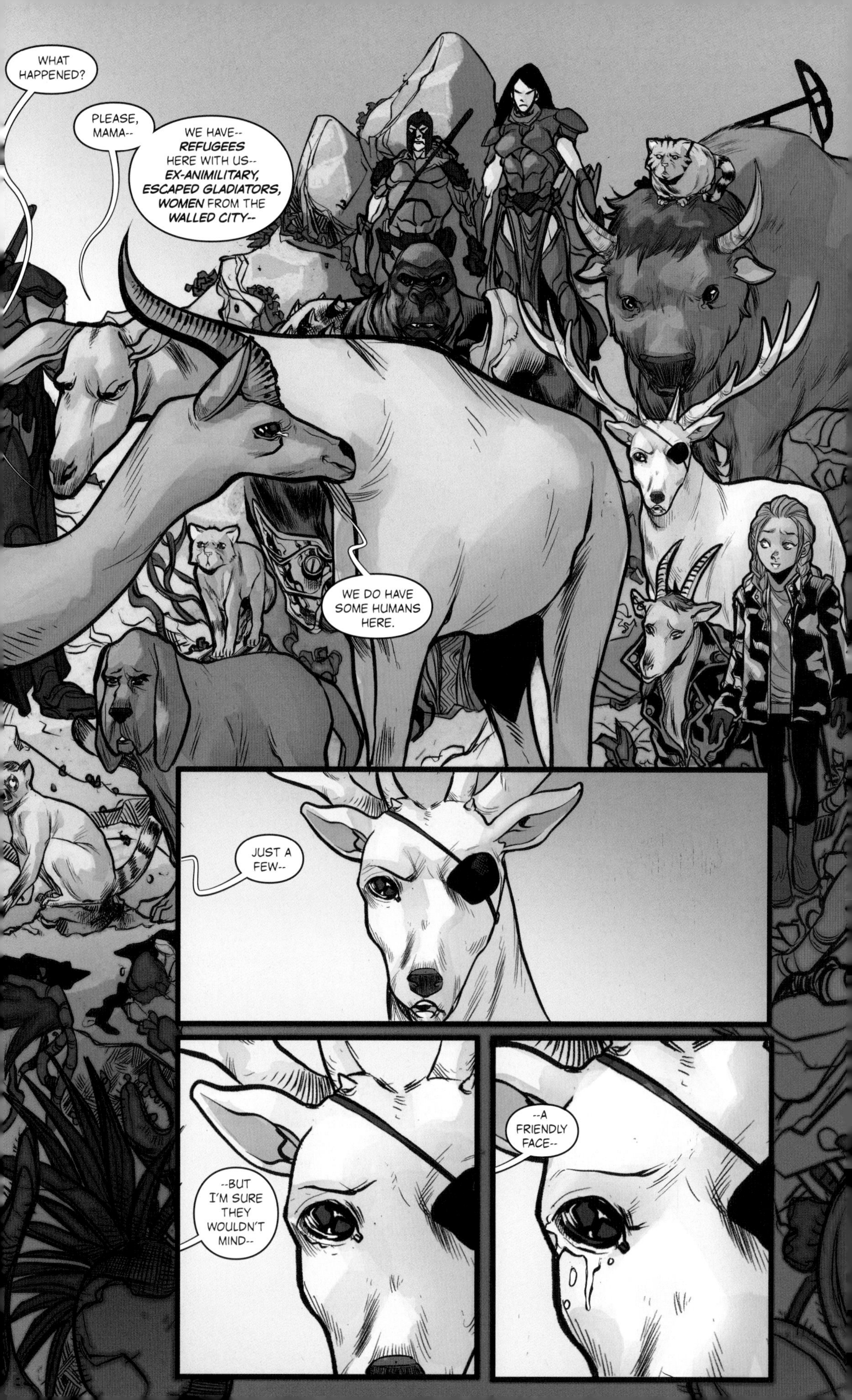
WHAT HAPPENED?
PLEASE, MAMA--
WE HAVE-- **REFUGEES** HERE WITH US-- **EX-ANIMILITARY, ESCAPED GLADIATORS, WOMEN** FROM THE **WALLED CITY--**
WE DO HAVE SOME HUMANS HERE.
JUST A FEW--
--BUT I'M SURE THEY WOULDN'T MIND--
--A FRIENDLY FACE--

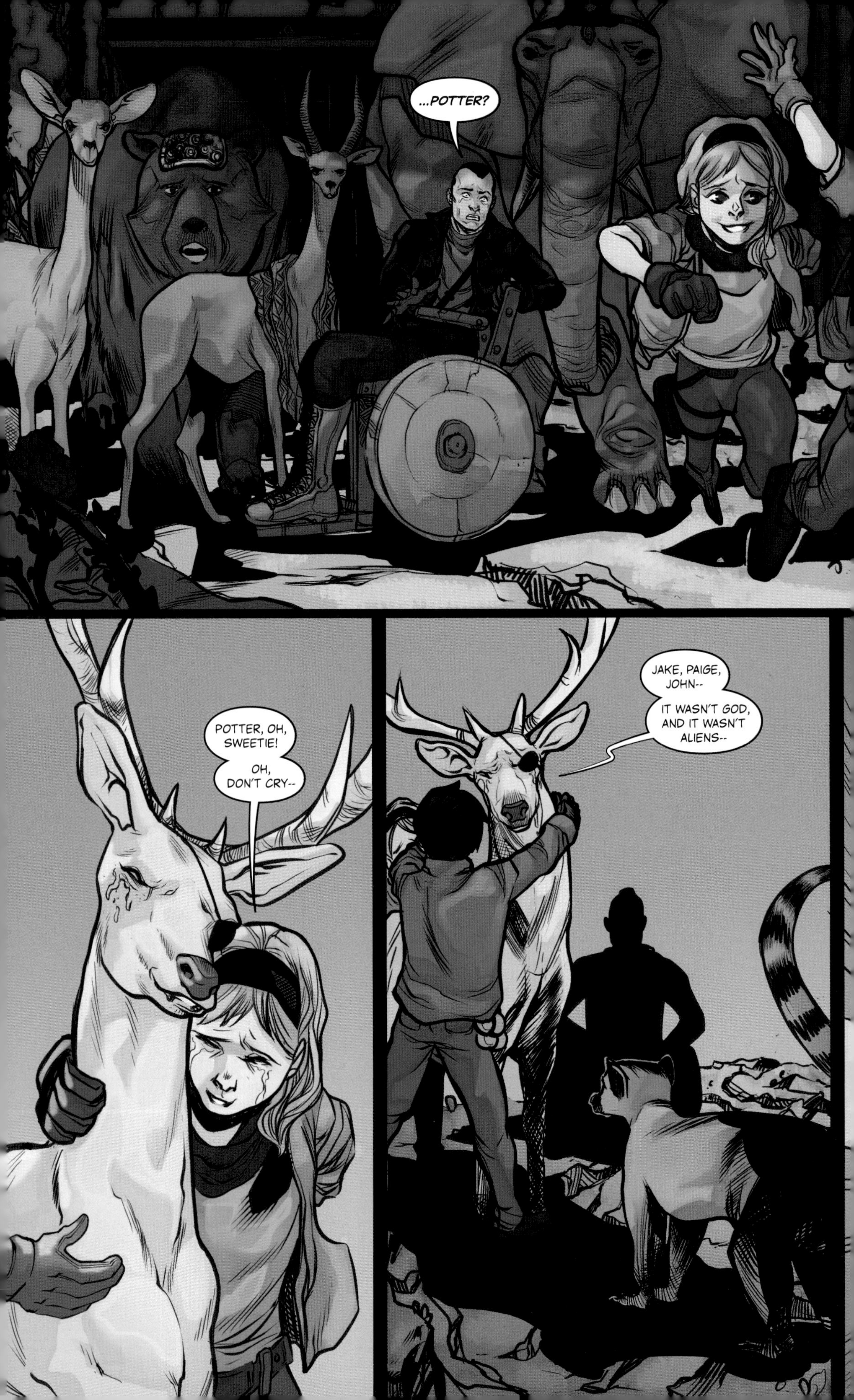
...POTTER?
POTTER, OH, SWEETIE!
OH, DON'T CRY--
JAKE, PAIGE, JOHN--
IT WASN'T GOD, AND IT WASN'T ALIENS--

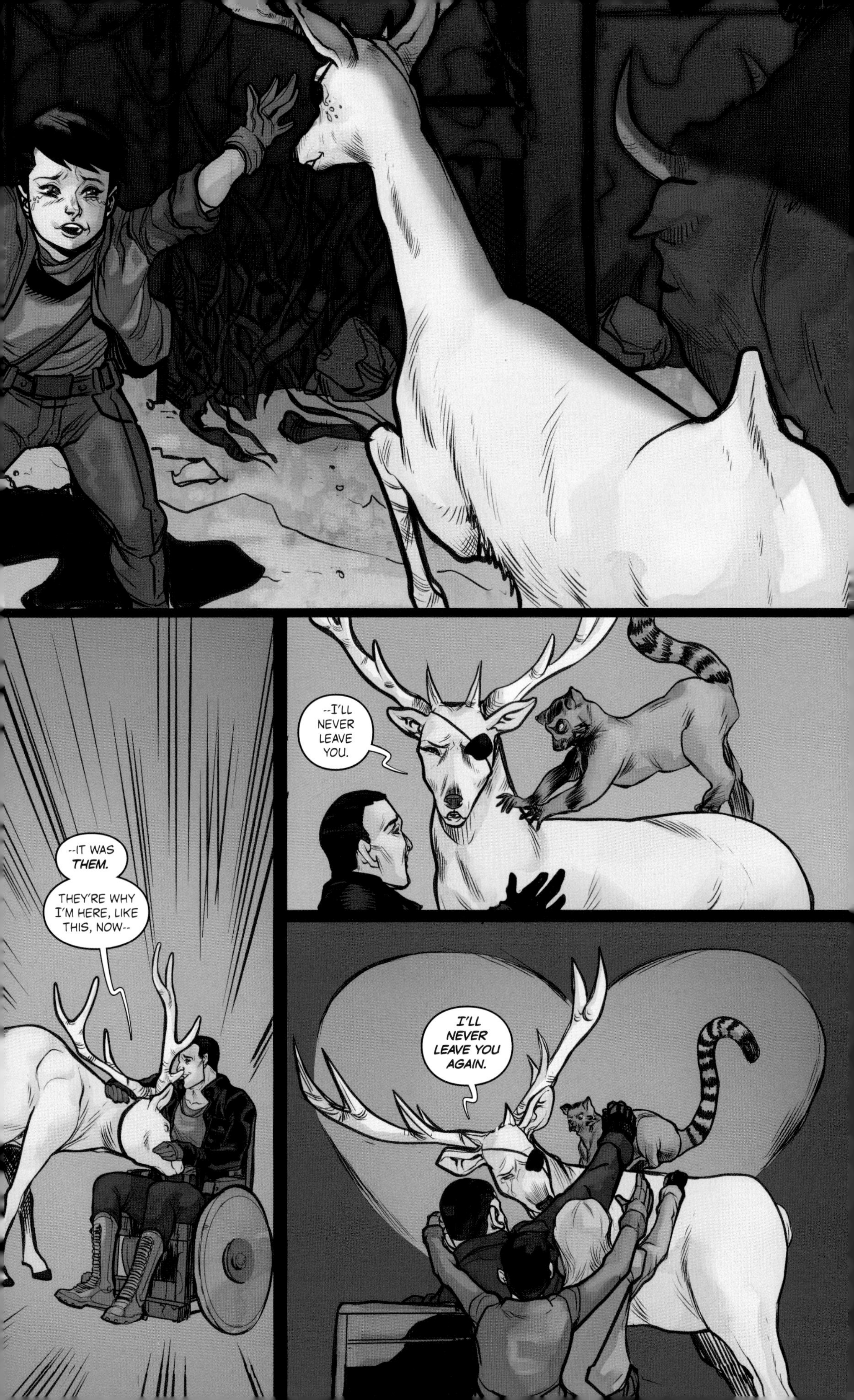
--IT WAS THEM.
THEY'RE WHY I'M HERE, LIKE THIS, NOW--
--I'LL NEVER LEAVE YOU.
I'LL NEVER LEAVE YOU AGAIN.

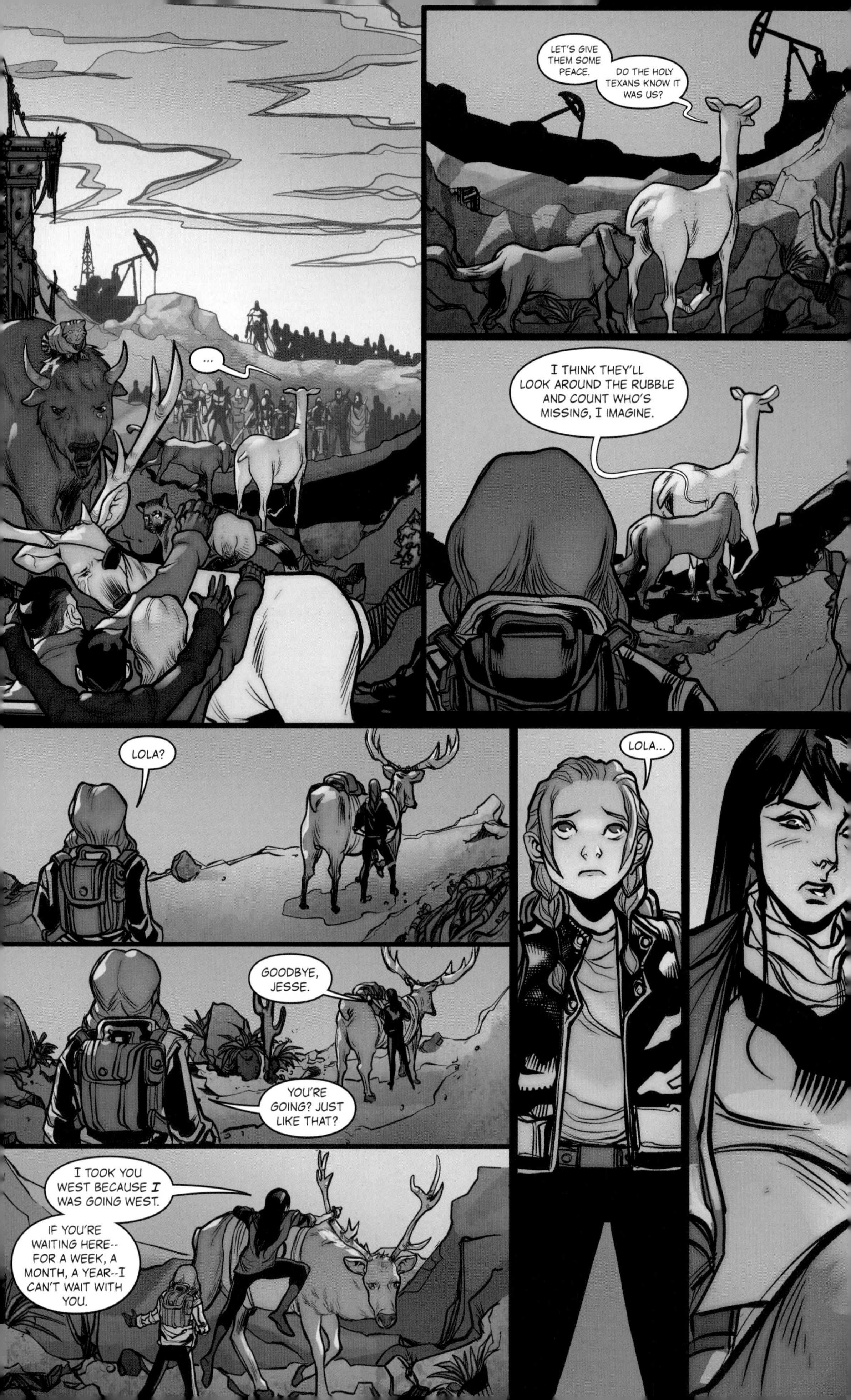
...
LET'S GIVE THEM SOME PEACE.
DO THE HOLY TEXANS KNOW IT WAS US?
I THINK THEY'LL LOOK AROUND THE RUBBLE AND COUNT WHO'S MISSING, I IMAGINE.
LOLA?
GOODBYE, JESSE.
YOU'RE GOING? JUST LIKE THAT?
I TOOK YOU WEST BECAUSE I WAS GOING WEST.
IF YOU'RE WAITING HERE-- FOR A WEEK, A MONTH, A YEAR--I CAN'T WAIT WITH YOU.
LOLA...

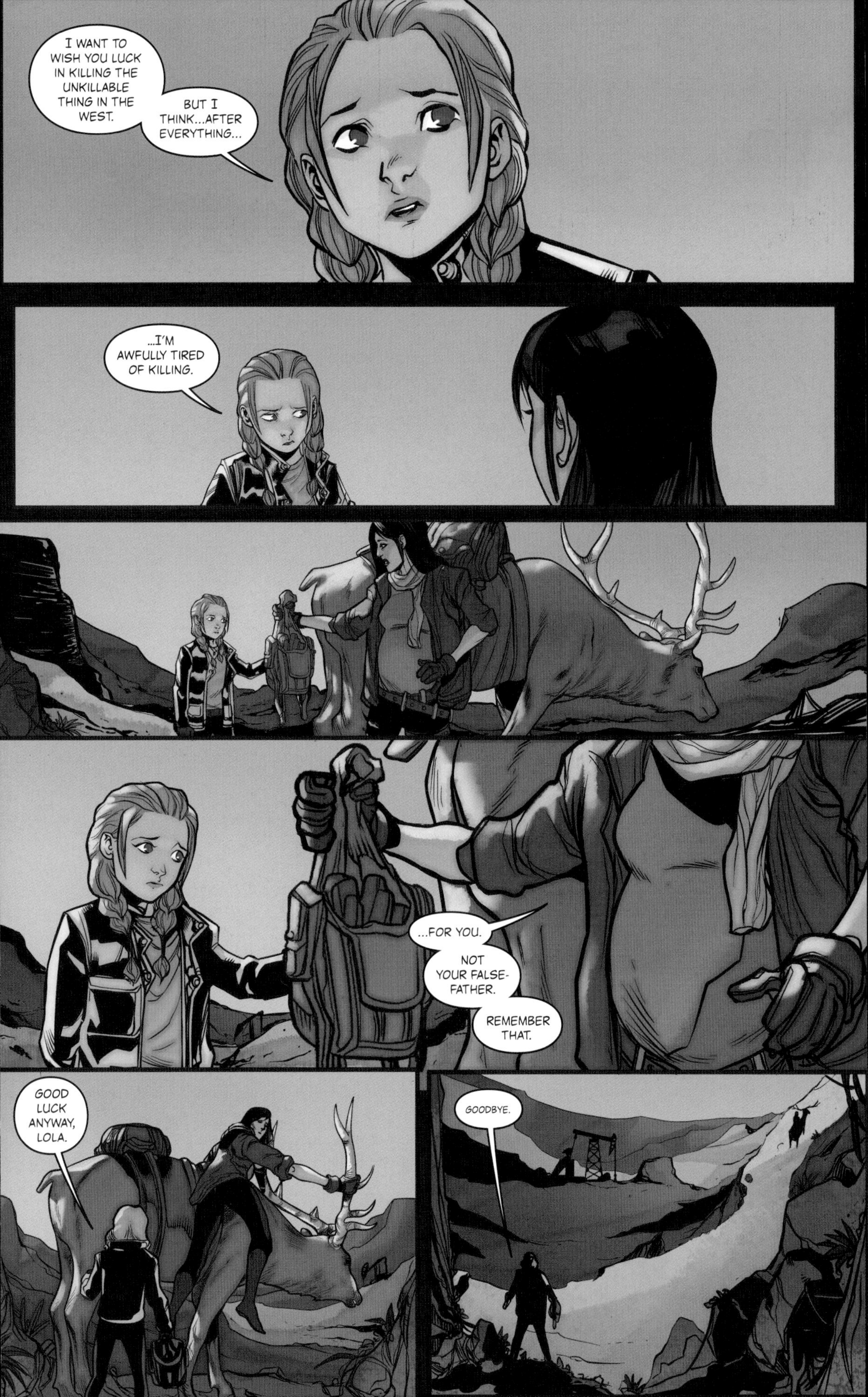
I WANT TO WISH YOU LUCK IN KILLING THE UNKILLABLE THING IN THE WEST.
BUT I THINK...AFTER EVERYTHING...
...I'M AWFULLY TIRED OF KILLING.
...FOR YOU.
NOT YOUR FALSE-FATHER.
REMEMBER THAT.
GOOD LUCK ANYWAY, LOLA.
GOODBYE.

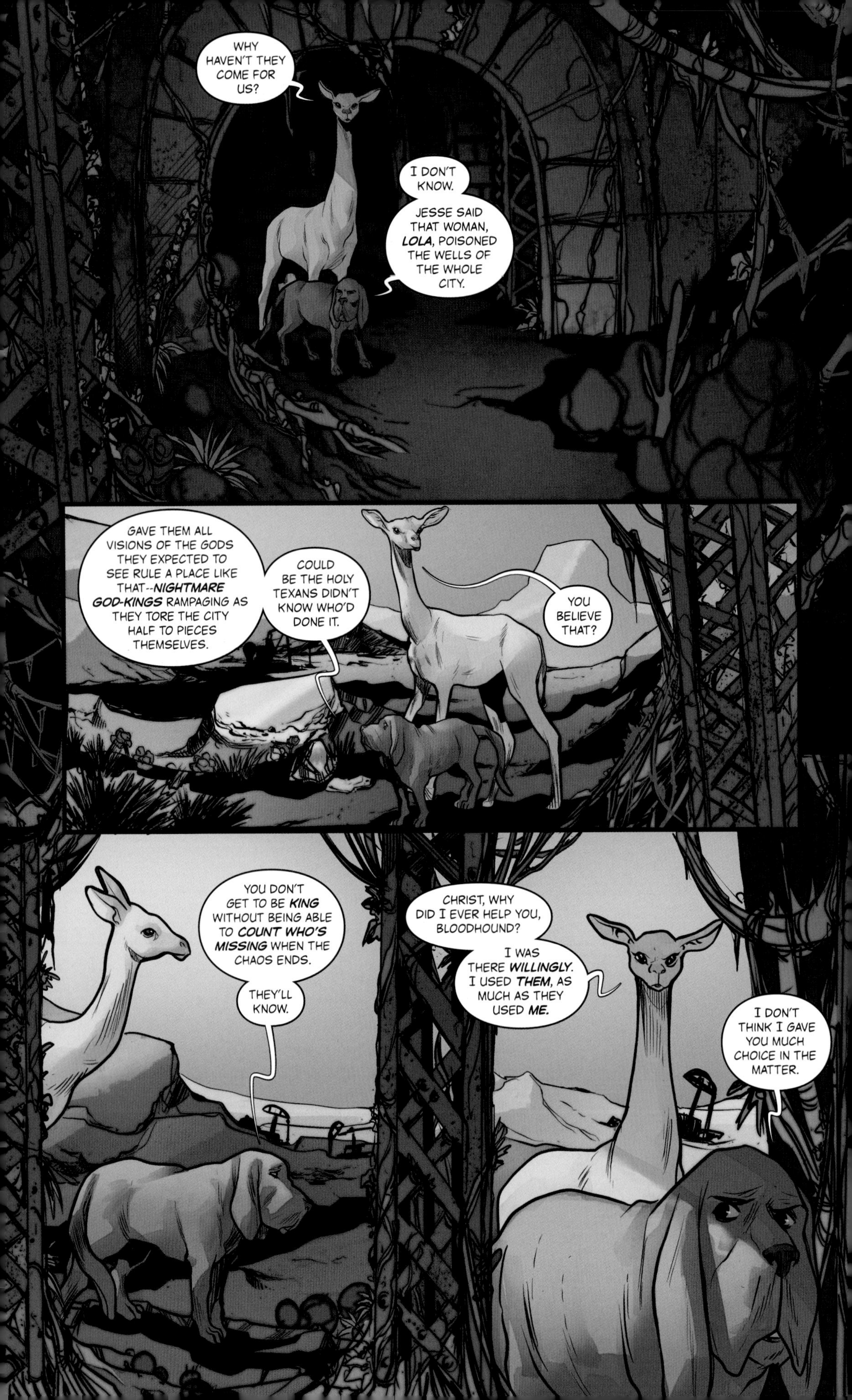
WHY HAVEN'T THEY COME FOR US?
I DON'T KNOW.
JESSE SAID THAT WOMAN, **LOLA**, POISONED THE WELLS OF THE WHOLE CITY.
GAVE THEM ALL VISIONS OF THE GODS THEY EXPECTED TO SEE RULE A PLACE LIKE THAT--**NIGHTMARE GOD-KINGS** RAMPAGING AS THEY TORE THE CITY HALF TO PIECES THEMSELVES.
COULD BE THE HOLY TEXANS DIDN'T KNOW WHO'D DONE IT.
YOU BELIEVE THAT?
YOU DON'T GET TO BE **KING** WITHOUT BEING ABLE TO **COUNT WHO'S MISSING** WHEN THE CHAOS ENDS.
THEY'LL KNOW.
CHRIST, WHY DID I EVER HELP YOU, BLOODHOUND?
I WAS THERE **WILLINGLY**. I USED **THEM**, AS MUCH AS THEY USED **ME**.
I DON'T THINK I GAVE YOU MUCH CHOICE IN THE MATTER.

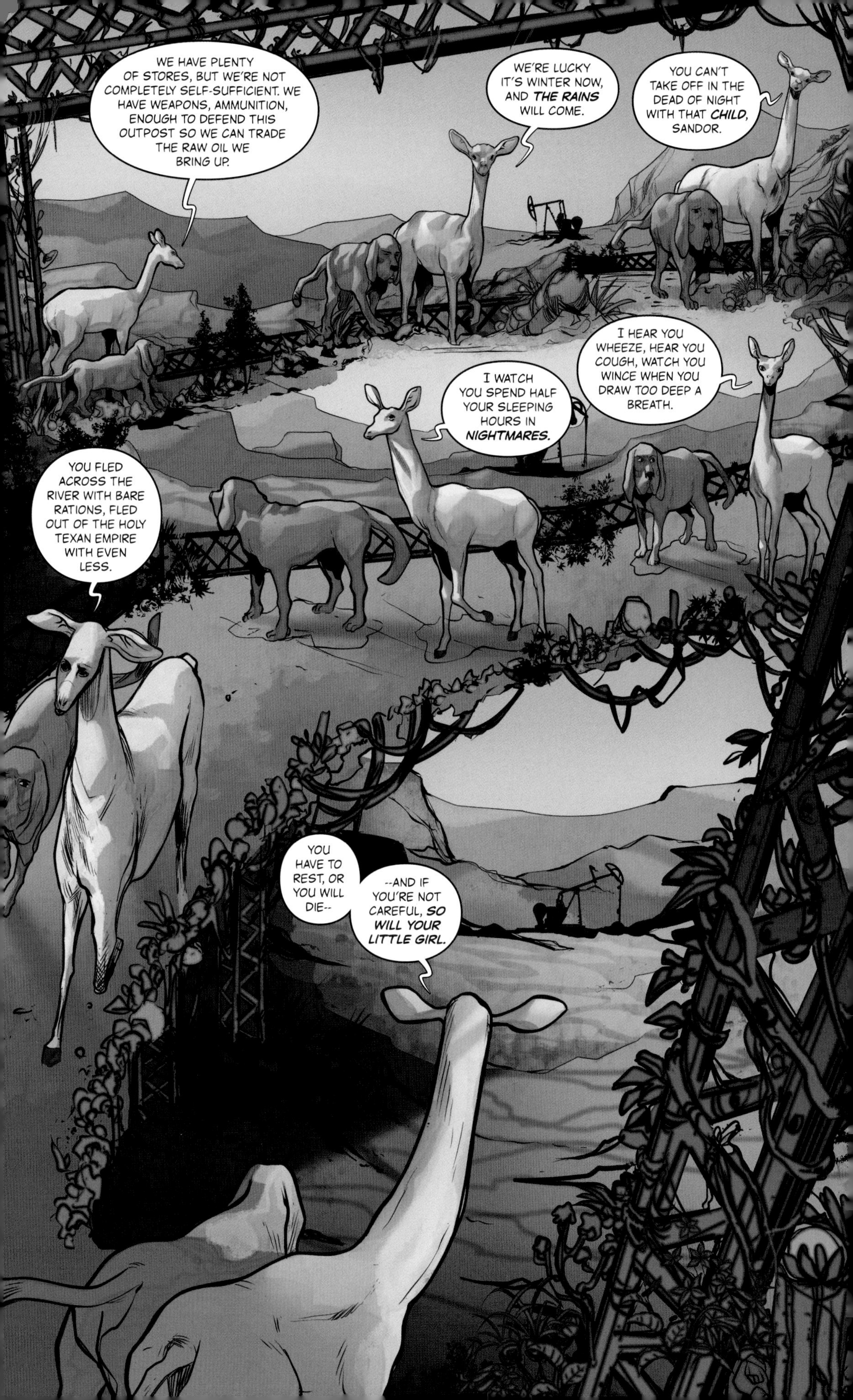
WE HAVE PLENTY OF STORES, BUT WE'RE NOT COMPLETELY SELF-SUFFICIENT. WE HAVE WEAPONS, AMMUNITION, ENOUGH TO DEFEND THIS OUTPOST SO WE CAN TRADE THE RAW OIL WE BRING UP.
WE'RE LUCKY IT'S WINTER NOW, AND ***THE RAINS*** WILL COME.
YOU CAN'T TAKE OFF IN THE DEAD OF NIGHT WITH THAT ***CHILD***, SANDOR.
I HEAR YOU WHEEZE, HEAR YOU COUGH, WATCH YOU WINCE WHEN YOU DRAW TOO DEEP A BREATH.
I WATCH YOU SPEND HALF YOUR SLEEPING HOURS IN ***NIGHTMARES.***
YOU FLED ACROSS THE RIVER WITH BARE RATIONS, FLED OUT OF THE HOLY TEXAN EMPIRE WITH EVEN LESS.
YOU HAVE TO REST, OR YOU WILL DIE--
--AND IF YOU'RE NOT CAREFUL, ***SO WILL YOUR LITTLE GIRL.***

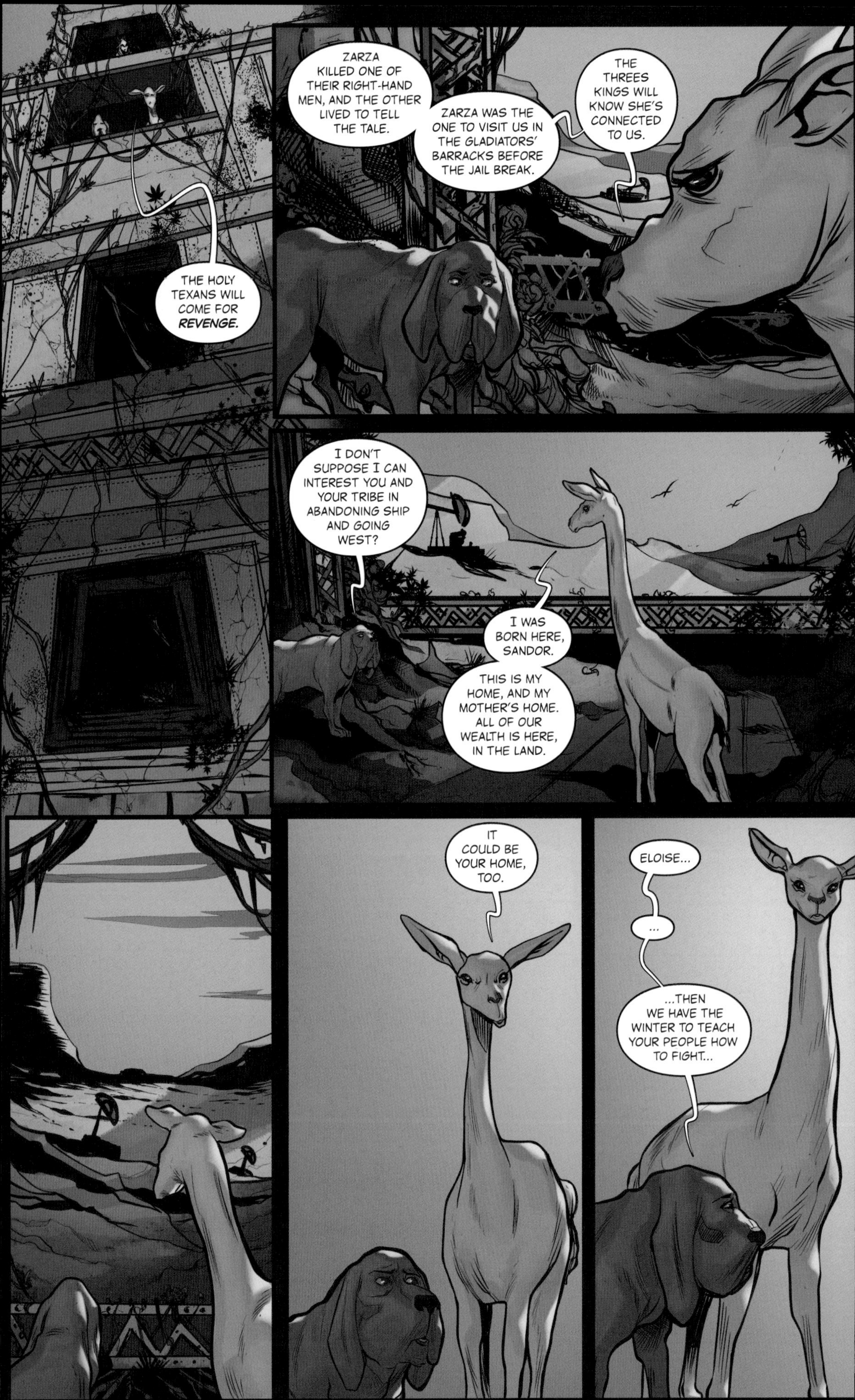
THE HOLY TEXANS WILL COME FOR *REVENGE.*
ZARZA KILLED ONE OF THEIR RIGHT-HAND MEN, AND THE OTHER LIVED TO TELL THE TALE.
ZARZA WAS THE ONE TO VISIT US IN THE GLADIATORS' BARRACKS BEFORE THE JAIL BREAK.
THE THREES KINGS WILL KNOW SHE'S CONNECTED TO US.
I DON'T SUPPOSE I CAN INTEREST YOU AND YOUR TRIBE IN ABANDONING SHIP AND GOING WEST?
I WAS BORN HERE, SANDOR.
THIS IS MY HOME, AND MY MOTHER'S HOME. ALL OF OUR WEALTH IS HERE, IN THE LAND.
IT COULD BE YOUR HOME, TOO.
ELOISE...
...
...THEN WE HAVE THE WINTER TO TEACH YOUR PEOPLE HOW TO FIGHT...

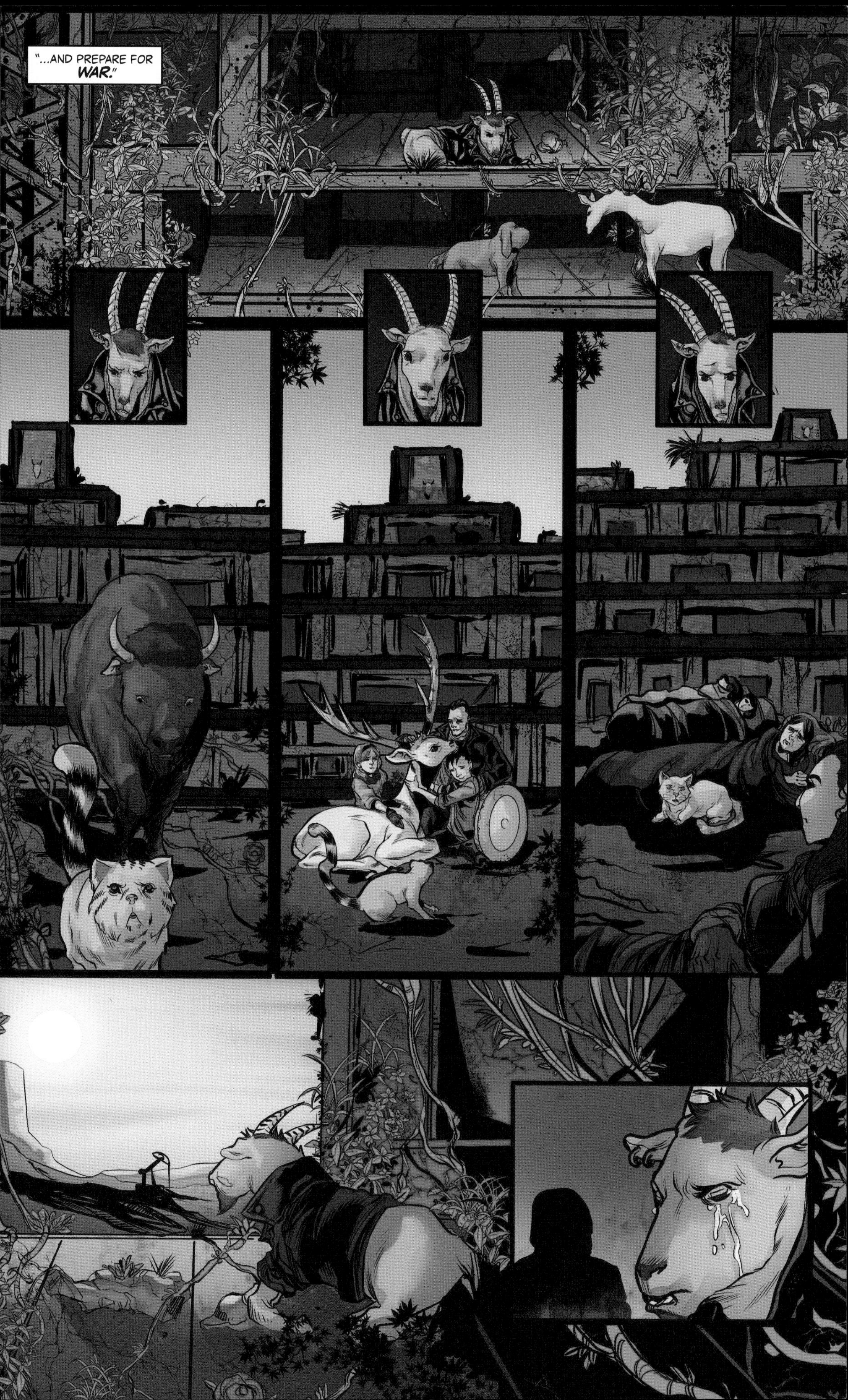
"...AND PREPARE FOR WAR."

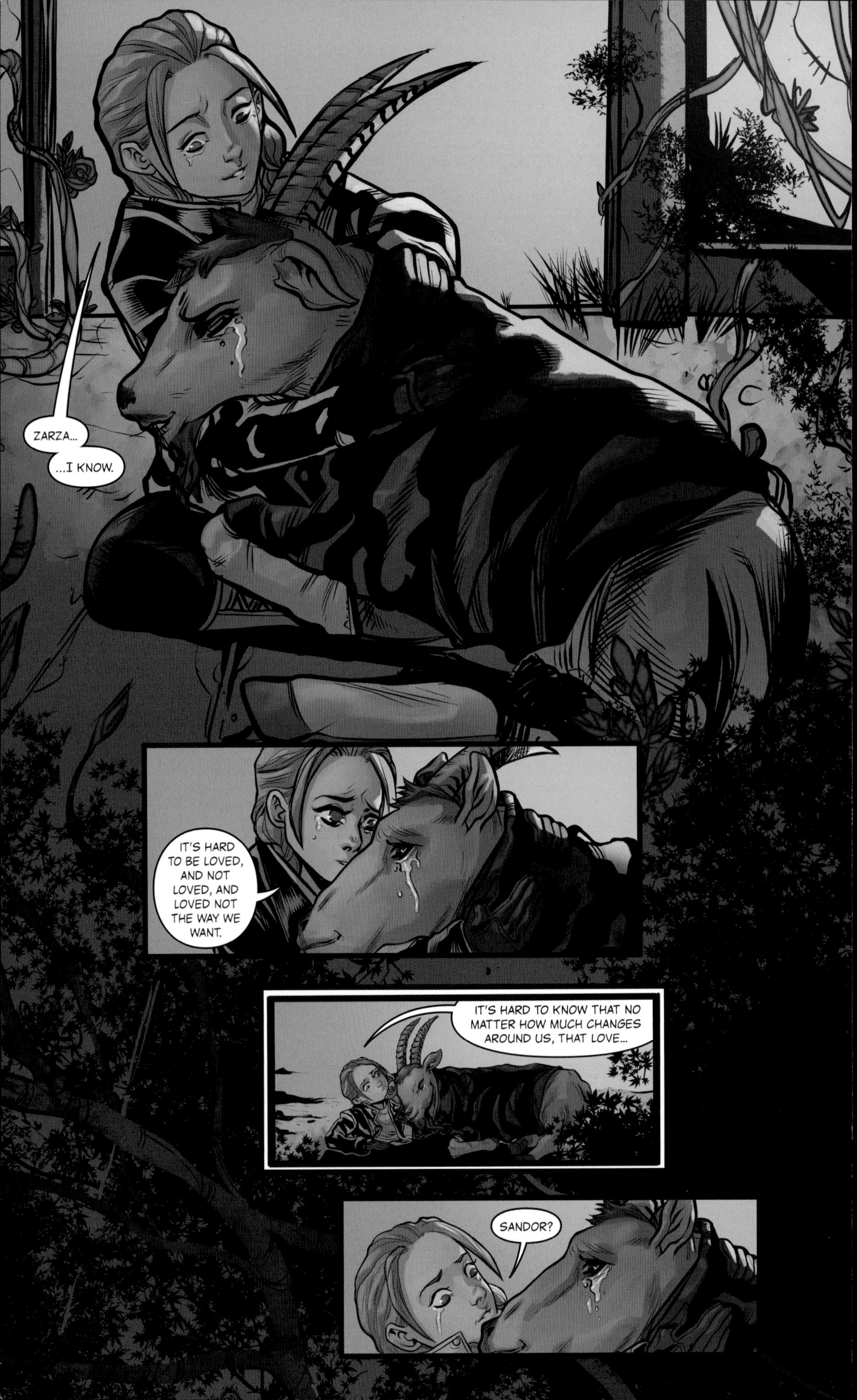
ZARZA...
...I KNOW.
IT'S HARD TO BE LOVED, AND NOT LOVED, AND LOVED NOT THE WAY WE WANT.
IT'S HARD TO KNOW THAT NO MATTER HOW MUCH CHANGES AROUND US, THAT LOVE...
SANDOR?

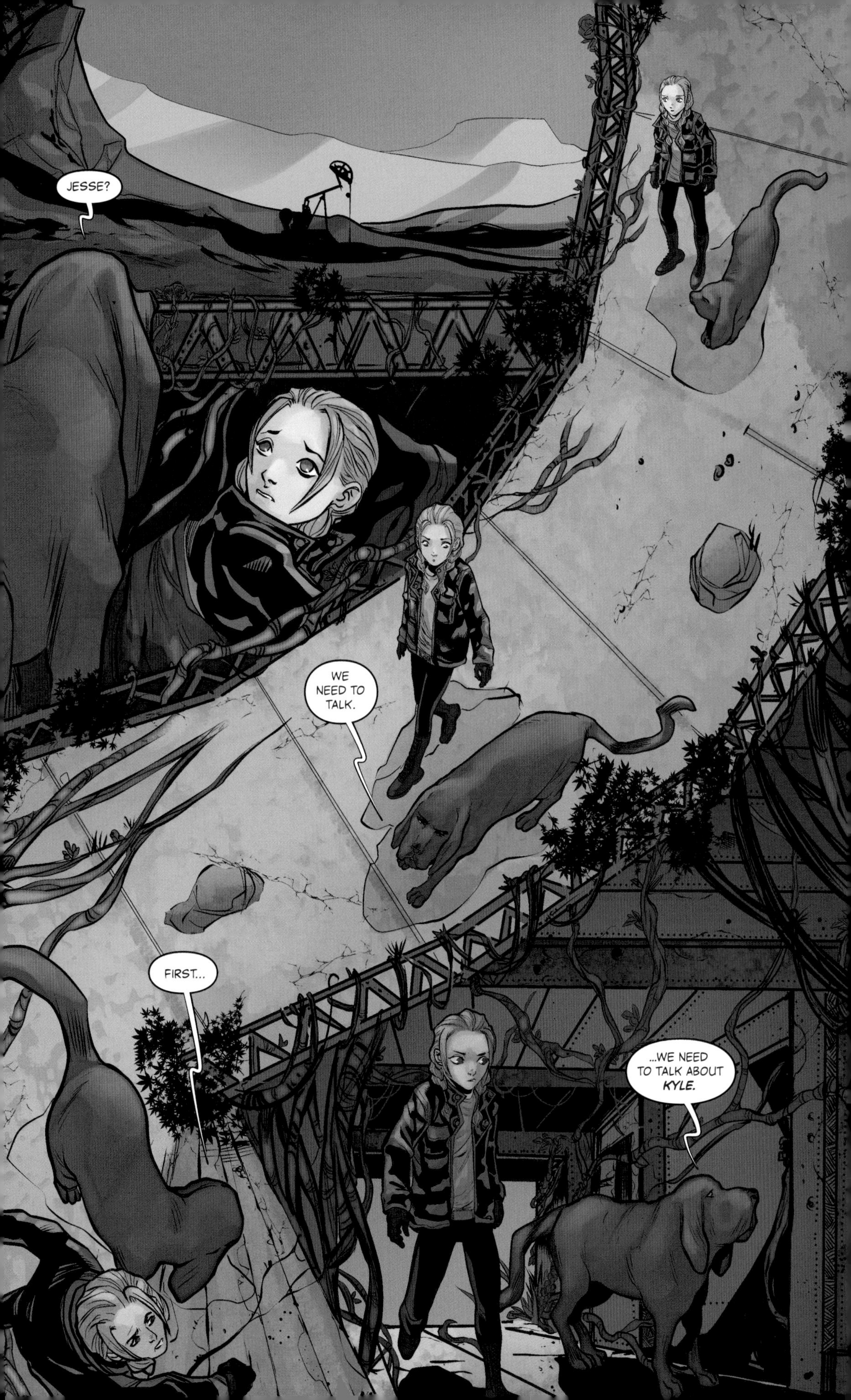
JESSE?
WE NEED TO TALK.
FIRST...
...WE NEED TO TALK ABOUT *KYLE.*

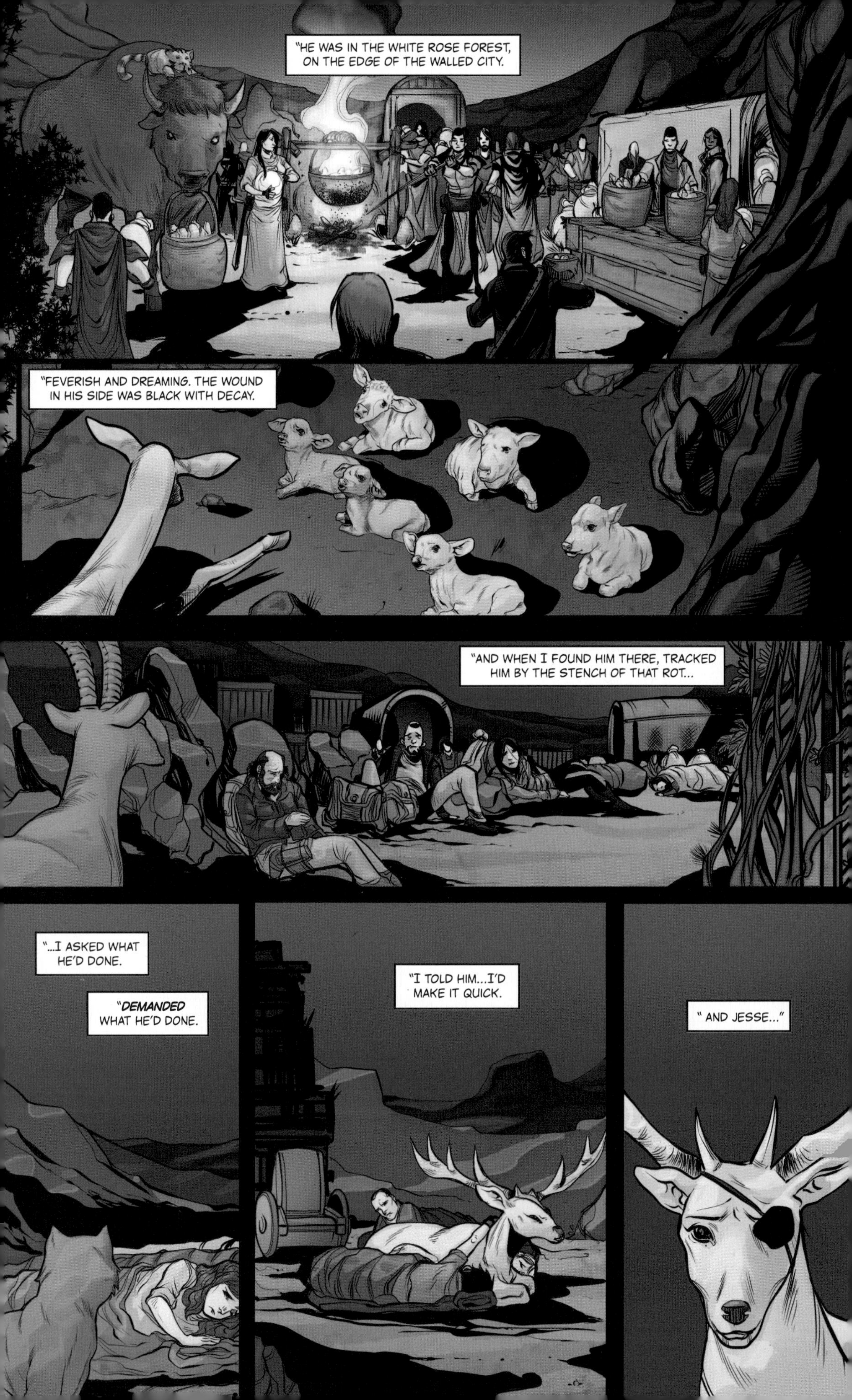
"HE WAS IN THE WHITE ROSE FOREST, ON THE EDGE OF THE WALLED CITY.
"FEVERISH AND DREAMING. THE WOUND IN HIS SIDE WAS BLACK WITH DECAY.
"AND WHEN I FOUND HIM THERE, TRACKED HIM BY THE STENCH OF THAT ROT...
"...I ASKED WHAT HE'D DONE.
"*DEMANDED* WHAT HE'D DONE.
"I TOLD HIM...I'D MAKE IT QUICK.
" AND JESSE..."

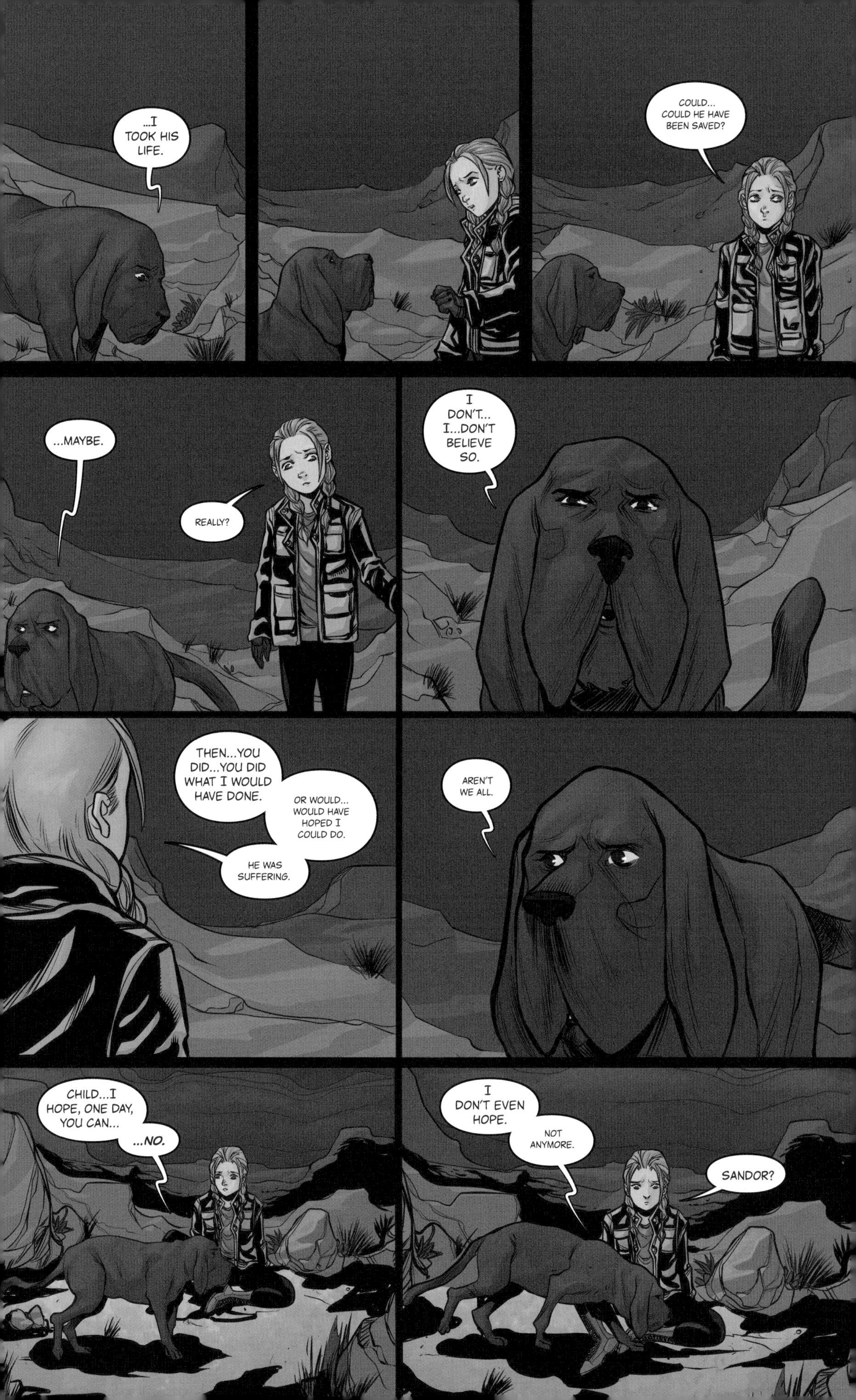

...I TOOK HIS LIFE.
COULD... COULD HE HAVE BEEN SAVED?
...MAYBE.
REALLY?
I DON'T... I...DON'T BELIEVE SO.
THEN...YOU DID...YOU DID WHAT I WOULD HAVE DONE.
OR WOULD... WOULD HAVE HOPED I COULD DO.
HE WAS SUFFERING.
AREN'T WE ALL.
CHILD...I HOPE, ONE DAY, YOU CAN...
...NO.
I DON'T EVEN HOPE.
NOT ANYMORE.
SANDOR?

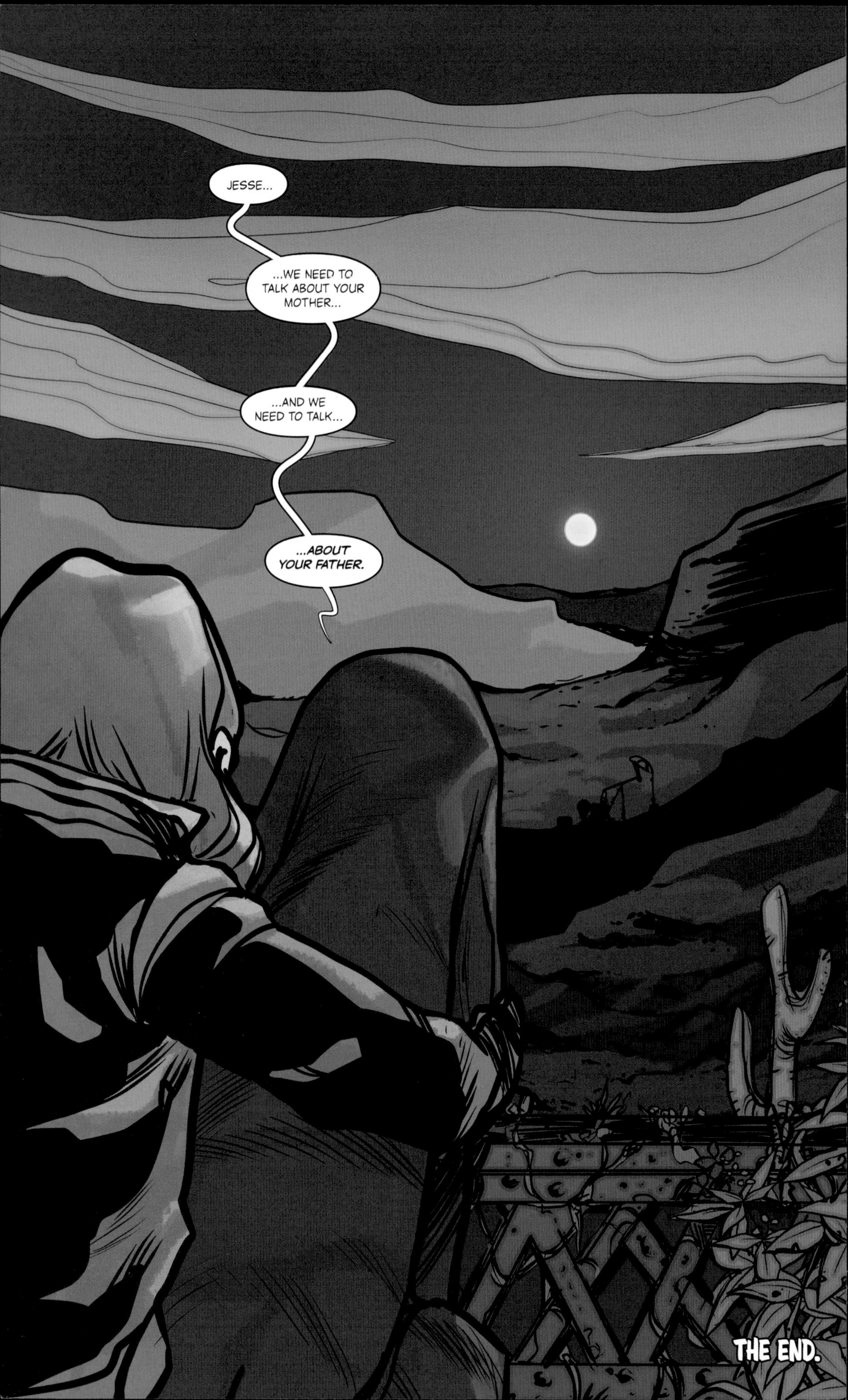
JESSE...
...WE NEED TO TALK ABOUT YOUR MOTHER...
...AND WE NEED TO TALK...
...ABOUT YOUR FATHER.
THE END.

ANIMOSITY™

BEHIND THE SCENES

ANIM⊘SITY™

#25

PAGES 10-11 PROCESS

ANIMOSITY #25
"BLOOD, SAND, AND OIL: PART ONE"
For Elton Thomasi and Mike Marts
From Marguerite Bennett
September 16, 2019

Page TEN – PAGE ELEVEN

Page 10-11/Panel 1.
LOLA and JESSE, on their mounts, come to a rocky outcrop above the CAPITOL. The OIL WELLS and the mad city lay before them.

1 SANDOR (VO): "Into *hell.*"

2 LOCATOR CAPTION: The Capitol of the New Holy Texan Empire.

3 LOLA: *Oil.*
4 LOLA: No wonder these bastards are rich as Croesus.

Page 10-11/Panel 2.
JESSE, anxious by LOLA'S SIDE, asks. LOLA looks cold and unimpressed, staring down at the city.

5 JESSE: Didn't he, *um*, have, *um*—molten silver—poured down his throat?

6 LOLA: To slake his thirst for wealth

Page 10-11/Panel 3.
SANCHO and JODY ride into the city with BEN strapped to the back of their motorcycle.

7 LOCATOR CAPTION: Three Days Ago.

8 LOLA (VO): If you know that, you know what oil's made of.

Page 10-11/Panel 4.
Larger panel. A towering NEON SKELETON of a dinosaur – a huge T-REX that has been strung up with gas station neon lights and made some sort of gaudy primal alien god.

9 LOLA (VO): *Dead dinosaurs.*

10 LOLA (VO): Bones and brains and meat and skin, tiny organisms floating in the soup of the sea.
11 LOLA (VO): Decomposing plant matter that rotted millions of years before the first ape came from the trees.

Page 10-11/Panel 5.
SANDOR, BETH, PALLAS, POTTER, and ZARZA enter the city, passing under the huge NEON DINOSAUR, passing by GUARDS (human and animal) dressed in a combination of COWBOY and ROMAN CENTURION gear.

12 LOLA (VO): Still animals. Animals still make the world run.
13 LOLA (VO): Animals are still the wealth that make humans king.

Page 10-11/Panel 6.
SANCHO and JODY make their way towards a modern COLISEUM, made of stone and scrap metal.

14 LOLA (VO): What would have happened if there had been dinosaurs at the Wake?
15 LOLA (VO): Can you imagine that world?

Page 10-11/Panel 7.
SANCHO and JODY make their way up the stairs to a royal dais.

16 LOLA (VO): Kings of the earth all become earth, in the end.

Page 10-11/Panel 8.
SANCHO and JODY make a show of presenting BEN to three unseen people on THRONES.

17 LOLA (VO): All become blood, and brains, and bone, and sand…

script by
MARGUERITE BENNETT

art by
ELTON THOMASI

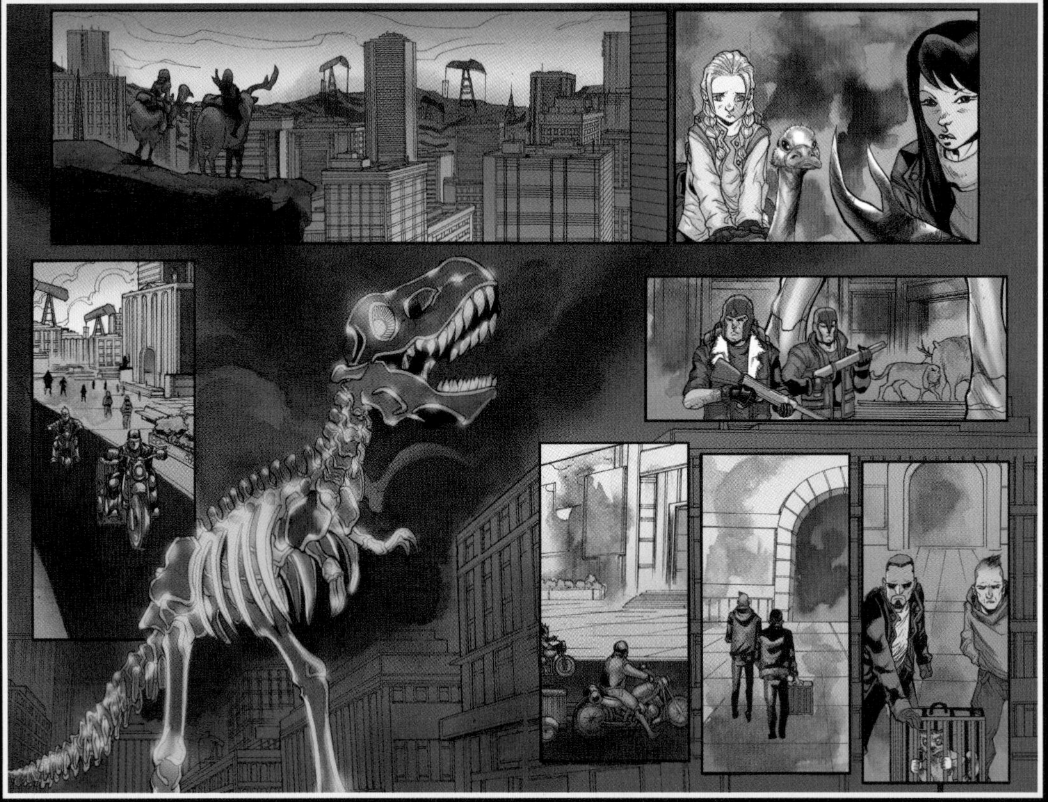

colors by
ROB SCHWAGER

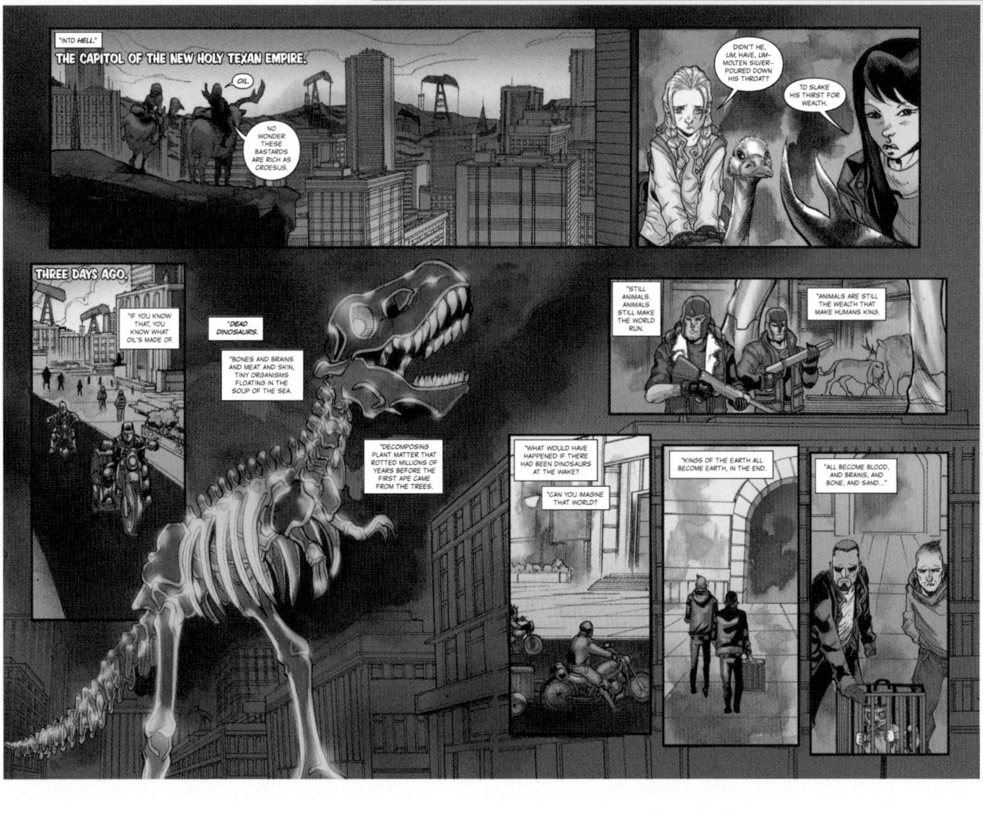
"INTO HELL."
THE CAPITOL OF THE NEW HOLY TEXAN EMPIRE.
OIL.
NO WONDER THESE BASTARDS ARE RICH AS CROESUS.
DIDN'T HE, UM, HAVE, UM-- MOLTEN SILVER-- POURED DOWN HIS THROAT?
TO SLAKE HIS THIRST FOR WEALTH.
THREE DAYS AGO.
"IF YOU KNOW THAT, YOU KNOW WHAT OIL'S MADE OF.
"DEAD DINOSAURS.
"BONES AND BRAINS AND MEAT AND SKIN, TINY ORGANISMS FLOATING IN THE SOUP OF THE SEA.
"DECOMPOSING PLANT MATTER THAT ROTTED MILLIONS OF YEARS BEFORE THE FIRST APE CAME FROM THE TREES.
"STILL ANIMALS. ANIMALS STILL MAKE THE WORLD RUN.
"ANIMALS ARE STILL THE WEALTH THAT MAKE HUMANS KING.
"WHAT WOULD HAVE HAPPENED IF THERE HAD BEEN DINOSAURS AT THE WAKE?
"CAN YOU IMAGINE THAT WORLD?
"KINGS OF THE EARTH ALL BECOME EARTH, IN THE END.
"ALL BECOME BLOOD, AND BRAINS, AND BONE, AND SAND..."

lettering by
TAYLOR ESPOSITO

ANIM○SITY

26

PAGES
18-19
PROCESS

ANIMOSITY #26
For Elton Thomasi, Mike Marts, and Christina Harrington
From Marguerite Bennett
November 1, 2019

PAGE EIGHTEEN - PAGE NINETEEN

Page 18-19/Panel 1.
SANDOR, emerges from the sewers, drenched in blood.

    1 LOCATOR CAPTION: New York. Then.

    2 MITTENS (VO): ...*radiation*.

Page 18-19/Panel 2.
SANDOR, in the barracks, murmurs to the GERENUK. BEN looks up blearily, looking ill and hungover.

    3 LOCATOR CAPTION: The Barracks. Now.

    4 SANDOR: >koff< This can't be...how I die...

Page 18-19/Panel 3.
In NEW YORK, in an alley, SANDOR shakes the blood free. It comes off in huge ropes.

Page 18-19/Panel 4.
JESSE in the present, is brought to an alley by LOLA and the ANIMALS.

    5 LOCATOR CAPTION: The Capitol. Now.

    6 SANDOR (VO): I have to...get Jesse to safety...

Page 18-19/Panel 5.
In NEW YORK, in an alley, SANDOR shakes the blood free. It comes off in huge ropes.

Page 18-19/Panel 6.
JESSE, in the present, is squatted down against the wall of the alley, rocking back and forth, clutching her head, while LOLA leans over her. LOLA is also squatting, with one hand (arm extended) on the wall over JESSE'S SHOULDER – it is both comforting, but also a gesture of authority and exclusion, the human Lola blocking the animals out, though BETH and POTTER look down in consternation, and PALLAS has crawled up beside her, ZARZA rubbing JESSE'S back with her forehead.

    7 SANDOR (VO): Then tell her the truth .

Page 18-19/Panel 7.
In NEW YORK, in an alley, SANDOR shakes the blood free. It comes off in huge ropes.

Page 18-19/Panel 8.
JESSE in the present looks up, tears running down her face. She fucked up. Exactly what Sandor said would happen has happened – she got him hurt, maybe killed.

    8 SANDOR (VO): And then he has to get to...

Page 18-19/Panel 9.
SANDOR walks away from the Rorschach of blood he left on the wall. It looks like fire and screaming people and demonic wings—like everything Sandor has left in his wake this entire trip, from the Animilitary to the Red Dragon to the Walled City.

    9 SANDOR (VO): She has to get to be the one...

script by
MARGUERITE BENNETT

art by
ELTON THOMASI

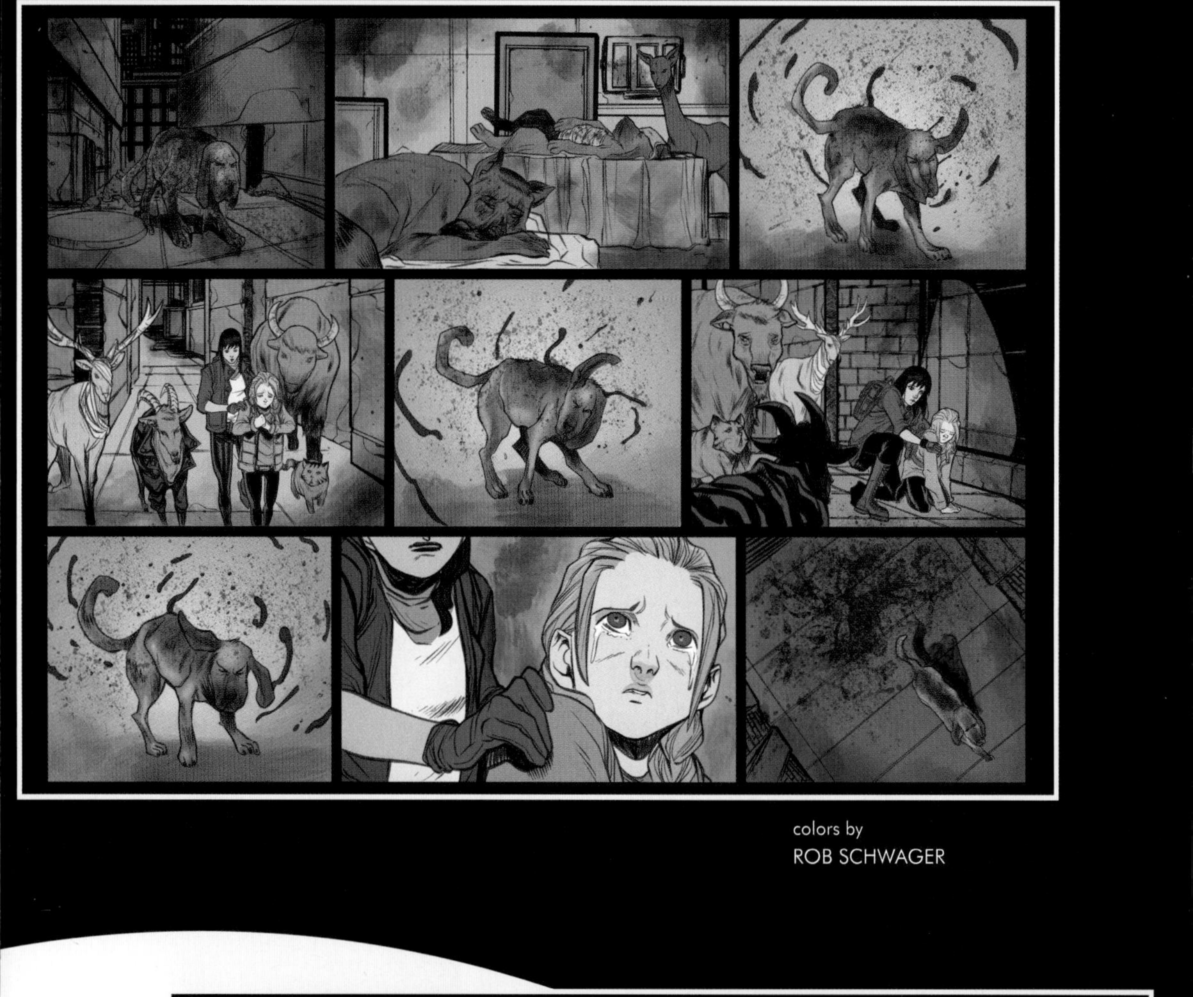

colors by
ROB SCHWAGER

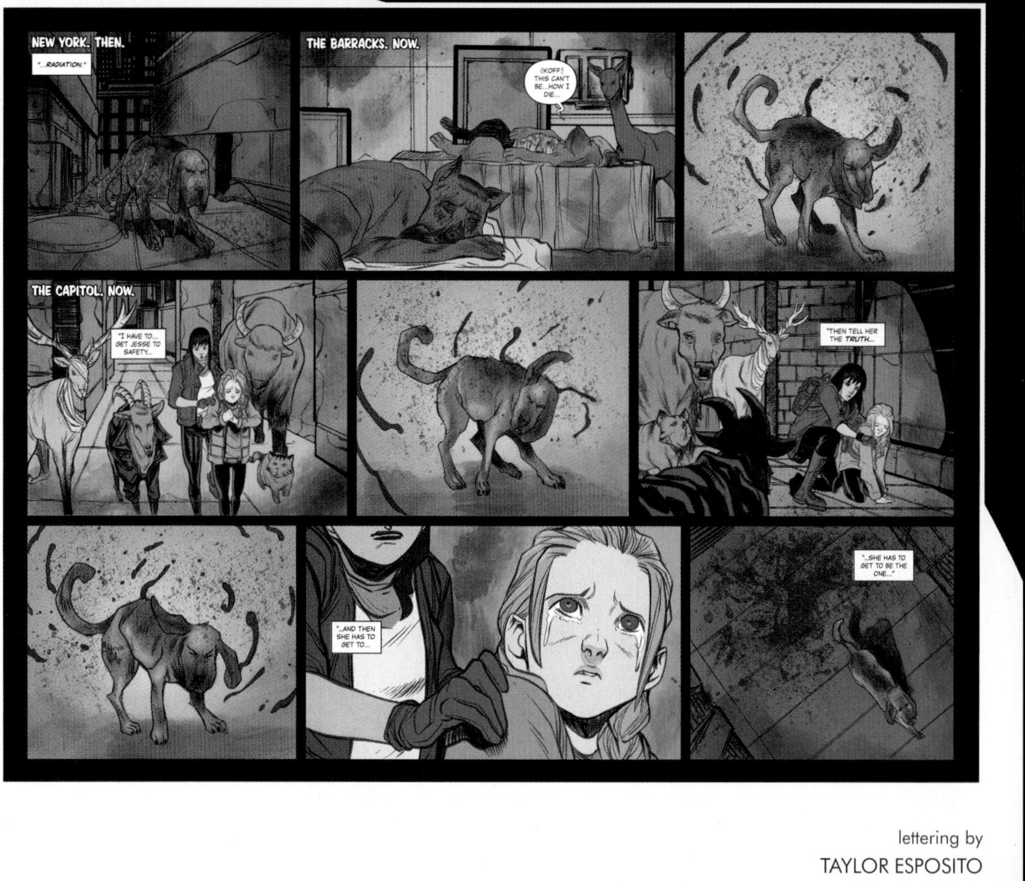
NEW YORK. THEN.
"...RADIATION."
THE BARRACKS. NOW.
¦KOFF¦ THIS CAN'T BE...HOW I DIE...
THE CAPITOL. NOW.
"I HAVE TO... GET JESSE TO SAFETY...
"THEN TELL HER THE *TRUTH*...
"...AND THEN SHE HAS TO GET TO...
"...SHE HAS TO GET TO BE THE ONE..."

lettering by
TAYLOR ESPOSITO

ANIMOSITY
#28

ANIMOSITY #28
February 20, 2020
For Elton Thomasi and Mike Marts
From Marguerite Bennett

PAGE SEVENTEEN

17.1
JESSE starts to stir as SANDOR'S PAW comes down to touch her arm. The sky is a dark blue that is beginning to lighten to gray.

　　1 SANDOR: Jesse?

17.2
In the pre-dawn gloom, JESSE and SANDOR walk down the overgrown iron ramparts of the OIL PUMP. Another classic comics intercut, like Page 13, as they descend the flowering beautiful OIL RIG together.

　　2 SANDOR: We need to talk.

　　3 SANDOR: First...

　　4 SANDOR: We need to talk about Kyle.

script by
MARGUERITE BENNETT

PAGE
17
PROCESS

art by
ELTON THOMASI

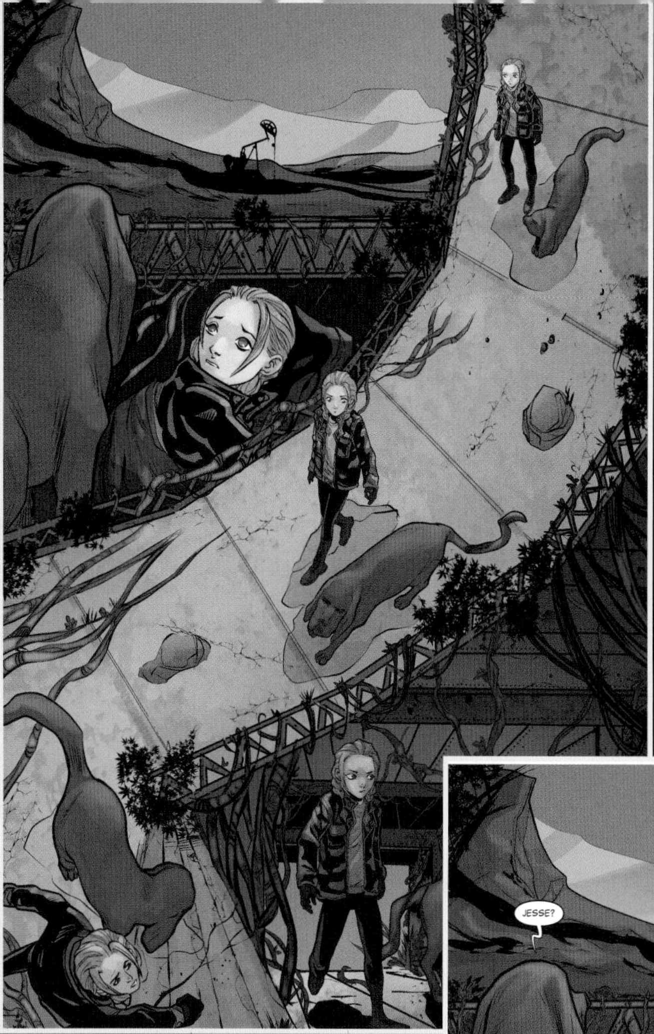

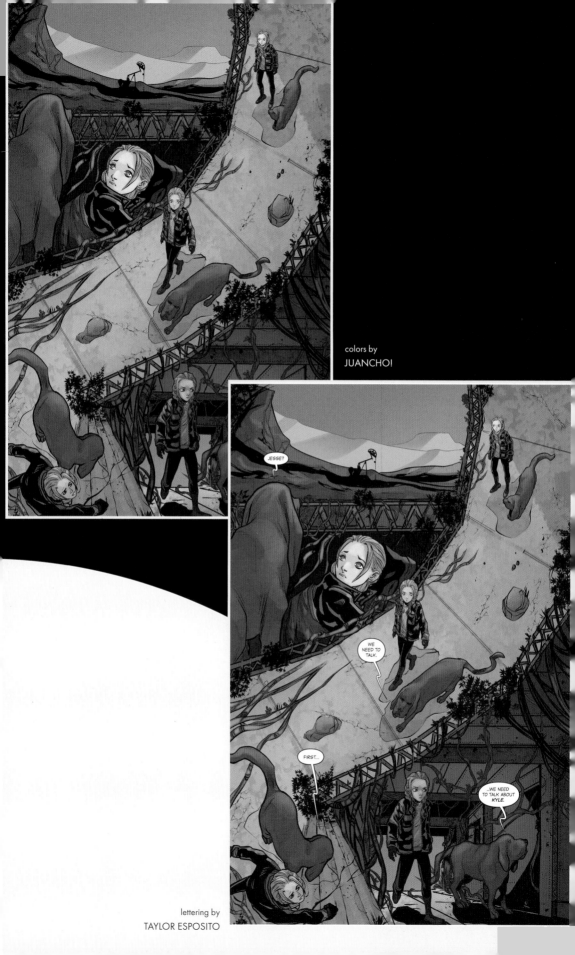

colors by
JUANCHO!

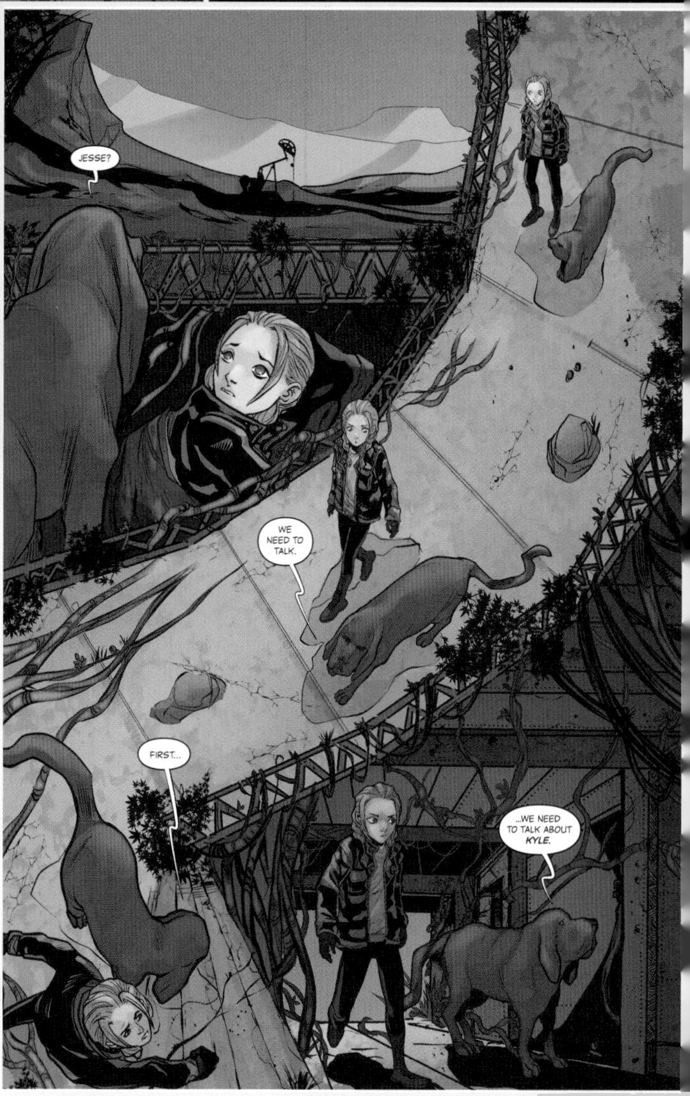
JESSE?
WE NEED TO TALK.
FIRST...
...WE NEED TO TALK ABOUT KYLE.

lettering by
TAYLOR ESPOSITO

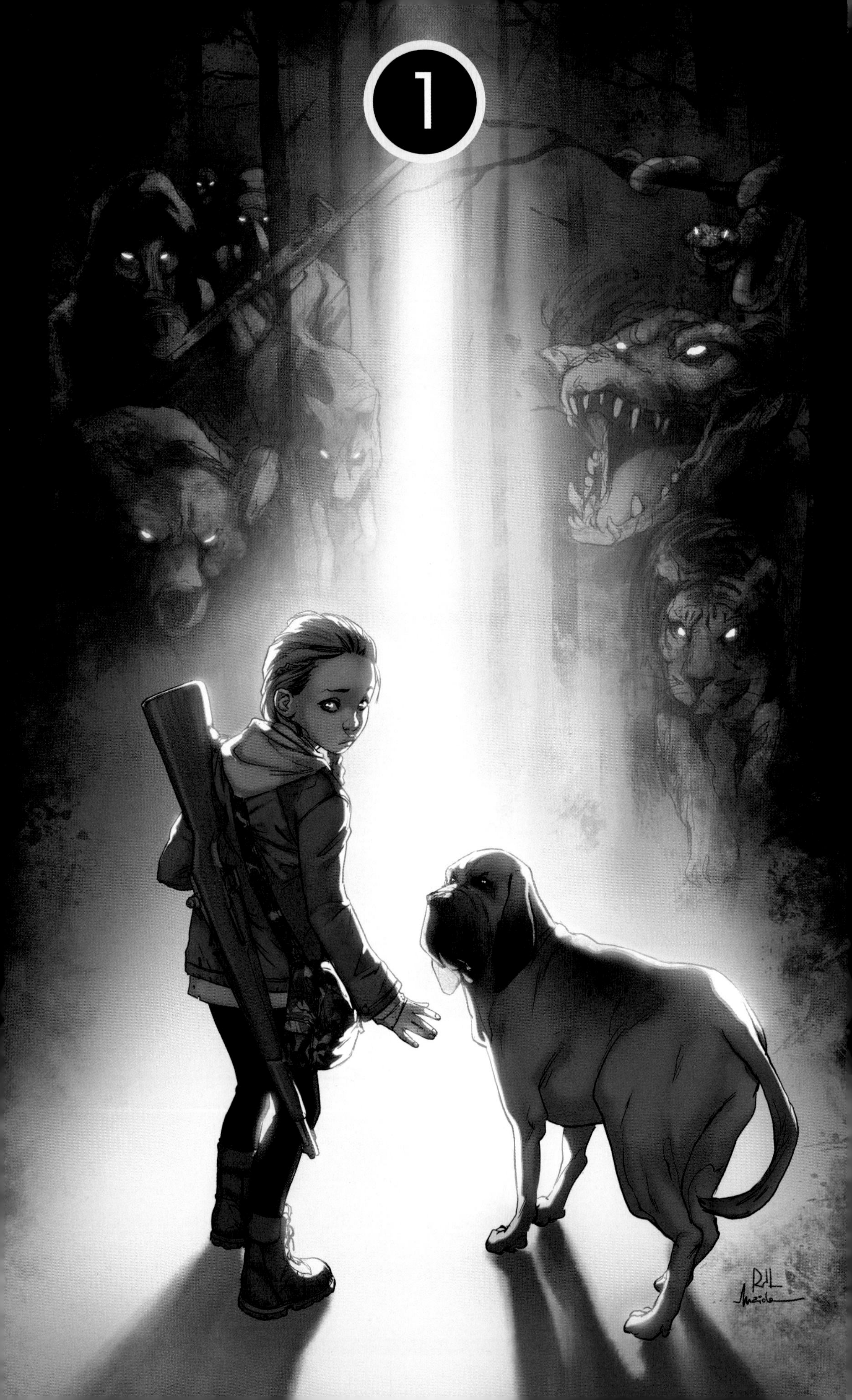
1

2

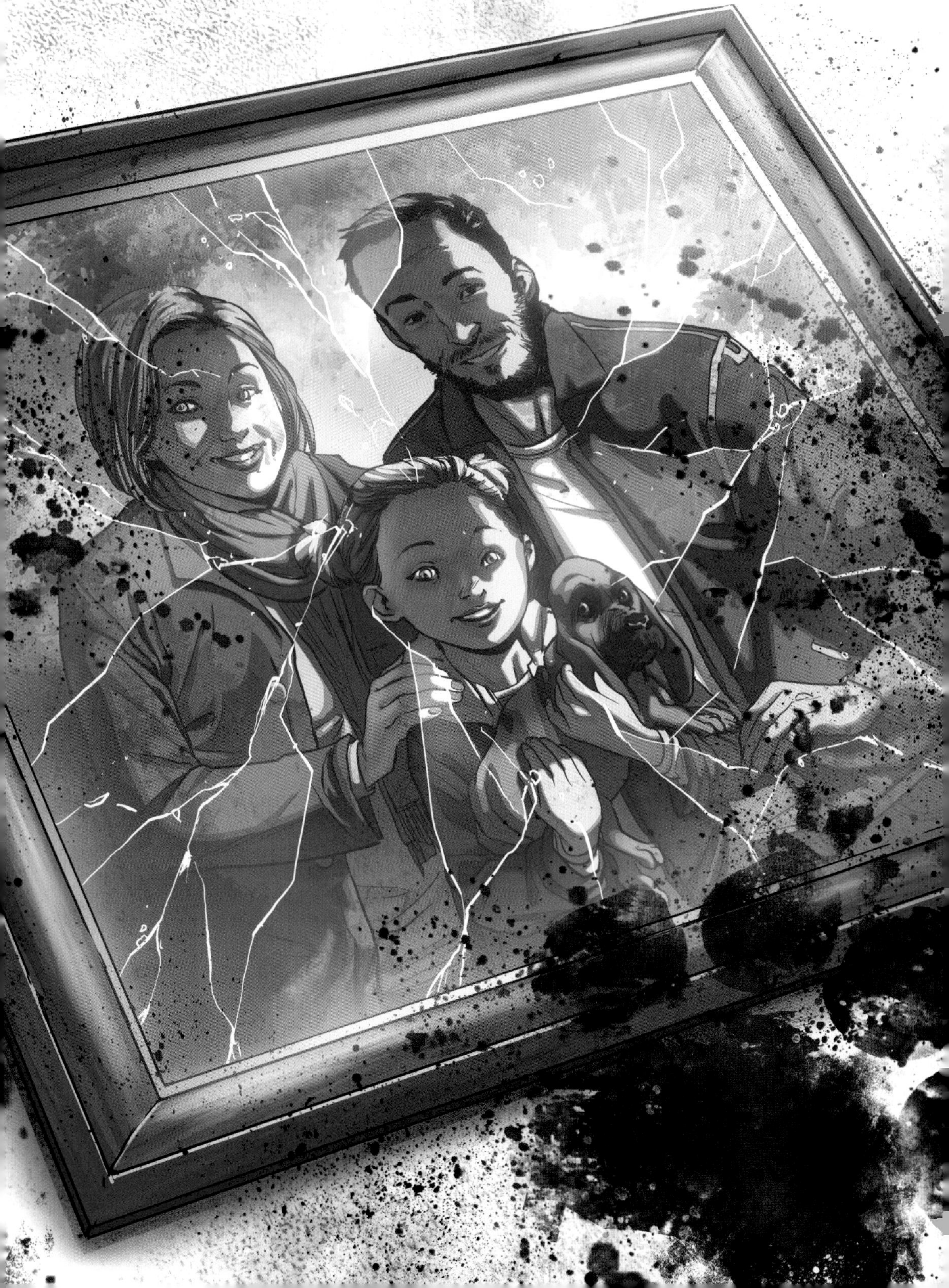

3

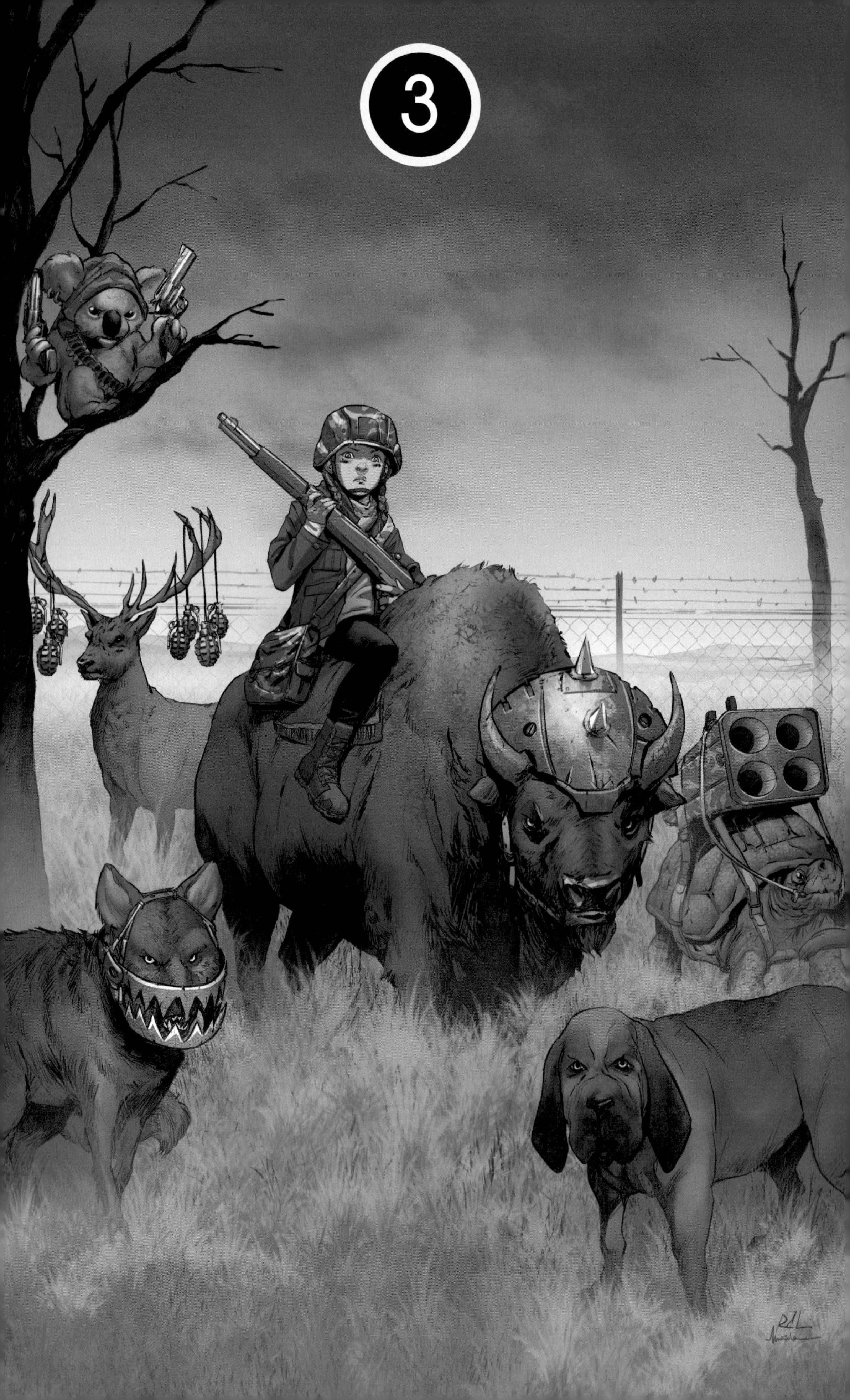

4

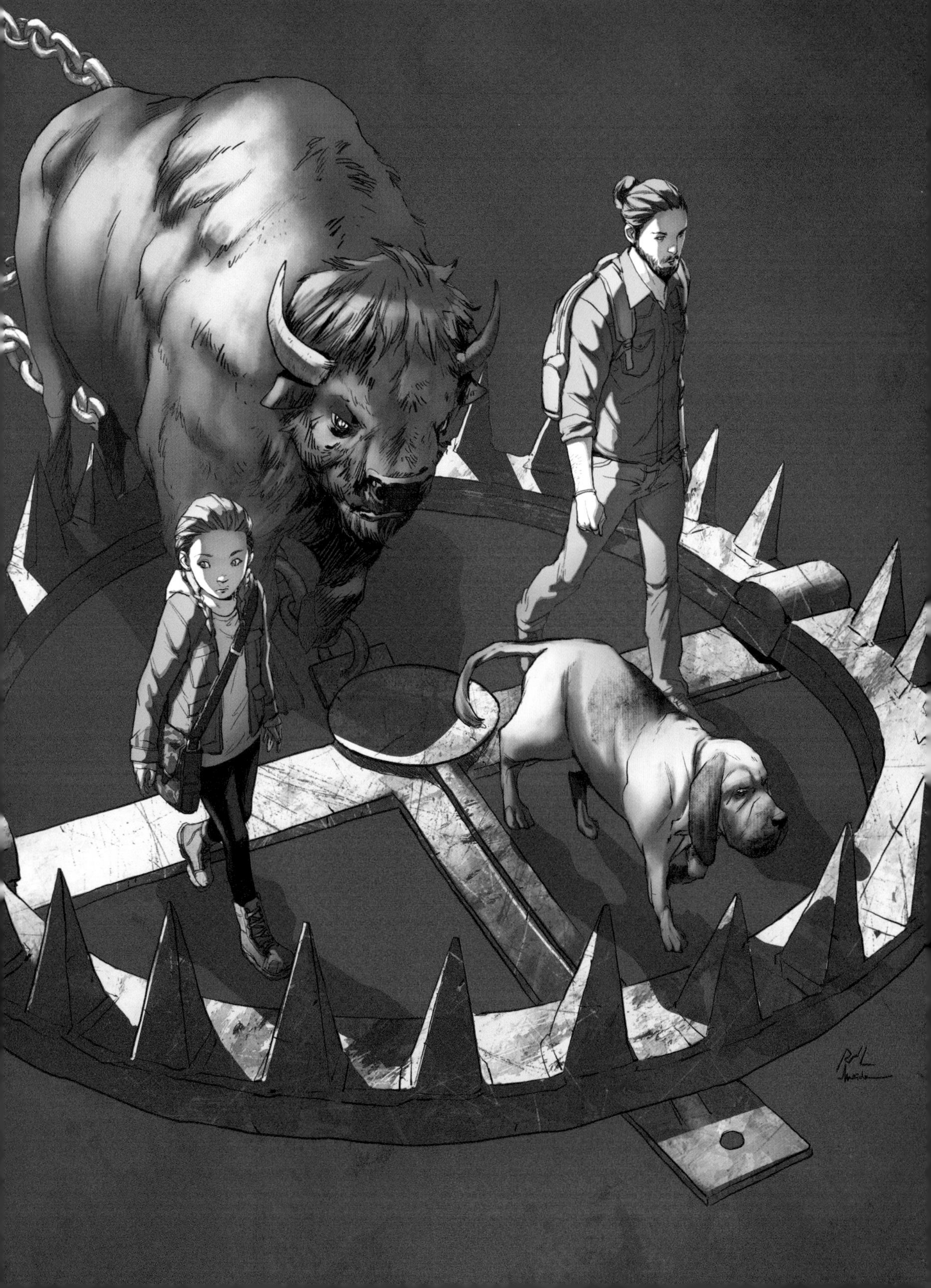

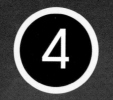

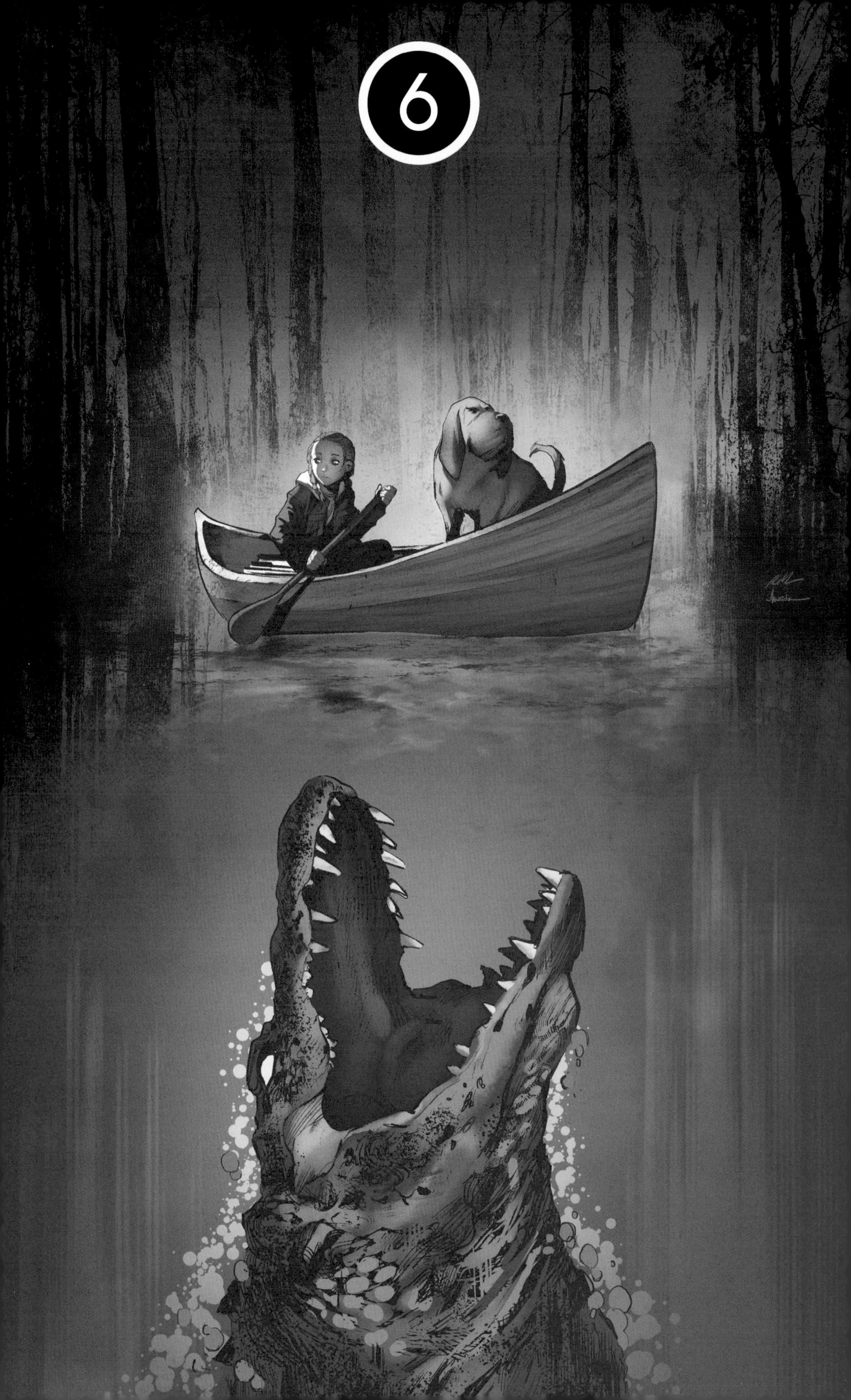
6

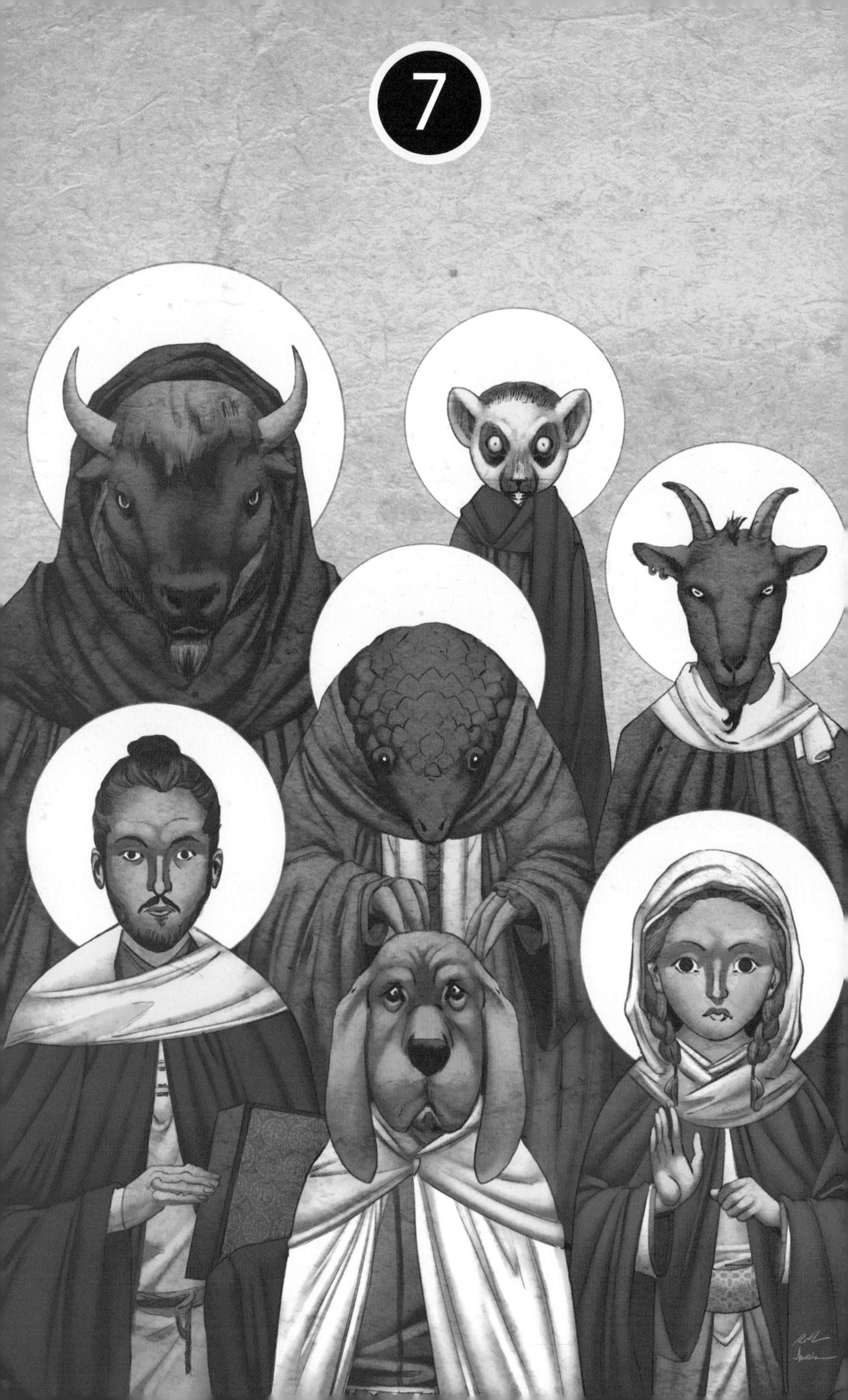
7

8

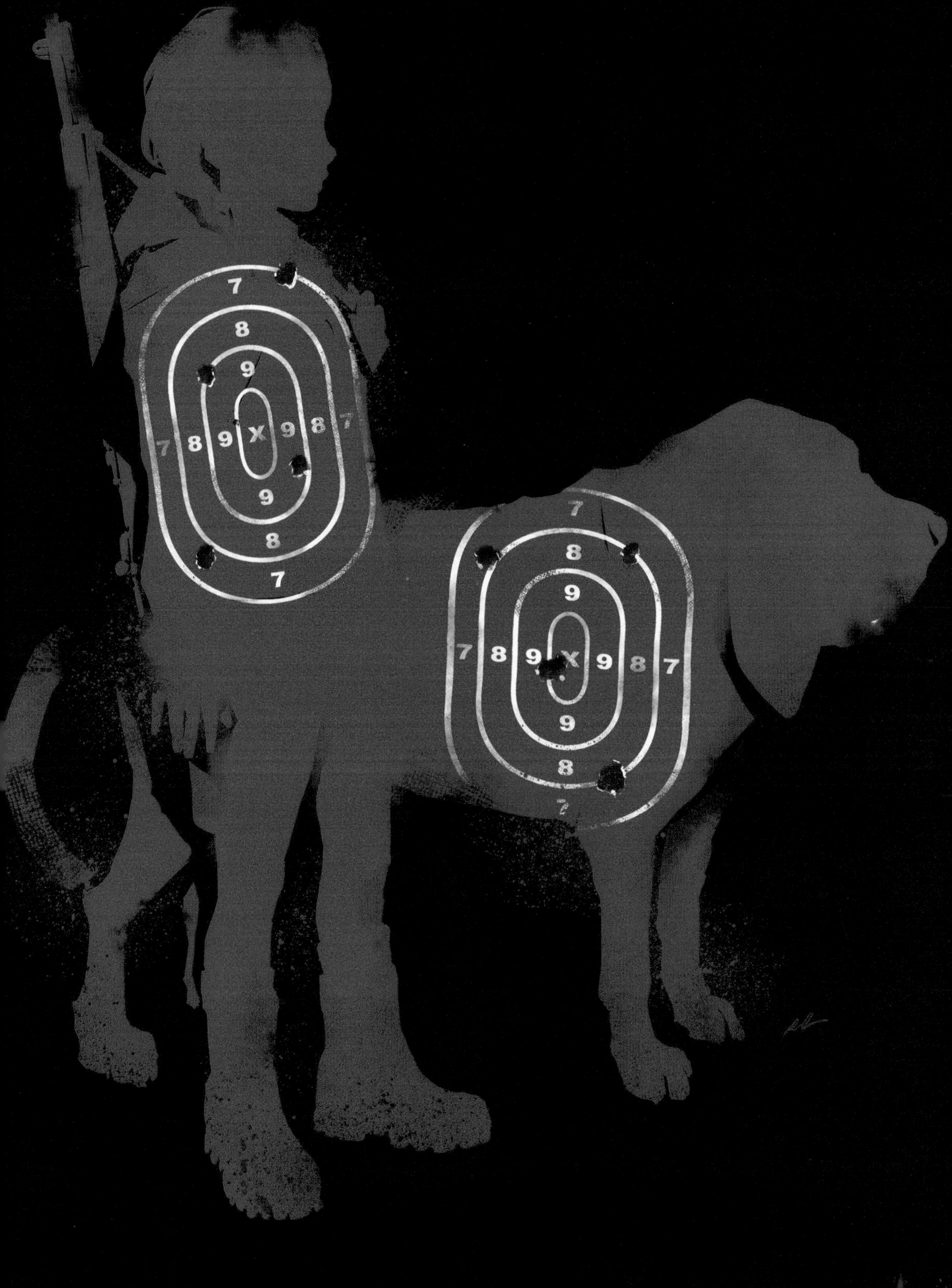
7
8
9
7 8 9 X 9 8 7
9
8
7
7
8
9
7 8 9 X 9 8 7
9
8
7

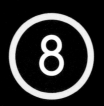

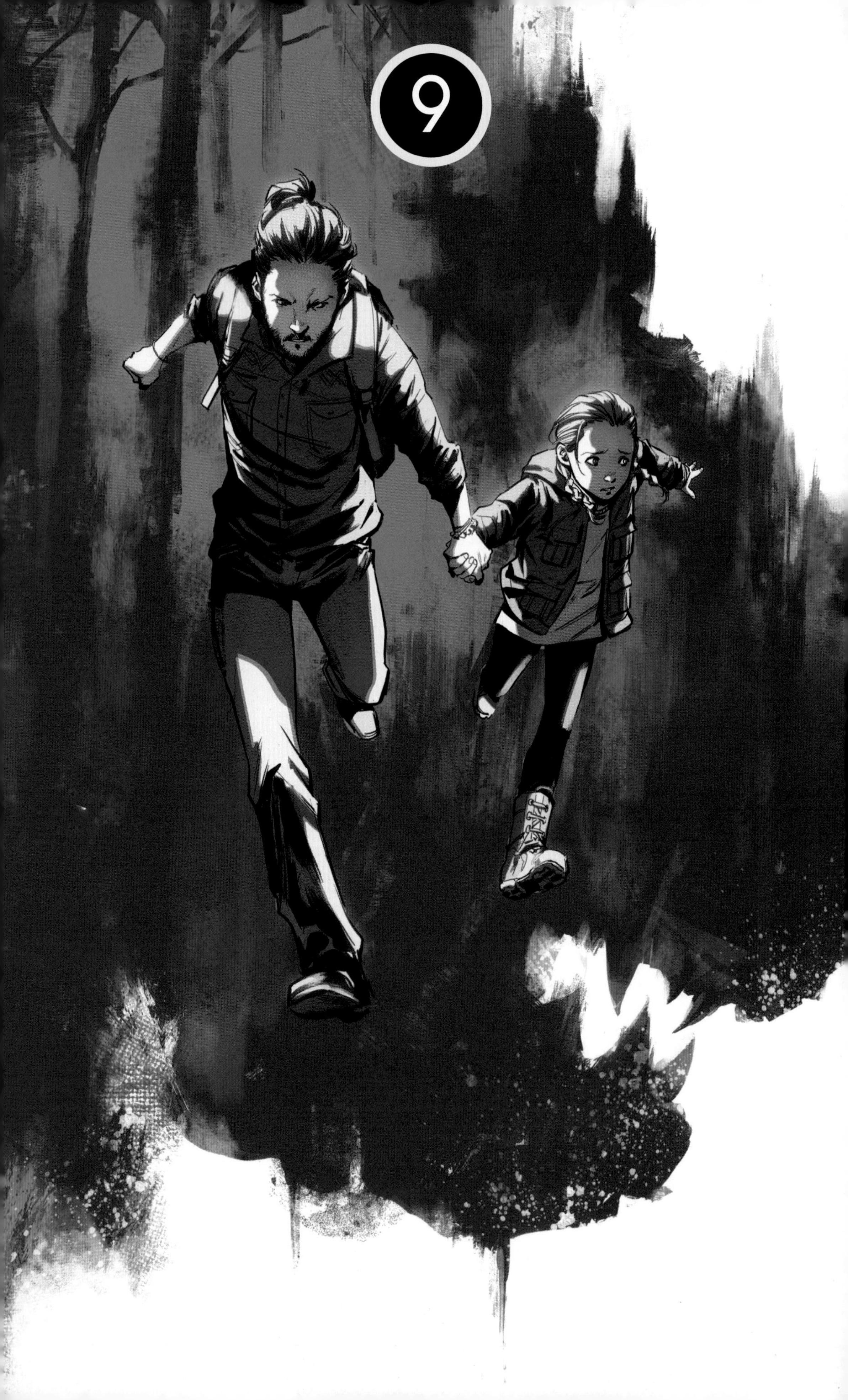
9

10

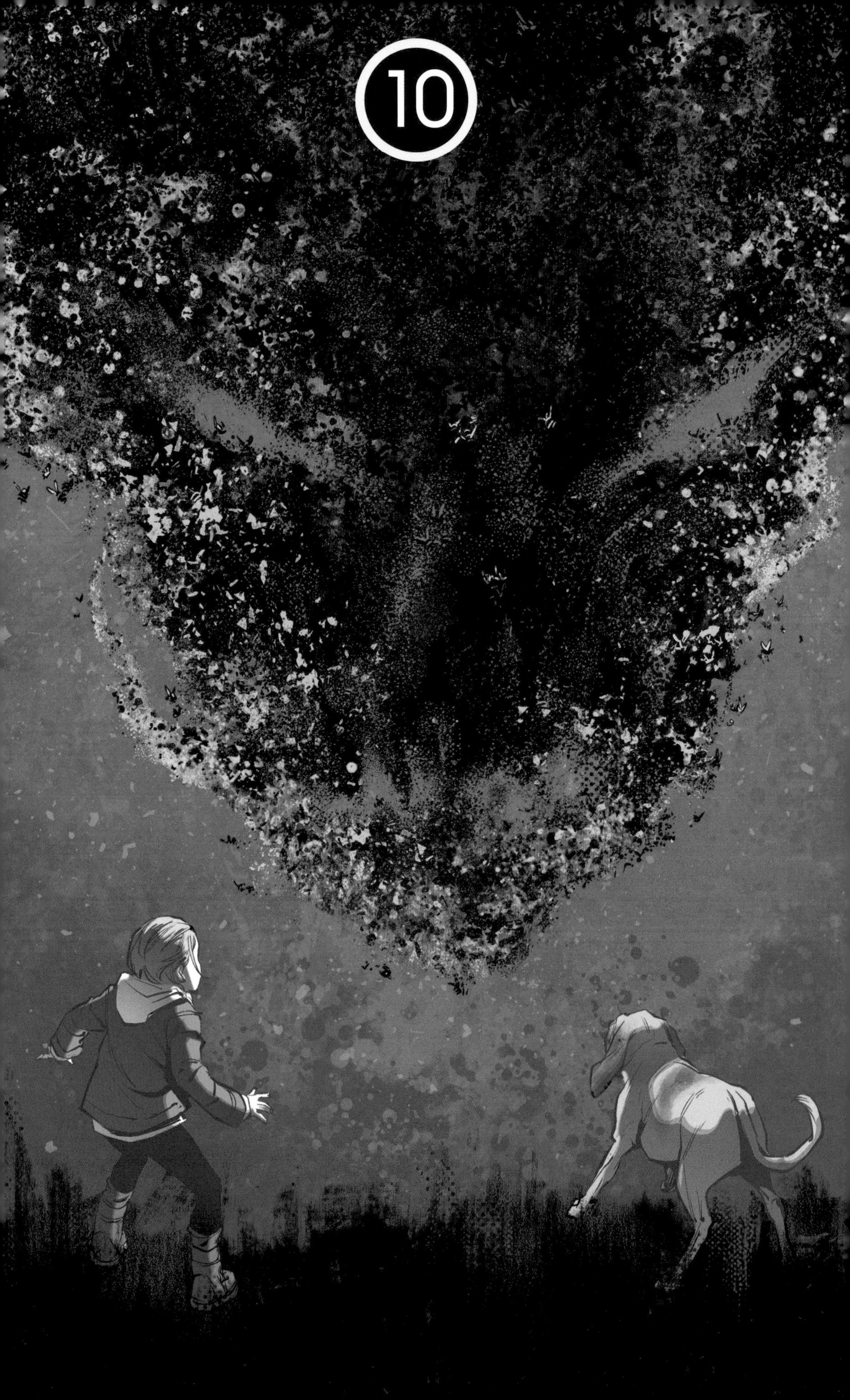

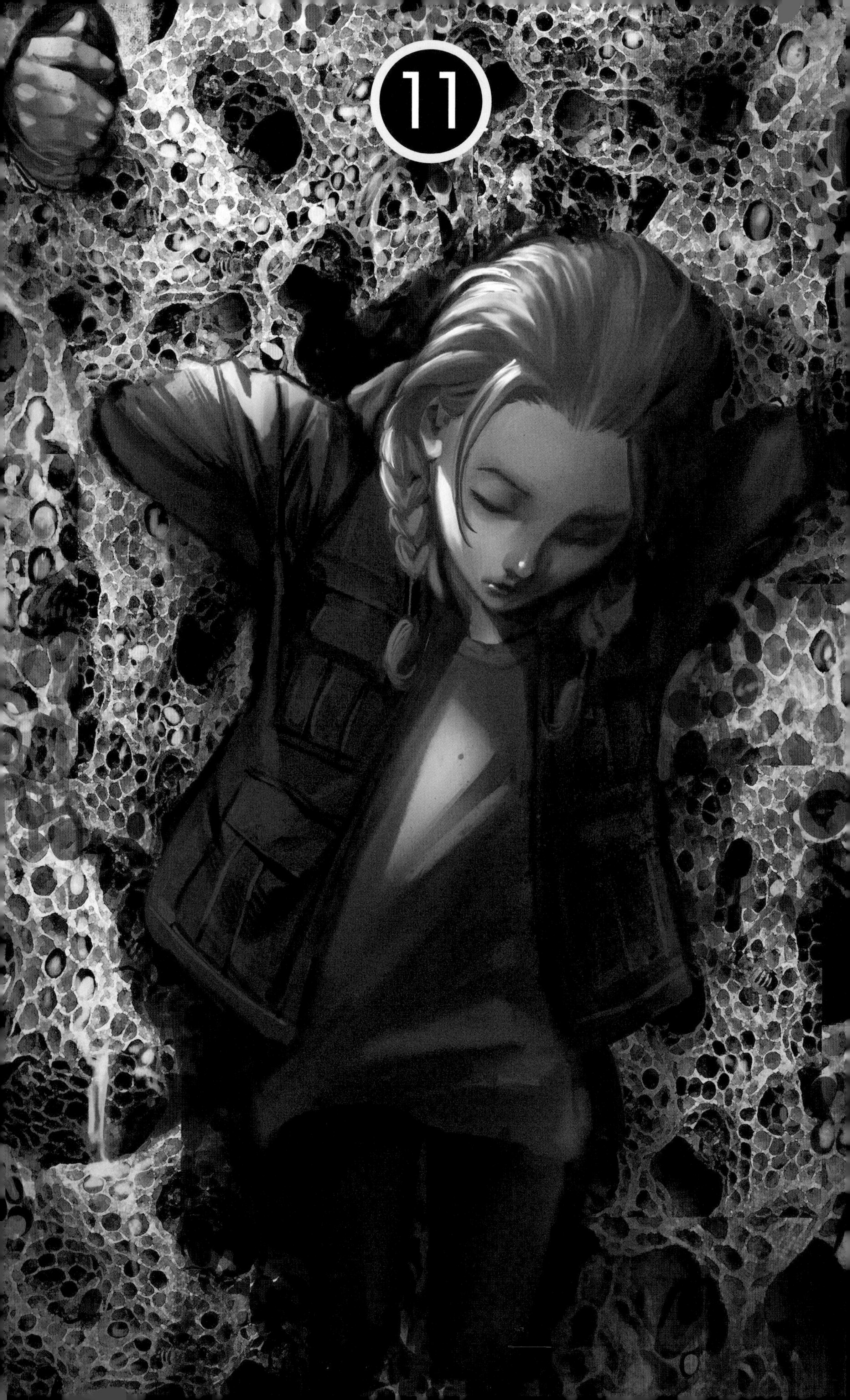
11

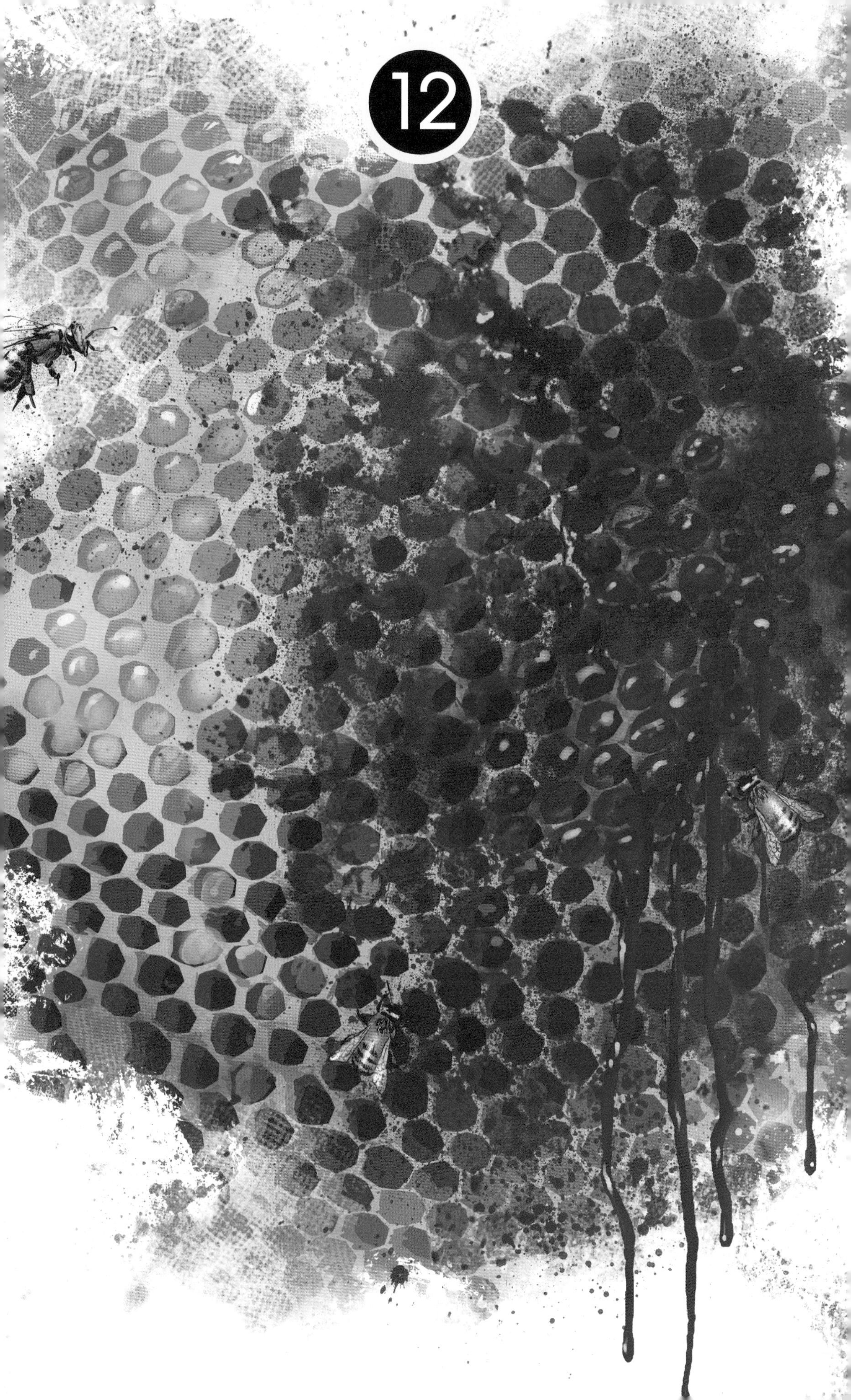
12

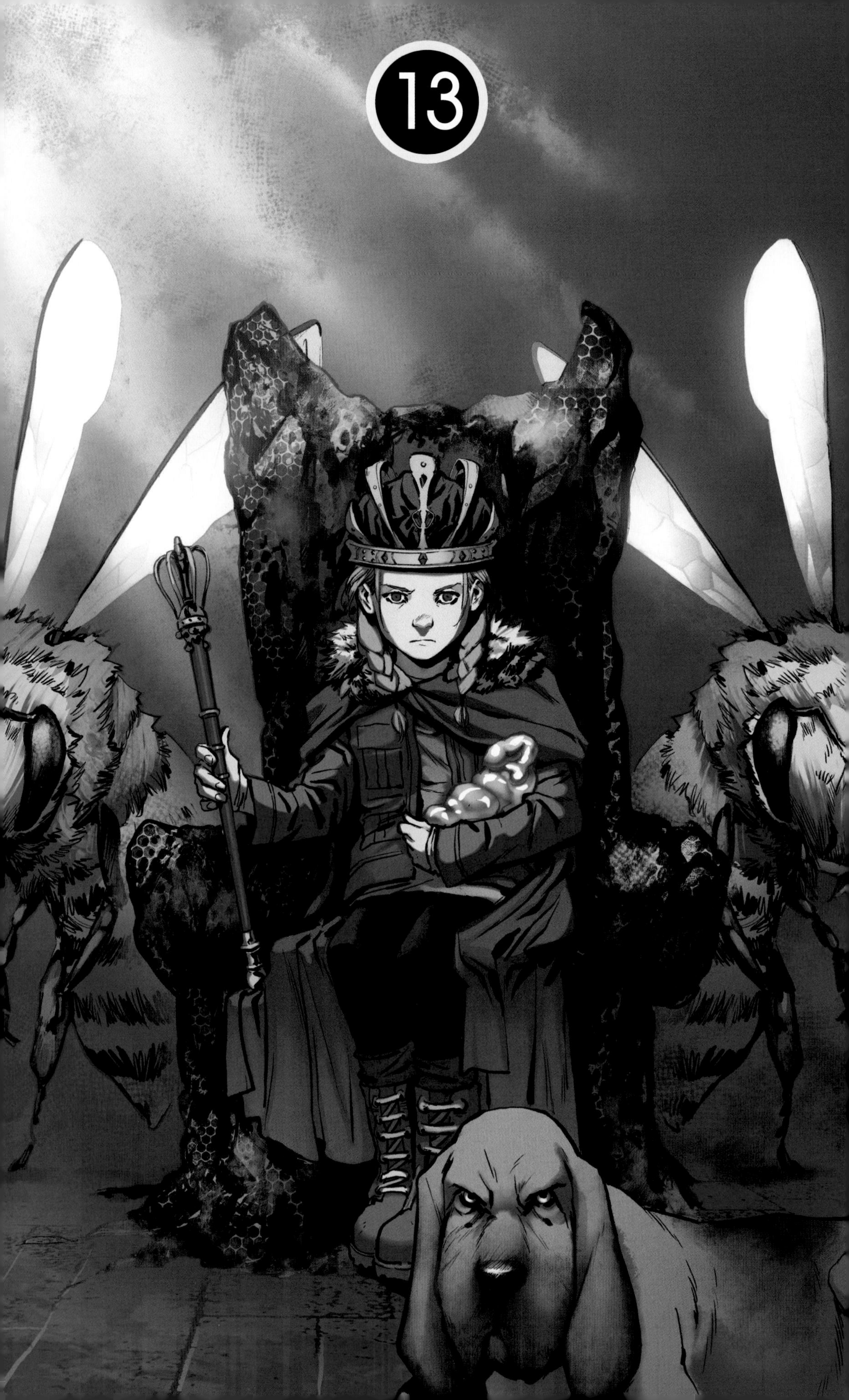
13

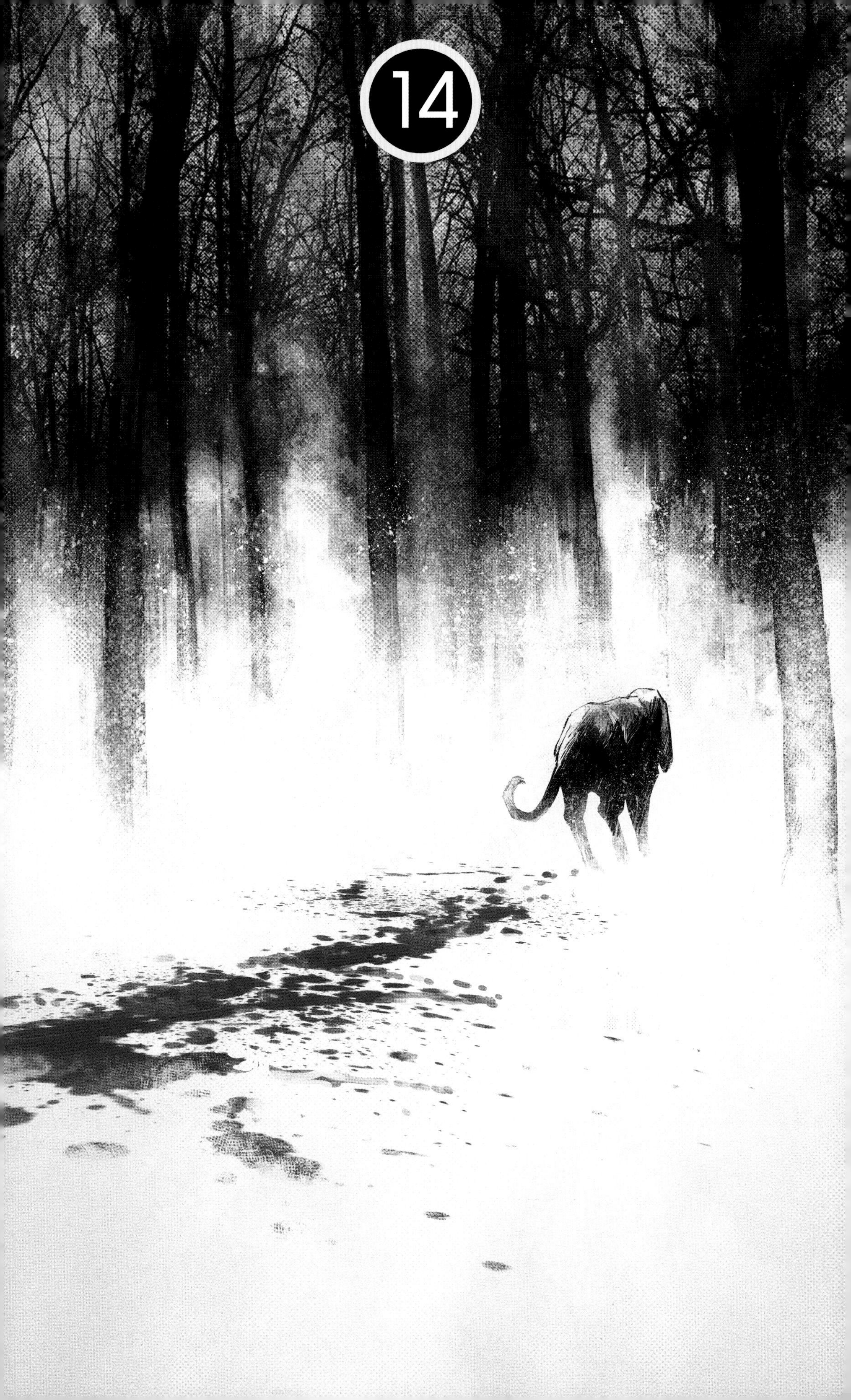
14

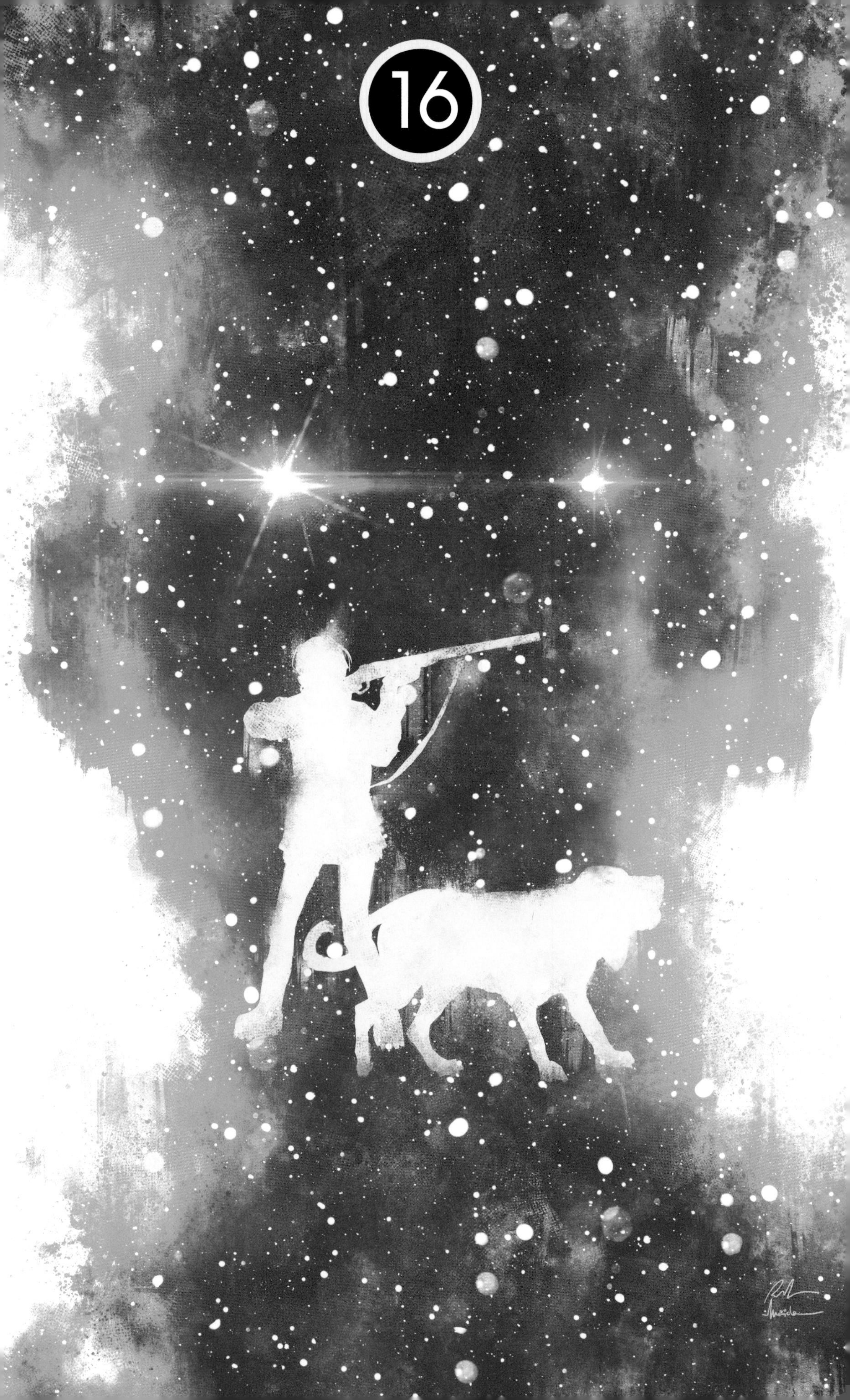
16

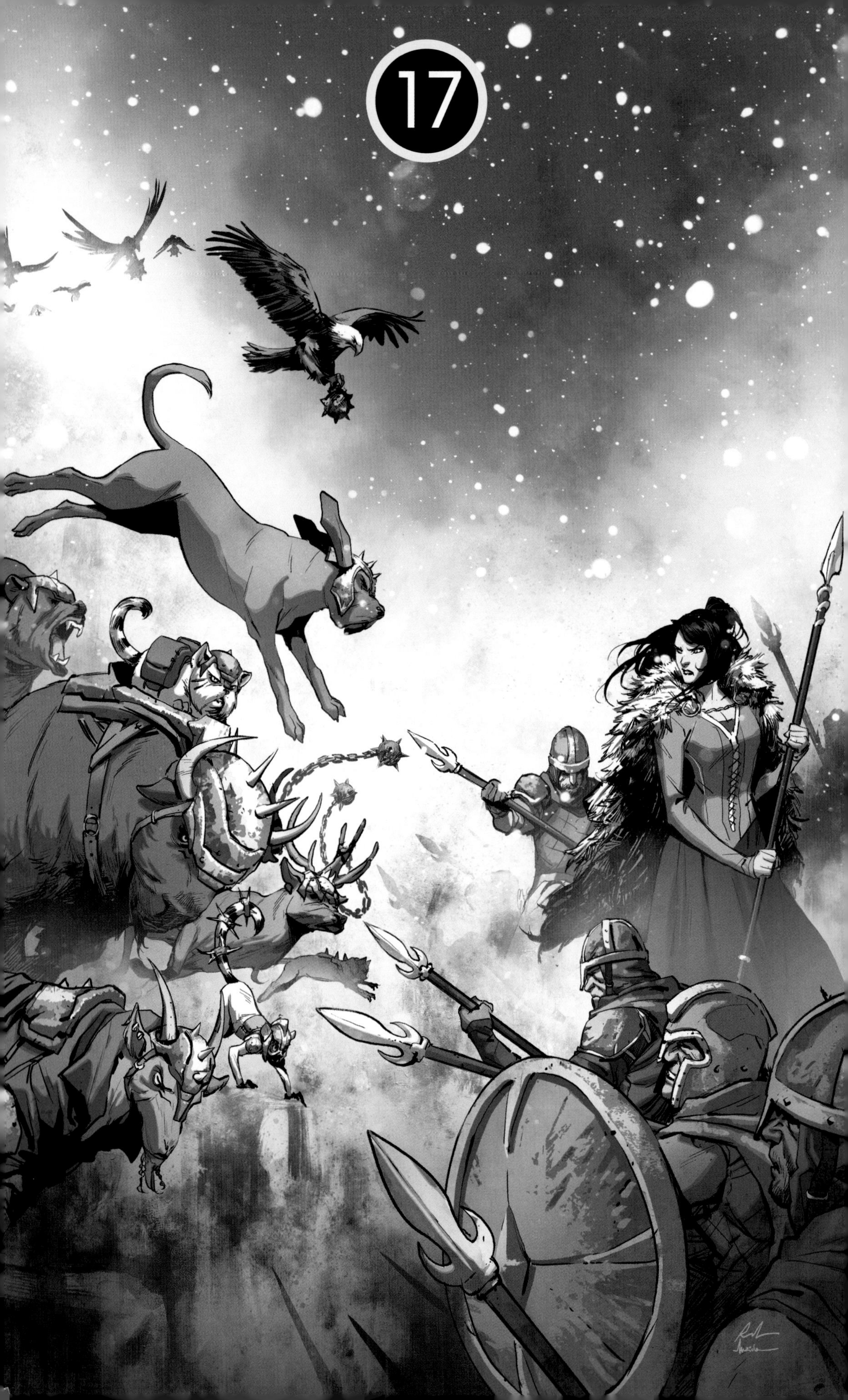
17

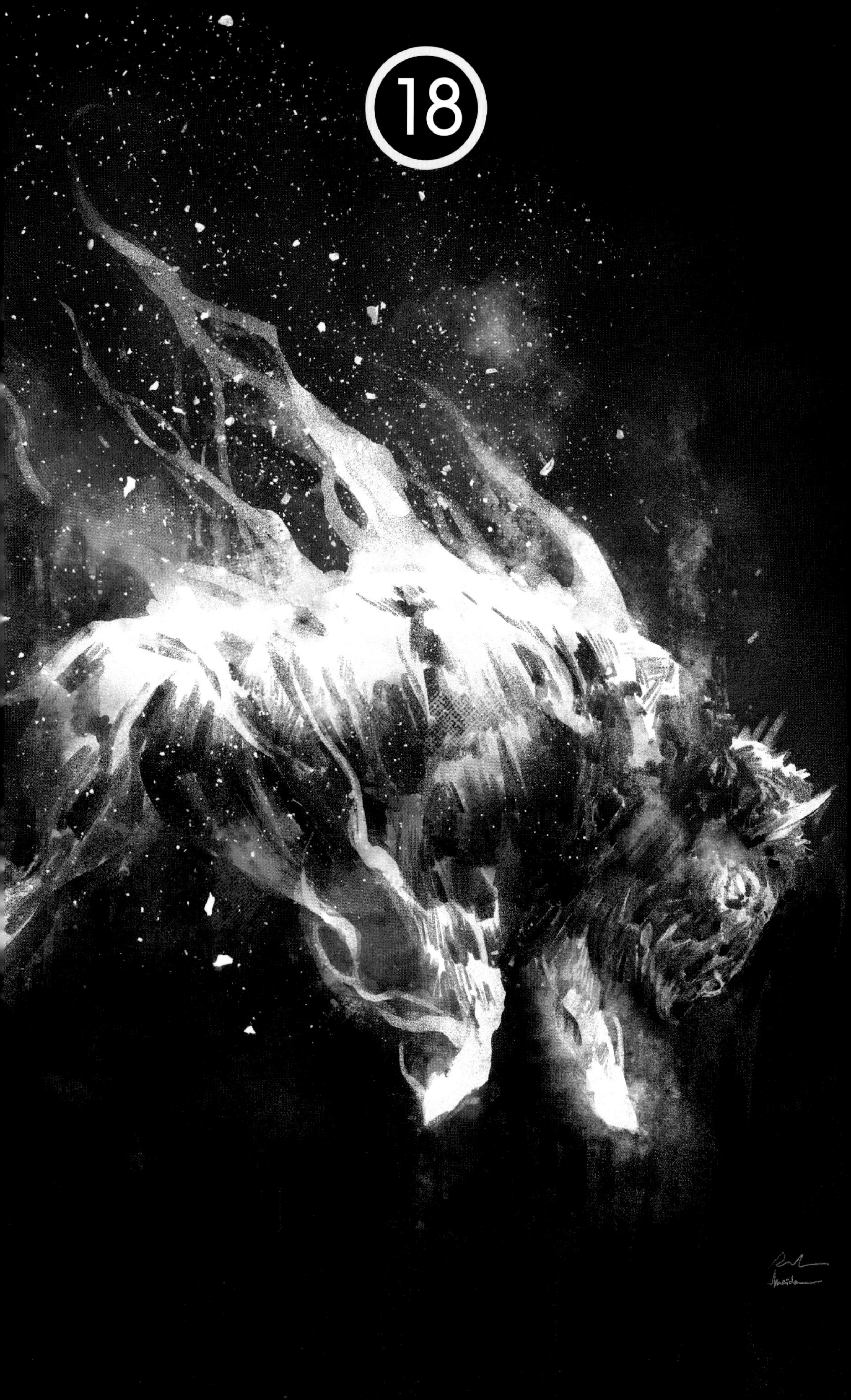
18

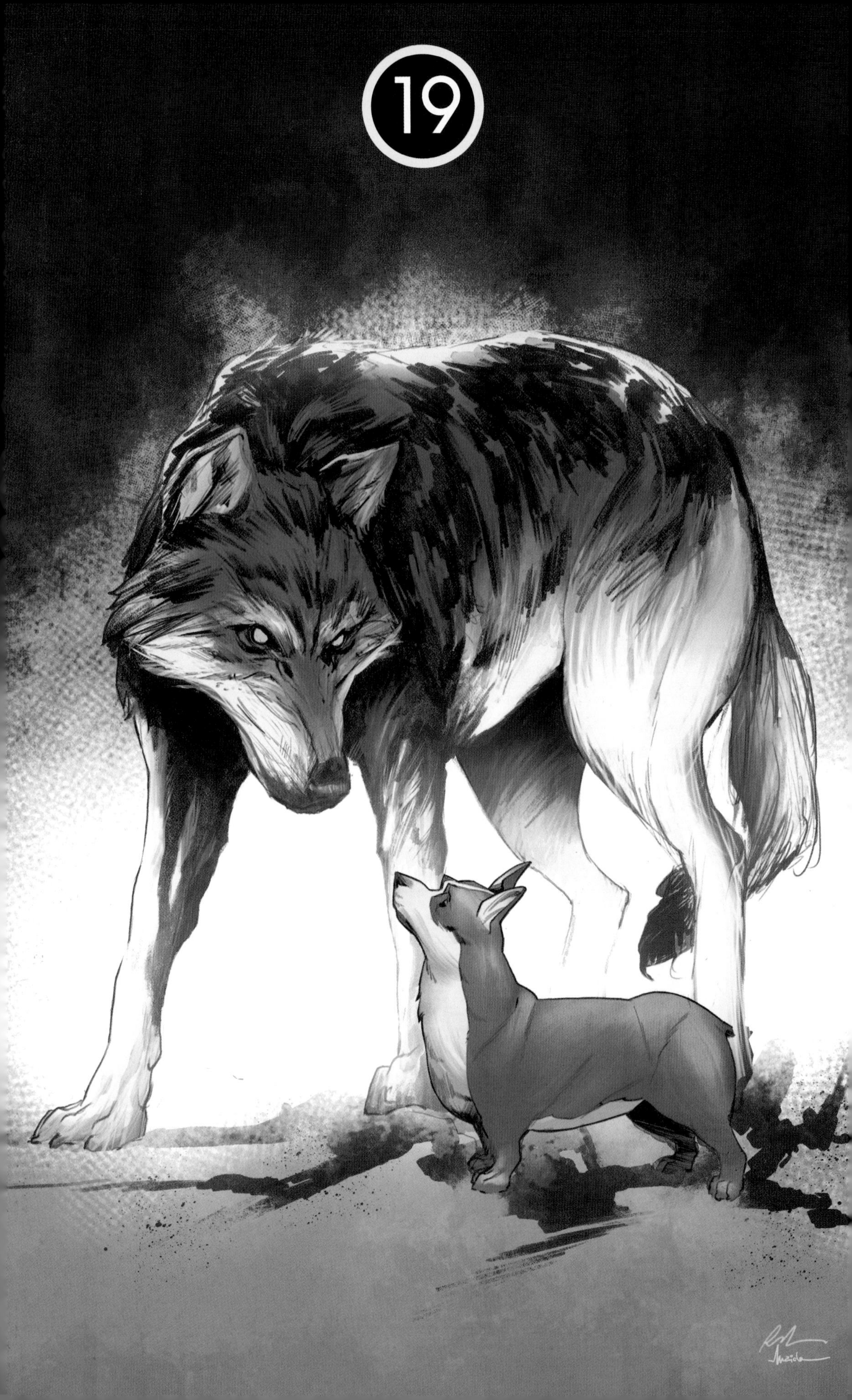
19

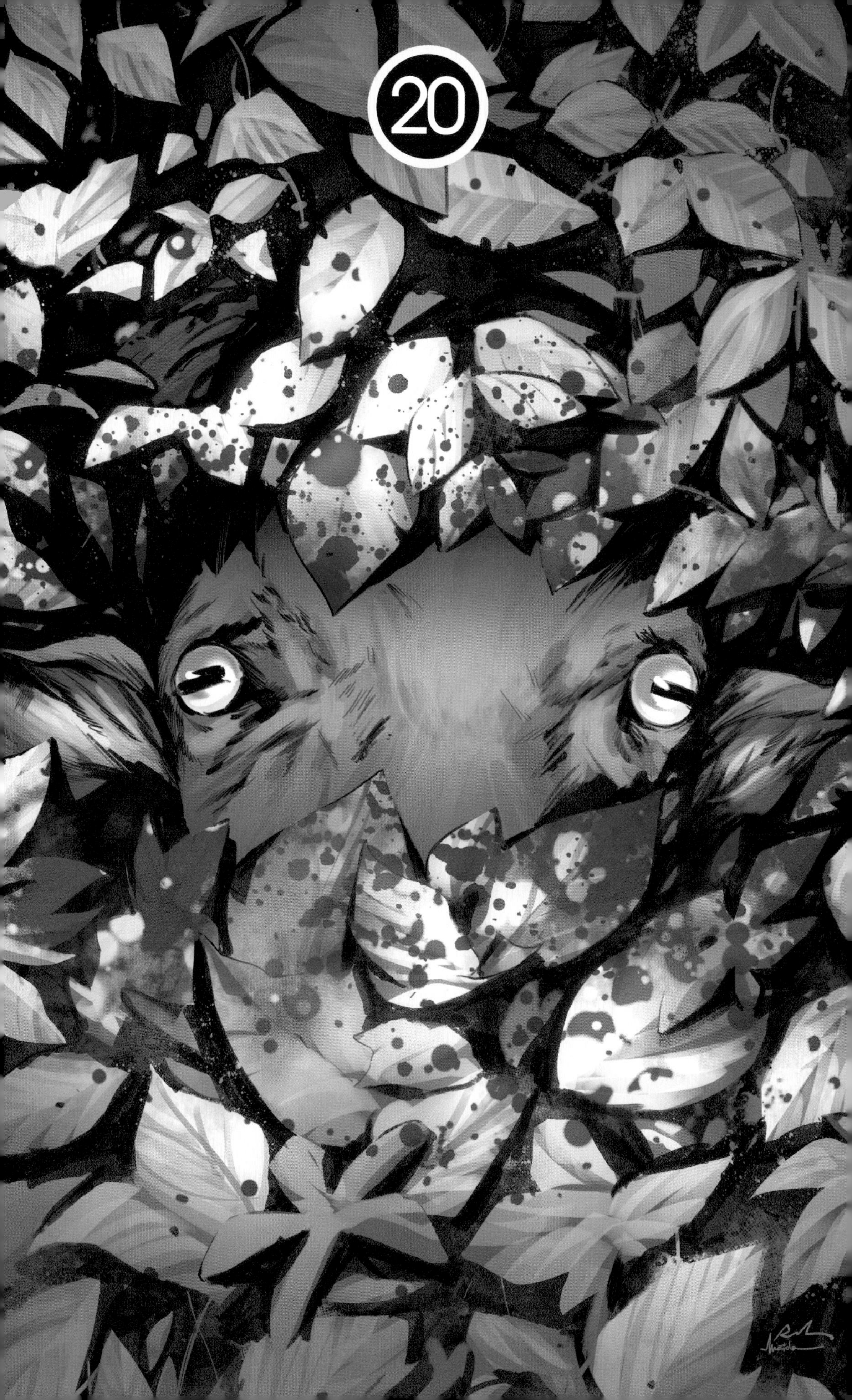
20

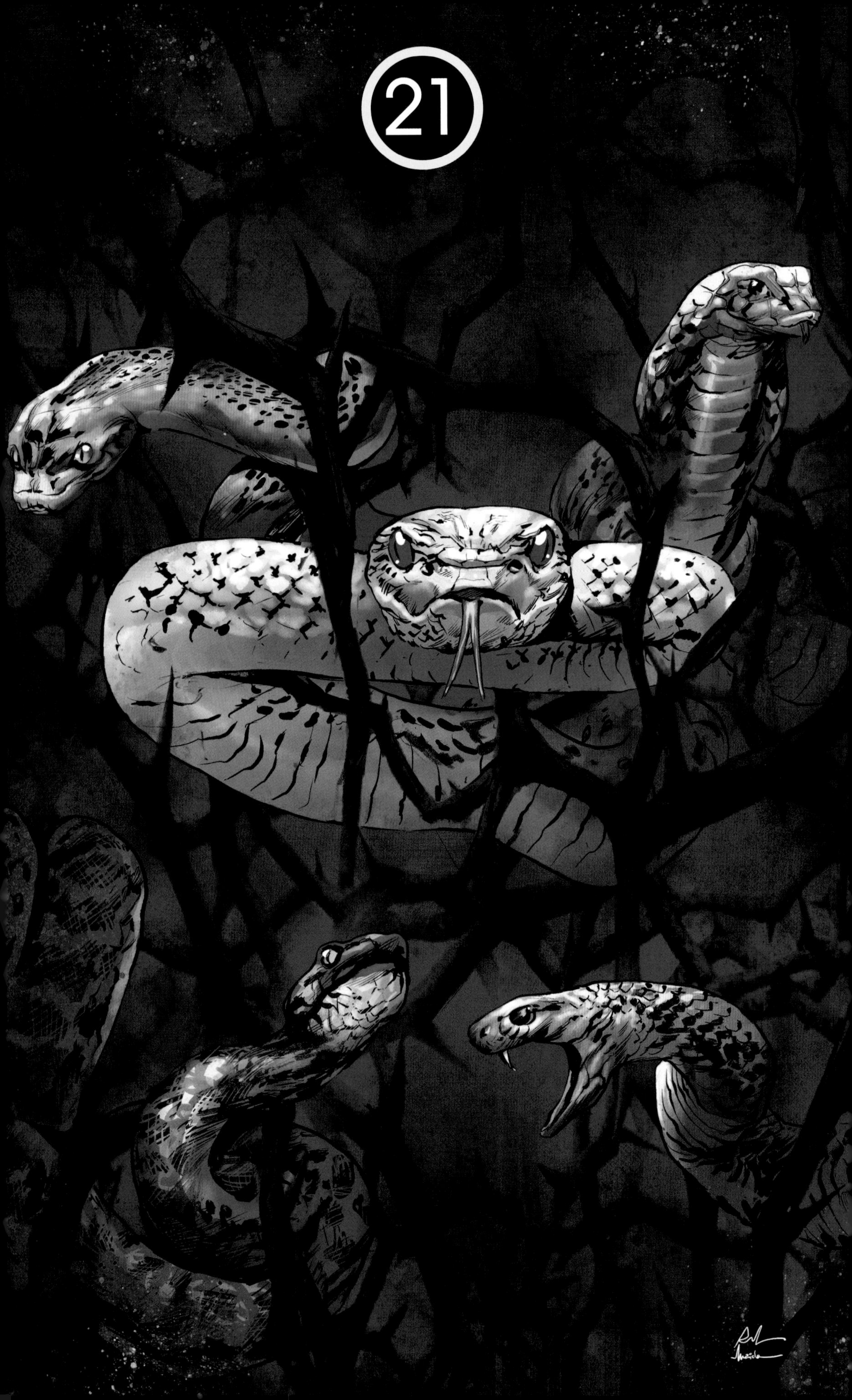
21

22

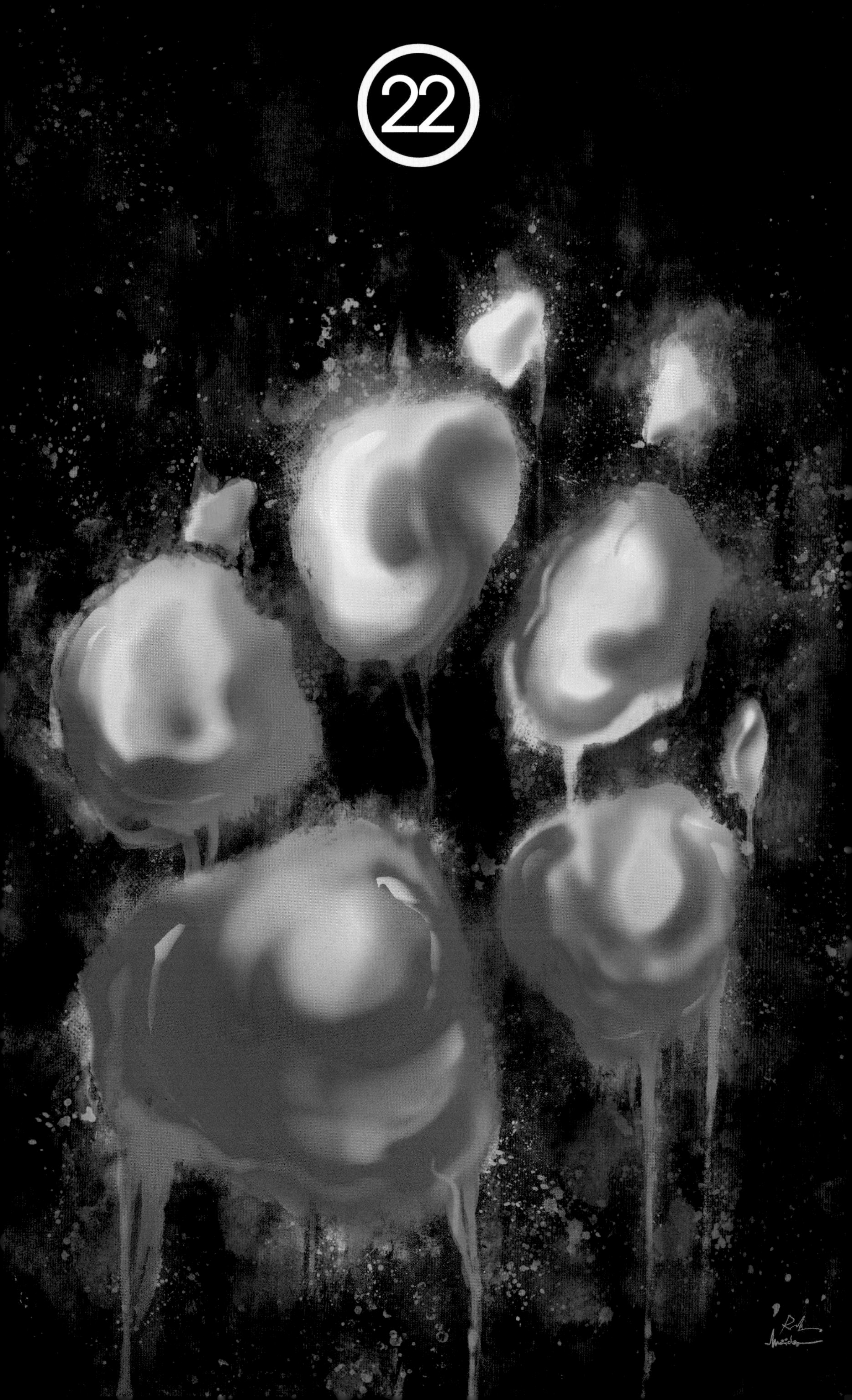

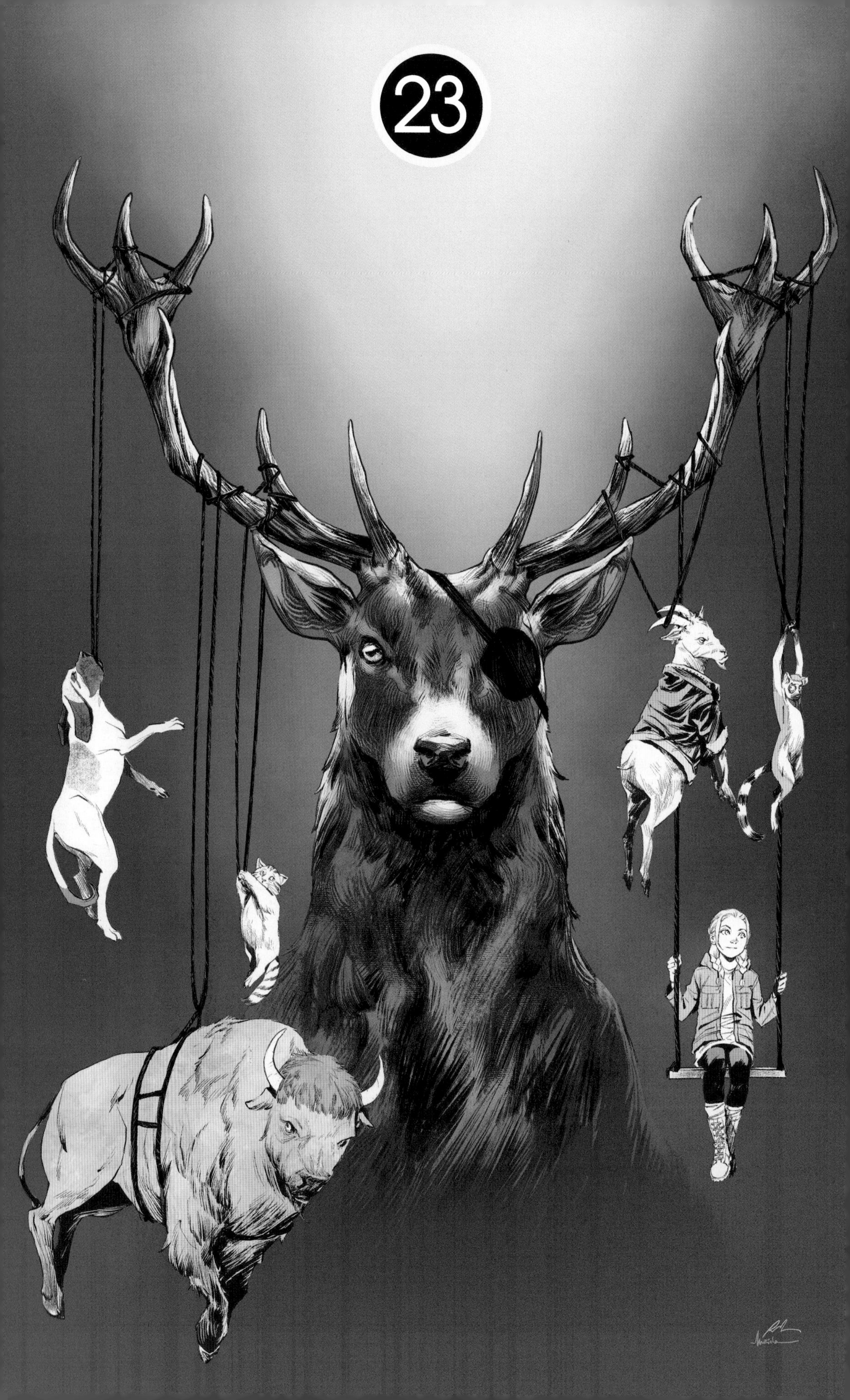
23

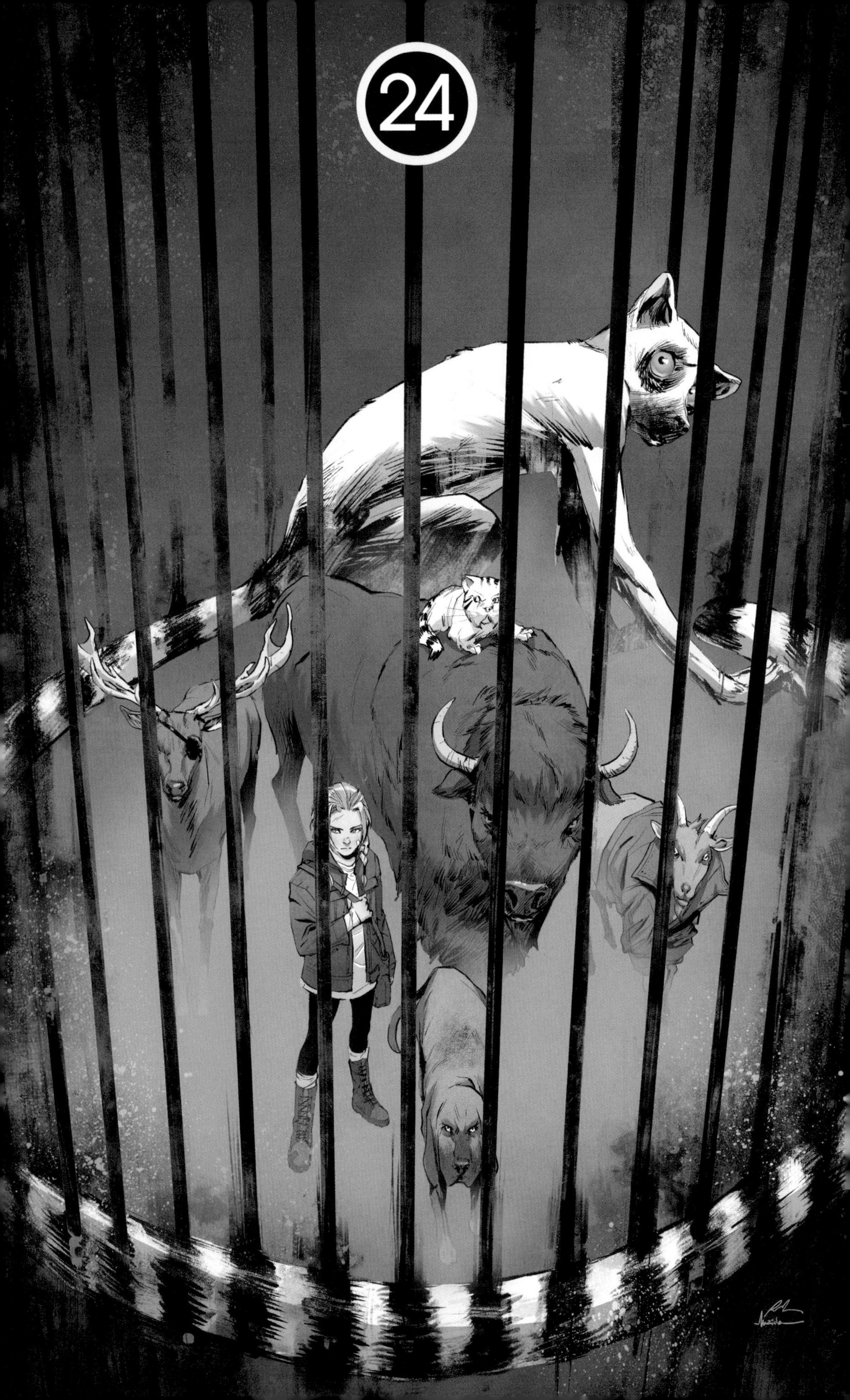
24

25

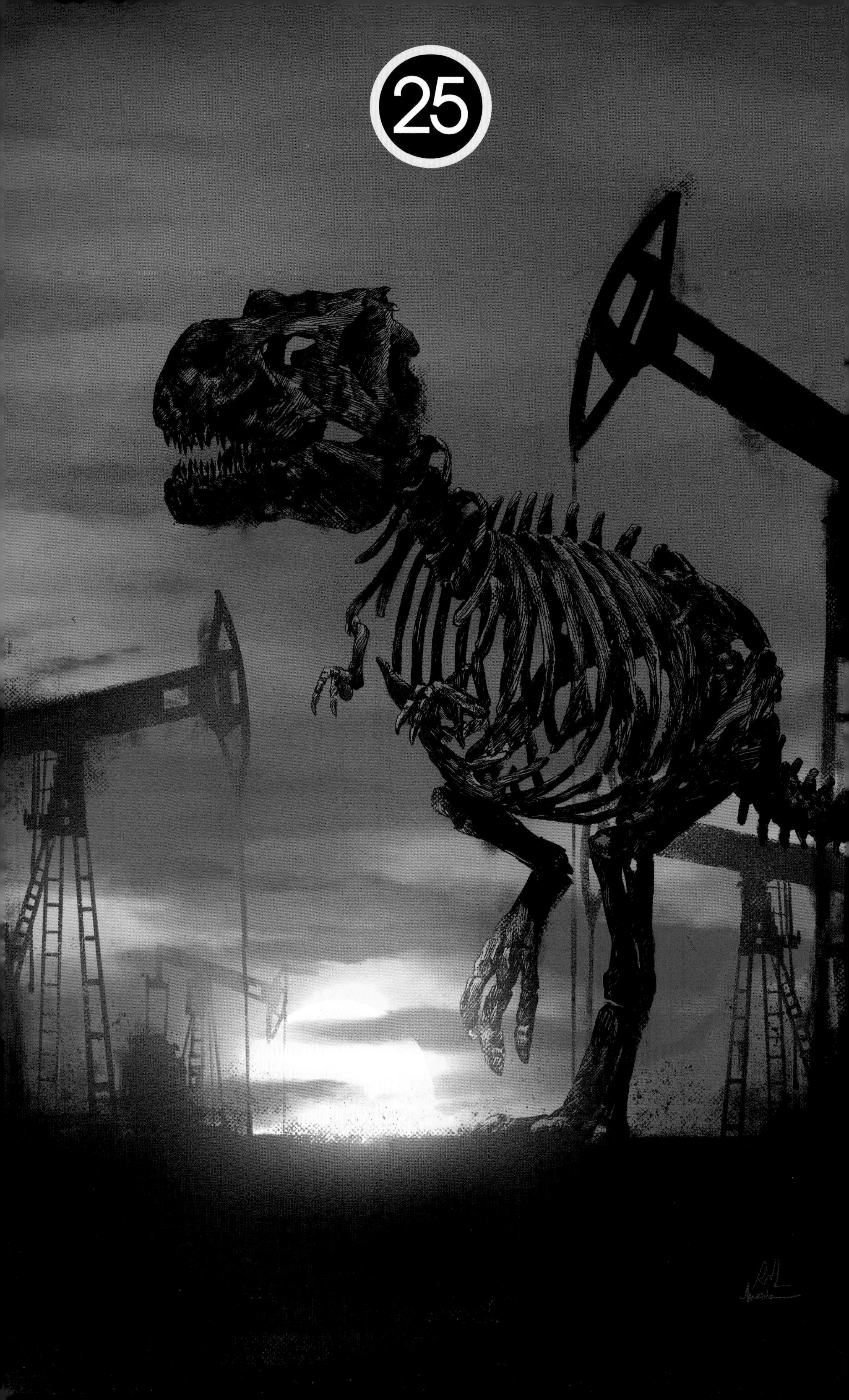

26

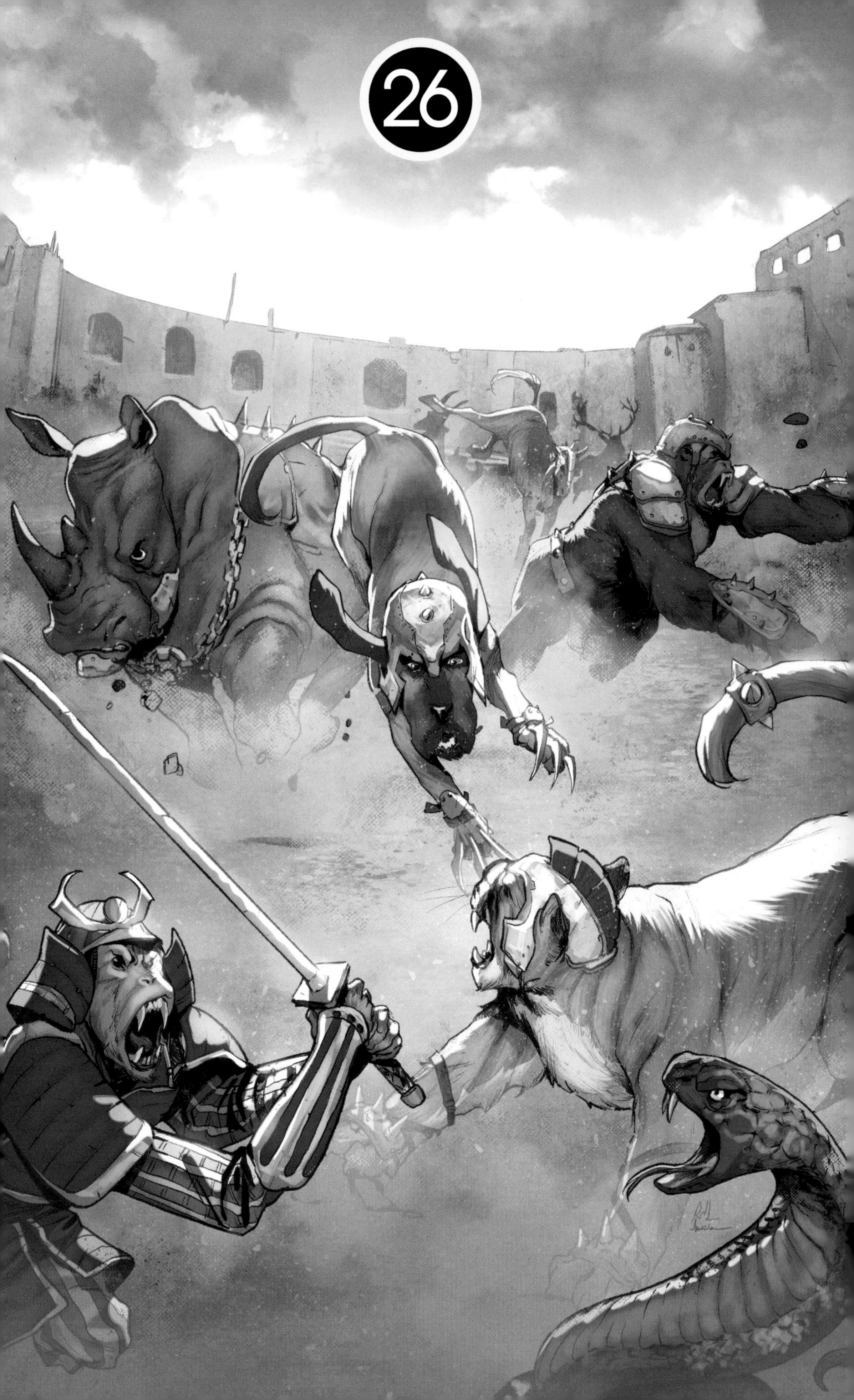

27

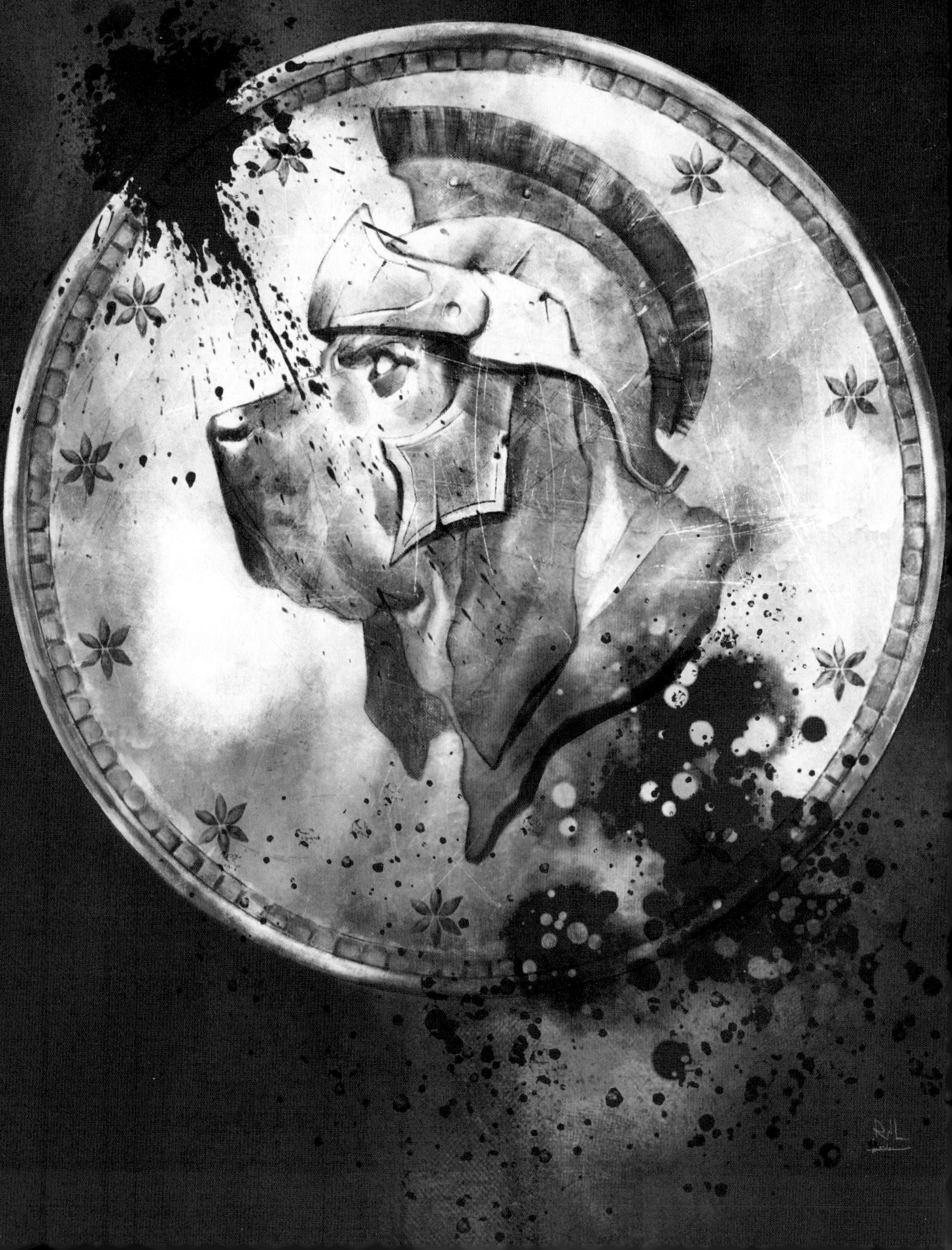

28

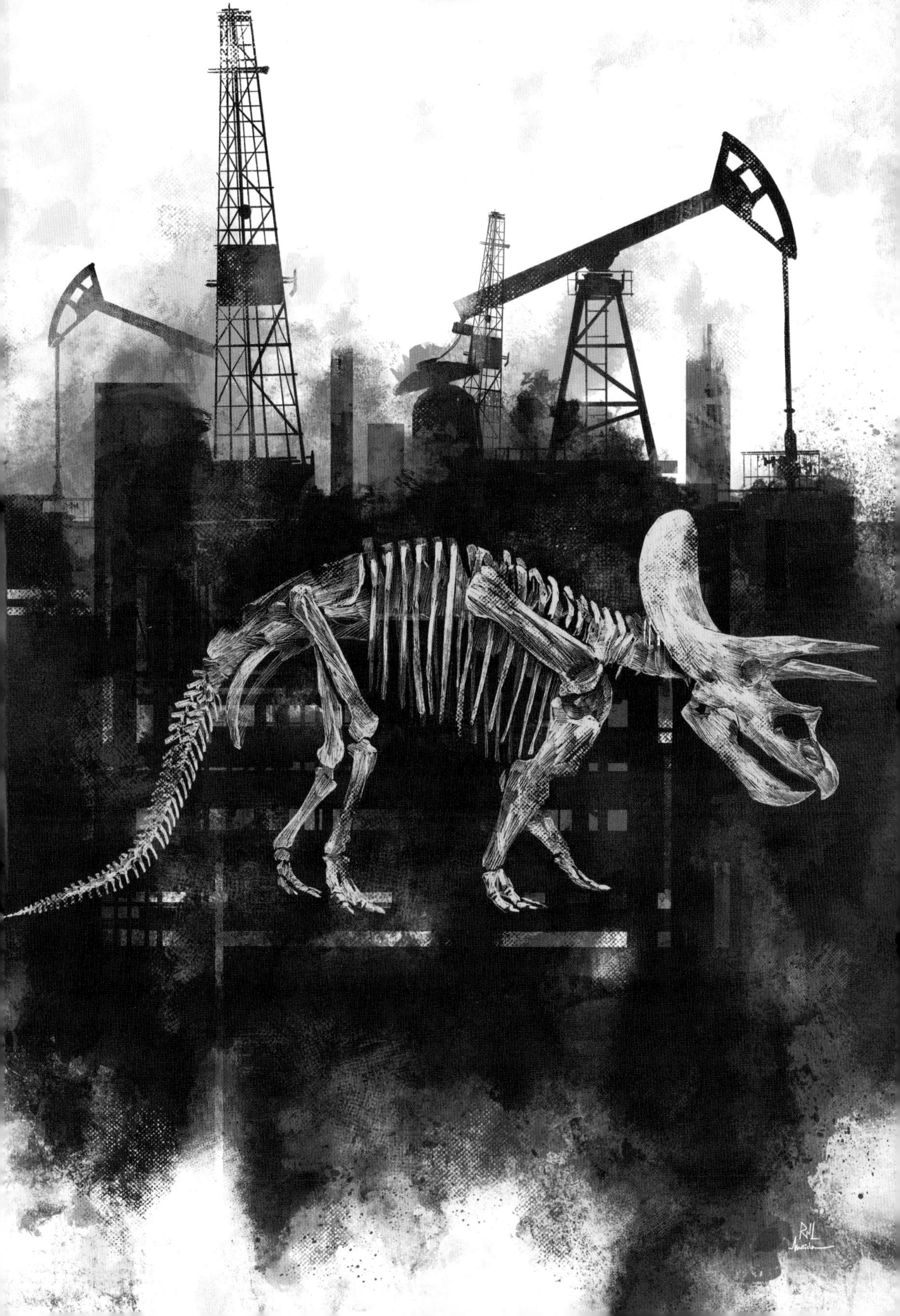

ABOUT THE CREATORS OF

ANIMOSITY™

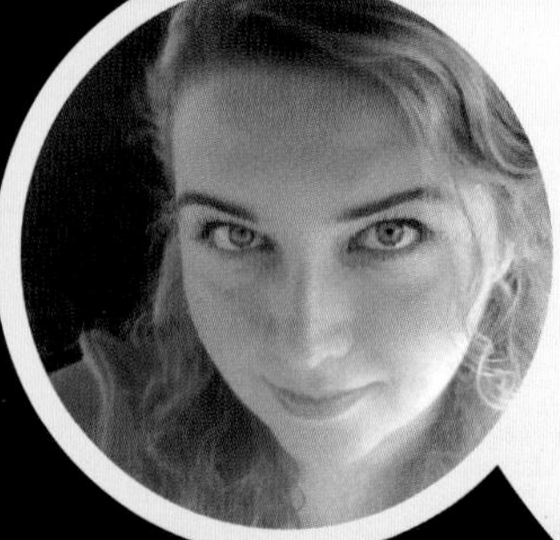

MARGUERITE BENNETT writer

@EvilMarguerite

Marguerite Bennett is a comic book writer from Richmond, Virginia, who currently splits her time between Los Angeles and New York City. She received her MFA in Creative Writing from Sarah Lawrence College in 2013 and quickly went on to work for DC Comics, Marvel, BOOM! Studios, Dynamite, and IDW on projects ranging from *Batman, Bombshells,* and *A-Force* to *Angela: Asgard's Assassin, Red Sonja,* and FOX TV's *Sleepy Hollow.*

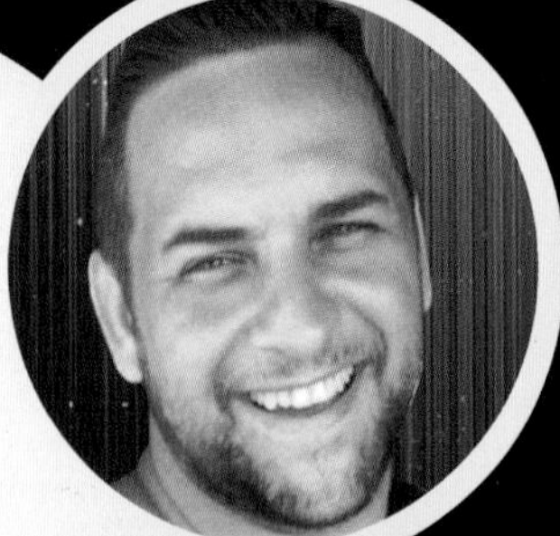

ELTON THOMASI artist

Elton Thomasi is an artist from Rio de Janeiro, Brazil. He started his artistic career in 2009, with the book, *Máquina Zero (Zero Machine).* From there, he's worked for other publishing houses, including Dark Horse *(The Sakai Project),* Titan Comics *(Doctor Who),* and doing sketch cards for Marvel and DC. Since then, he's worked in partnership with his friend and comic book creator Mike Desharnais on a comic book named *Marshal Strong,* which will debut in 2019 at New York Comic Con.

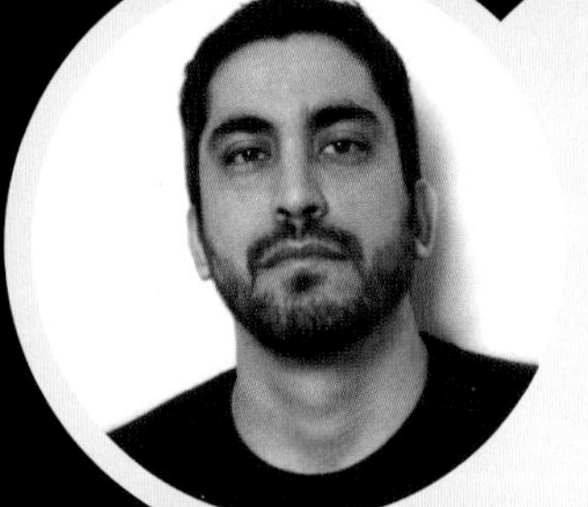

RAFAEL DE LATORRE artist

@De_Latorre

Rafael De Latorre is a Brazilian artist who has worked in illustration and advertising since 2006. His first comic book was *Fade Out: Painless Suicide,* which was nominated to the HQMix award in Brazil. He also worked on *Lost Kids: Seeking Samarkand* and *321: Fast Comics.*

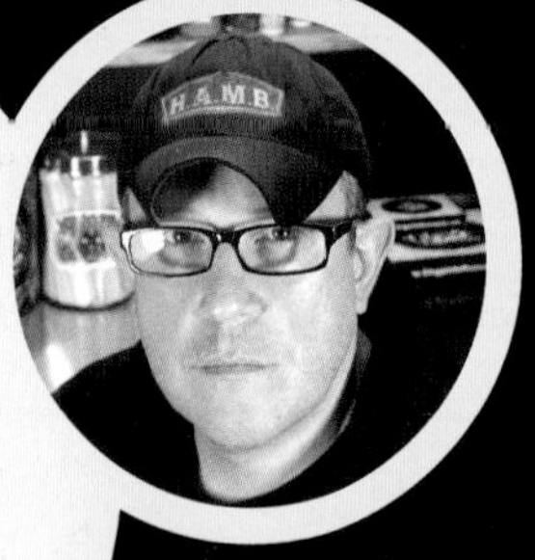

ROB SCHWAGER colorist

@robschwager

Rob Schwager is a self taught artist with over twenty-five years experience as a colorist in the comic book industry. He's worked on such iconic titles as *Batman, Superman, Green Lantern, Jonah Hex, Ghost Rider, Deadpool, Spider-Man, X-Men* and many others. He currently resides in the Tampa Bay area with his wife and three children and is extremely excited to be part of the AfterShock family of creators.

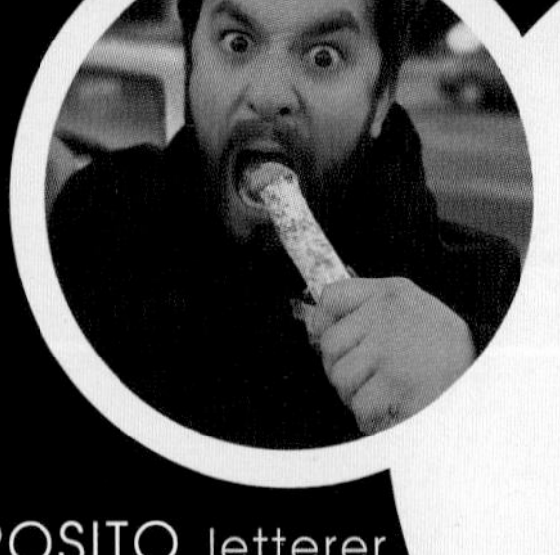

JUANCHO! colorist

Juan Ignacio Vélez, aka JUANCHO! is comic book colorist/illustrator from Bogotá, Colombia and a Kubert School graduate. His past comic book experience stretches all the way from North American to European publishers. He currently lives in Barcelona, Spain, where he splits his time between eating fuet with guacamole and freelance color duties.

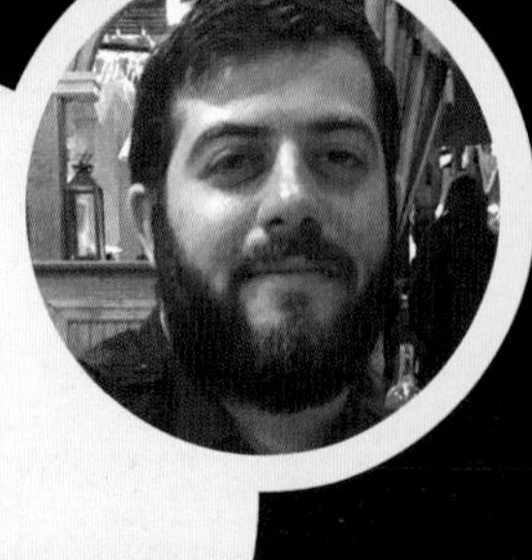

TAYLOR ESPOSITO letterer

@TaylorEspo

Taylor is a comic book lettering professional and owner of Ghost Glyph Studios. As a staff letterer at DC, he lettered titles such as *Red Hood and The Outlaws, Constantine, Bodies, CMYK, The New 52: Future's End* and *New Suicide Squad.* He's also worked on creator-owned titles such as *Interceptor, The Paybacks* (Dark Horse) and *Jade Street Protection Services* (Black Mask). He is currently working on *The Sovereigns* and related books (Dynamite), *Heroine Chic, Dents, Mirror,* and *Firebrand* (Line Webtoon). Other publishers he has worked with include Image, Zenescope, BOOM! and Heavy Metal.